## Ernest L. Norman
**Author, Philosopher, Poet, Scientist,
Director-Moderator of Unarius Science of Life**

# UNARIUS
**UNiversal ARticulate Interdimensional
Understanding of Science**

# INFINITE

# PERSPECTUS

By

## ERNEST L. NORMAN

Published By
UNARIUS, SCIENCE OF LIFE
P.O. Box 1042
El Cajon, Calif. 92020

# INFINITE PERSPECTUS

ISBN 0-9724710-2-2

Third Edition

*

# CONTENTS

cont.

# Contents (Cont'd)

# PREFACE

It will be conceded by all those who read this book, that it excels, both in quality and quantity, any other expressive element in the curriculum of Unarius. It is also presented without compromise or apology, for none is needed, despite what might seem to be revolutionary concepts aimed at destroying all conformities.

It is, as with all other vehicles of Unariun concepts, a book created as a tool, which can be used by any individual to dig himself out of the burrow of his material existence. It is a book which compounds within itself, all of the vastness of Infinity. It is at once provable in the dimension of present-day science and in personal relationships to the world; yet terminates at no point—either here or hereafter. The breadth, depth, and scope of its contents cannot and will not be more fully realized by any reader, even after a lifetime of study! Indeed he will be vitally concerned with its message even into the most remote corners of Infinity.

It may be interesting to note that unlike most other Unarius books and lesson courses, it did not start as a preconceived effort in a book form, but started rather as several taped lectures which could be utilized in group meetings which were forming all over the country. However, spirit was not to be denied; the two or three original lectures grew into thirty-three, and aside from this indicative number, the net content is not only a summation of past presentations, but also contains many new and technical abstractions, not previously presented.

After these lectures were so recorded, they were presented to the Unarius student as a means to more thoroughly acclimate him with the entire procedium. It was felt that through the recorded Voice, new power could be projected to the student when he listened to the Message. The response to these taped Messages, individually speaking, was very great; all persons who so listened to them, reported great progress, as well as more paranormal realizations, activities and manifestations.

It was at this point that Ruth began to realize the importance of these taped Messages in the written word or book form, and so they were thus transcribed, word for word, followed by the usual process of varitype setting performed by Velma—editing etc., and have finally found their way into the covers of this book.

Perhaps it might be well to interject a final note of introspection; the presentation of the Infinite is indeed under any circumstances an extremely difficult if not impossible task especially when it is considered that such vehicles of transposition, human speech, word forms, etc. must be used—at least autosuggestively—to activate the mind of the student. This mind or consciousness, too, is not a very suitable place to transplant the breadth and scope of Infinity; as every human has lived the singular, chain-like, reactionary sequence form of life, it is extremely difficult to transpose this vision of Infinity—and even more so to grasp its entirety. Nor is it reasonably supposed that this prodigious feat can be accomplished, but rather a more evolutionary pattern of life, which integrates these factors into future lifetimes and their evolution-ary phases should take place.

This book must also try to accomplish its purpose with people from many strata of life. It must appeal to the scientist, the pseudo religionist, the agnostic, and the illiterate. It must be provable in all aspects, in all dispensations, and especially with the future. Read, therefore, its contents with an open mind, *freed, as much as possible*, from personal opinions and preju-dices. Its contents were compounded and delivered by those who have advanced far beyond the necessity of earth life; people who, at one time, like you are now doing, passed through these various phases of third dimensional evolution.

They present to you, this, the Unariun concept, the entirety of Infinity compounded together with a vast intellectual power which will permeate your consciousness, and into your psychic anatomy, and will help you in all ways, manners, and forms to accomplish your most ultimate destiny—to progress progressively and infinitely into the future.

# INFINITE PERSPECTUS

## CHAPTER 1

## Beginning A Constructive Evolution

Greetings friends: This is indeed a most joyous and happy occasion, and so far as my own personal feelings are concerned, this joy is not some selfish joy in which I may be vindicated in my personal beliefs, or that I gain satisfaction in some such manner or form; but rather the joy I feel is for each and everyone of you, for I know, as you are seeking further knowledge of Unarius you have taken at least one positive step forward in expressing a certain quotient in the dynamic expression of Infinite Creation.

This in itself, is most important, and something which you should always remember throughout the coming years and in the times when you are troubled or emotionally distressed; that always there must be a consciousness of this infinite expression which is working directly in a regenerative principle, to constantly recreate for you, the form and substance of your lives, and rather than to continuously indulge yourselves in past emotional reflex experiences born from out other worlds and other times, it is most imperative that you learn to recognize this Infinite Creation which is above and beyond the immediate horizon of these various reactionary and emotional experiences.

In other words, there is always a positive and creative motion involved even though it may apparently seem to you that such happenings or intents at the moment are destructive in nature. When this more positive and most necessary attunement and introspection begins to be attained, you will realize that there is infinitely much more in progressive evolution than you have heretofore imagined. Not only that, but you will actually begin a constructive evolution which will automatically, in itself, express into your outward or exterior life, the better quotients and qualities of life as they have, up until some point, only been dreamed of by yourself.

This point could perhaps be best illustrated by telling you a story, one which has possibly happened in innumerable cases and in varying situations. It concerns a small child who was being scolded by her father for being naughty; after the scolding, the child looked up at her father with innocent eyes and expression and asked this question: "Why can't I be naughty, Daddy?" You can well imagine what the father thought at that particular moment and how his intelligence was taxed to come up with a suitable and direct answer to this very naive question. Perhaps he used the number one stock answer, which most fathers give to such questions; "Because God doesn't want you to be naughty."

Now, this is all well and good to a certain point, but it must be remembered that from that moment on, the child would pass through life with more or less of a subconscious sense of fear that some god was looking over her shoulder at every moment in

2

her life. In this respect we can easily visualize adults as grownup children, and they have passed through their lives, in a sense, feeling subconsciously or consciously, that some god or some deification has, in a mysterious way, been looking at their various actions.

Under pretense of moral codes or ethics, we can say that such constructive motivations which may arise in the daily intercourse of human beings among themselves, must, primarily be spurred and motivated or instigated by such thoughts and actions, or such visualizations as can be considered creative in nature. In the personal interpretation of thought into action, some element or quotient of this Infinite Creative Principle is expressed, rather than doing something simply because it was necessary, or it was expected of us—or that in some way we were being intimidated by an unseen deification.

It is at this point, when we evolve into that state of consciousness in which we are beginning to express in our daily thoughts and actions a certain creative quotient of the ever-regenerating Infinite expression, that our lives begin to change. This consciousness will, in itself, supplant and replace the old reactionary elements which we have heretofore been practicing and by which we have been victimized in the past.

To further enlarge our introspection, let us see that humanity as a whole, has been living, not only the immediate or physical life as it so appears, but individually every person has lived many hundreds of lives and passed through the same temporal experiences and these things in themselves have only assumed new forms, new derivations, and new expressions; but basically all remained, categorically speaking, in the realm of the emotional reflex. There was not at any time a direct consciousness or a connotation to a higher and heretofore unknown principle of life.

3

Today our modern 20th century science has created a great paradox. This, in itself, is simply the general extraction of science or abstraction as it so concerns our material world and is reducible into certain principles of creative and expressionary energy. Even the atoms of mass itself are so subdivided into energy particles known as electrons and protons. It is therefore a great and rather obvious mystery that man has not, up to this moment, applied the same creative principles of reconstruction and reconstructive infinity into his own daily life, as it concerns the more immediate function of such daily action and thought as can be considered psychological in nature; and here again, man is still at the present moment being victimized and is practicing the same subversive elements as he has always done.

Religion in itself—and to define a religion according to Webster's dictionary—is merely a code of ethics by which we conduct ourselves from day to day; this is rather a broad frame of reference and one which gives considerable latitude in interpretation. To the religionist there is somewhat of a different classification inasmuch as religion is more purely confined to such expressionary elements as can be found and seen being practiced in various temples and churches throughout the world. In analyzing these diverse religions and their backgrounds of historical interpretations, it is always found that these various religions are merely extractions and readaptations of older existing beliefs, which had their origin in more barbaric or pagan eras of time.

So far as the existing 20th century science is concerned such deifications and the suppositions which are concurrently being expressed by the many religious orders, are purely fictional in nature, and as of this time and place cannot be verified in a scientific manner. This difference between science and religion, so far as the existing multitudes of the world are concerned, poses a great and rather confusing problem, and until the individual becomes more thoroughly acquainted with science in a more universal or inter-dimensional aspect, he is hopelessly lost in the maze of conflicting opinions and expressions which are so concurrently being expressed. It is for this purpose that Unarius is now being presently expressed on the planet earth; and while this movement has not yet gained the proportions or the strength which it will have in the future, it is the beginning of an era, or an epoch of time, through which man will take definite and progressive steps into a more comprehensive understanding of interdimensional factors which concern his everyday life.

Every day we can read accounts of various rockets or intercontinental missiles being fired by our scientists in an attempt to probe space. Around the outer fringes of our atmosphere there are also numbers of satellites which have been, and are being used by science in the same effort to probe the vast unknown. These are all healthy symptoms and show man's curiosity, in an evolutionary way, to comprehend the more fundamental aspects of a creative and universal intelligence, such as has heretofore been largely supplied by religious beliefs in their various deifications.

To serve a more ultimate purpose therefore, in the science of Unarius you are taking a direct short cut into the future, to a time and place when the scientist and the general populations of the world will understand, to some degree and in some like manner, the principles of science which you are now reading in your Unarius books and lessons. It is therefore logical to assume, that by the same level of reference and in viewing your evolution, as it is concerned with so many past lifetimes, that you have been, in a sense, saved from innumerable karmic earth lives and the attendant untold suffering which always goes hand in hand with these various expressionary factors.

In this respect, in viewing such constructive evolutionary factors with which you are now primarily concerned, I can only urge you to continue in whatever manner and form is best suited to serve this purpose and with the greatest possible strength, to constantly maintain within yourselves, the same constructively minded evolution which I have tried to describe to you. Ever and uppermost in your minds must remain that principle of constructive evolution; regeneration in such a constructive manner and form is the *paramount* principle of the Creative Intelligence.

Always this is a progressive, forward, dynamic movement which is constantly regenerating itself into new and different forms, yet always with the same basic similarities which have previously been manifest. This is a relationship of positive and negative cyclic forms which has been explained to you in the lesson courses. You, as individuals, in your daily lives, are constantly expressing certain quotients or various expressionary forms of these different wave lengths of energy which are not only stemming from your psychic anatomy, but which are constantly being harmonically linked and relinked, through consciousness, into your exterior world.

Bearing in mind this progressive principle of contructive evolution, it is therefore of the utmost importance that your evolution into the future shall maintain an equilibrium. This equilibrium consists of equal portions of knowledge which you so acquire in the study of these Infinite principles, compounded together into equal portions of practical usage and application. In this prescription, you will find that magic elixir of life which has long been sought after by the ancients, and which composes some very vivid portrayals of historical accounts, some fictional, some true.

But in the compound of your future lives, if they are so integrated with equal portions of knowledge of the future, and of the interdimensional principle of regenerative action, compounded with equal portions of positive useful application, then indeed you will have compounded that magic elixir of life, and it will surely give you eternal life; life lived in far off distant planets and in conditions which are beyond your present comprehension. This is not to be feared, but rather it is to be looked forward to, with joy and anticipation; for if this evolution is so constructively compounded, in the manner which I have described, then indeed, there is nothing to fear.

At this point, it might be well to more properly define these two important ingredients which we must enter into our compound of the magic elixir. The various books and lesson courses of Unarius explain quite adequately the knowledge which must be used; while the nomenclature and diverse depictions are, to some extent, part of our modern classical 20th century science, yet they in themselves, are inviolate; that is, in whatever particular perspective we wish to describe them, they could ultimately be resolved into these configurations, and at whichever point we wish to discern ourselves in arriving in some future spiritual evolution, we will be involved with these principles regardless of nomenclature or the idiom of the time.

So far as action is concerned however, here is a distinct departure from what has heretofore been considered action in a third dimensional way. For action is usually associated with some physical manipulation or some prescribed mental extrusion. This is far from that which can be more correctly discerned as true spiritual action; for indeed we must make a complete departure from all past customs, observances, and various conscious or physical expressions which related action to us in our past lives. Under no circumstances should we continue to indulge ourselves in such conscious expressions of action as are generally associated with the material world.

So far as the metaphysical teachings or religions of this time are concerned, these too, are utterly false and without basic scientific origin or concept. It must always be remembered that the physical mind is merely an extrusion of the psychic anatomy, a sort of surface place where certain energy configurations, reassume in their various confluxions a regular pattern which, in its reverse phase, constitutes a thought. A thought is, as is done in photography, sort of a negative, then a reprint of the positive. This is what most people call thought; therefore such actions, mentally speaking, as are associated with concentration, prayer, supplication to various fancied deities, the visualization of some particular physical attainment, such as a new car, a new home, or other such particular dimensional aspects is also quite false and is merely another assumed form of the age-old practice of witchcraft, sorcery, and numerous other paganistic expressions.

Action in its pure sense, resolves into a fourth dimensional aspect, associated as a culminated effort between the Superconscious Self, which is a polarized abstraction of the Infinite, in conjunction with various mental and subconscious dimensions of the psychic anatomy. In this respect, it can be rightfully assumed that power is originating in its proper place from whence all things originate, in the higher dimensions—sometimes called the fourth or fifth—thus correctly stemming, as it were, into the person's life. Should such a person indulge himself in the capricious practices of mental projections or any of the many such concentrated efforts which are supposed to give him power and dominion over the physical world, then he will surely be obstructing the true flow of power from the inner or higher self.

Action must always be superimposed on the consciousness as a function of the Infinite which is flowing into the person from the higher abstract Super-consciousness. It is polarized most properly with various perspectives in the individual's immediate life so that this power will appear upon the surface in his daily life as the correct perspectives of personal relationship. It is therefore immediately seen that such appearances will be well-ordered; they will be quite miraculous in nature in many instances. There is *no* preconceived, meditative, concentrated, or projected effort made in this direction. All things will be harmoniously attuned and will appear at the precise moment when they are needed. Such sundry other attributes as mental telepathy, attunement with not only the entire physical world, in all its various transpositions, but an attunement with the higher worlds will also be quite possible and entirely feasible, and will become an actual reality.

To properly instigate such mental consciousness as an action into your daily lives, simply resolves into a formula in which you must realize that you are actually engaged in its infinite number of ingredients. Your daily physical life is the appearance of form and substance from another world at another time and so cyclically interposed as to have some definite meaning with you in the present. It is also realized as correct attunement is made with various perspective relationships with the Higher Worlds, that they in turn, can manifest and re-manifest in certain perfected cyclic movements within your daily life.

Such attunement is, of course, hard to come by. You have, as a creature of evolution, sustained your different lives from one life to the next, just as you do your daily life—a subconscious association and reassociation in the memory consciousness of the subconscious part of the psychic anatomy. This also has been adequately described to you in the second lesson course. It is only fair to state at this time that you cannot hope to achieve this new attunement, this

9

new perspective of consciousness, in a few hours time; nor can you do so in one lifetime. It will remain a challenge with you for many thousands of years to come and their subsequent lifetimes. It is the challenge of the future; it is one way in which you attain infinite knowledge. For, in that theoretical supposition of time and place when you have achieved a direct relationship with the Infinite, to such a perfected degree that you are no longer reactionary in any sense or manner, then indeed you will be endowed with all of the god-like propensities and proclivities.

For the present however, there are a few rules to remember: do not resort to any of the mind practices which are commonly associated in your present time, such as concentration, prayer, or in the supposed belief that you regulate fate in any sense of the word; purely because fate, as it is generally supposed, is nonexistent. True fate is the direct extracted derivation of various cyclic movements which occur within your psychic anatomy, and in which, to a large extent, you, in the past, instituted and relegated this so-called fate by your previous actions; so does the future hold the same promise, that as of today you are relegating yourself into whatever particular dimension to which you so aspire.

It is conceivable therefore, in your study of Unarius you are making a serious and concerted effort to aspire into a higher dimension of interpretation. While it is well and good to have certain idealisms or aspirations, it is much more logical if we can possess the power of perception within ourselves to attain these various idealisms.

Principally, the way to a higher life is never achieved from selfish reasons; that is, we have some ulterior motives within our subconscious selves which have been born from out the old insecurities of the past lives; we are still creatures of a primitive world living under the law of survival of the fittest, the carnal law of the jungle. Aspirations and idealisms must be born from an entirely new concept: that you are beginning to function as an integral part of the Infinite Consciousness; that your ultimate destiny is participation in a universal reconstructive and regenerative infinity. You cannot do this if you are motivated by selfish reasons, by ulterior motives, or by reasons which are mandated by some of the subconscious fears of insecurity. Participation in the Infinite and becoming such a universally participating element or entity, mandates an obvious fact; that you must learn of this Infinity, learn of it, its function, and its relationship to even greater Infinities.

Mark Twain once said, "Everybody talks about the weather but nobody does anything about it." This is quite true about the general philosophical idealisms, religions, etc., of our time; everyone is talking about survival after death, as is posed in various religious orders. Everyone yearns for eternal life. To the average earth individual nothing is more fearsome than the sudden extermination of his physical life. The person who is more securely indoctrinated in the higher expressionary principles of infinite regeneration, does not have such fear; but rather he knows that life is supported as a continuity from one cycle to the next, and carries with it, an agent of transmission—the entire entity of being—the reason within itself, the knowing of certain unalterable basic principles of life. These, in themselves, are the immortal elements that refuse to perish with the passage of time, or the advent of (so-called) death.

Any person who wishes to survive this life, and in an intelligent manner, without incurring the usual karmic impregnations which come through lack of knowledge, must do so by becoming acquainted with the principles of function as they concern the Infinite. So far as the sciences and religions of this day are concerned, there is much talk about these things, as

11

to the sustaining of life beyond the third dimension, and to the possibility of life on distant planets; yet apparently no one seems to know how this is done, or what really exists beyond the mortal ken.

This is the purpose of Unarius, to supply these missing ingredients. And like the little girl who asked her father, "Why can't I be naughty?", so people have in their past evolutions through time and space, to the present, in their many lives, reincarnated back into a terrestrial life which has fostered their very beginnings. These people, too, are beginning to learn that they can't be naughty. The reasons are not, as they are generally supposed, but are based entirely upon a constructive presentation of evolution as it concerns the personal entity in traveling into time and space; traveling into a higher dimension of consciousness where the physical life is no longer lived in the customary manner, mandated by the laws of the jungle.

Therefore, it would be well at this time to go within yourselves, to make a solemn vow, that as of this moment, as of this time, you will spend your life, your eternity in learning of the Infinite; you will know that in the learning, there will come a higher sense of consciousness which will supercede any voluntary conscious mind function which you might make. You will cease to resort to the common paganistic practices which smack of age-old superstitious witchcraft, sorcery, and various other spirit practices used in the barbaric past. Instead there will come within yourself the gradual realization, the consciousness of the great and vast Infinite; and with this consciousness there will be relayed into your life a certain proportion of perfection; idealisms will come about in a natural functionable manner which is most perfect and miraculous to see; and you will know, at that time your identity, your personal being as an integrating participant in the function of universal

12

consciousness will be sustained through eternity.

So let us go forward; each moment, each hour, each day is precious; we must use all this time remaining to us in this third dimension to do all we can to further or progress our evolution into a higher consciousness. This we must do or we shall surely perish.

# CHAPTER 2

## Obsession—A Scientific Fact of Life

In various places throughout the works of Unarius, great emphasis has been placed upon the concept of obsession, and because of its importance to us in our daily lives and in our future evolution, it might be well at this time to enter into some more extensive and technical aspects of this all-important subject. No doubt all of you have at one time or another, seen pictures such as TV or motion pictures depicting witch doctors or medicine men adorned with sundry feathers, beads, and trappings, who were shaking bells or rattles and other numerous noisy instruments, and were dancing around some sick person in an attempt to scare out the evil spirit or spirits which were obsessing this person.

The man of medicine or the psychiatrist of our civilization does not recognize this type of obsession. There are, psychologically speaking, certain kinds or classifications of obsessions which are more purely related to the general subconscious terminology of pure psychology, in a sense, that they are obsessive thought forms.

So far as the witch doctor or the medicine man is concerned, he is perhaps, in one respect, more intelligent than is the doctor or the psychologist; for while

14

both of these individuals may be right and wrong, neither of them has entered into the more purely interdimensional aspects of what they are trying to do. While the witch doctor is right in recognizing the spiritual obsessions, he is very unrealistic in trying to frighten the obsessing entities from out of the body of the sick man by making weird sounds.

Likewise, the psychologist or the doctor in our modern medicine is equally ignorant of the various fourth dimensional aspects of his present-day practice. He cannot and does not have sufficient insight into these numerous interdimensional factors to make a relative and concisive psychology in our present-day dispensations.

To understand obsessions means that we have to carry our introspection far beyond the point of the very primitive aspects of the medicine man, or the witch doctor. An obsession can be said to be any kind of a thought form or a compulsion which, seemingly without rhyme or reason, makes any individual a victim of the various expressions in attempting to re-enact whatever constitutes this particular obsession.

In a pure and more general classification therefore, it can be safely said that all things which mankind does are, in themselves, technically speaking, obsessions. The obsessive thought of death creates in man many obscure compulsions as well as some of the more factual continuities whereby life can be sustained on the surface of this planet earth. The fear of death does relate man to many processes of his physical life which are obsessive in nature, because they have, as their common source, the fear of death which is unrelated in a pure sense, inasmuch as death does not really exist. When man has developed the consciousness to exist in spiritual worlds without the body, then the compulsion of death will cease to exist.

Therefore, the numerous obsessive thought forms

15

which are always, directly or indirectly, related to death will consequently cease to exist. Obsessions also can run the gamut, so to speak, of various astral entities which are actually people without physical bodies, who have, in some way, succeeded through vibration in connecting themselves to various people or groups of people in this present day.

All people who are living in the world today, just as people who have lived in the past, can be said to be obsessed to some more or less degree by these diverse spiritual entities that inhabit the astral worlds which are part of these fourth dimensional or inter-dimensional aspects about us. The fact that these spiritual entities cannot be seen or sensed by most people does not mean that they do not exist. We know that a TV transmitter can transmit or radiate into the surrounding atmosphere a certain wave form which carries sound and picture; and it can be interpreted by the TV set in such a manner and form that it becomes a realism in our minds when we watch this re-enactment.

Therefore, an obsession must be reduced in the way and manner in which it expresses itself; whether it is an astral entity, or whether it is an obsessive thought form, is therefore reducible to the pure scientific concept that it is a radiated form of expression which succeeds, through the correct attunement, in remanifesting itself into our consciousness. The principles of science, as they are related to vibration, attunement, and harmonic interplay are just as valid and valuable to us here in this aspect as they are in any other relationship of science and the manner in which these aspects assert themselves as part of our daily lives.

If a woman goes to a psychiatrist and says, "I am all upset and need help," he will therefore try to analyze this woman on the basis of psychosomatic medicine. He will suggest to her that she go back, mentally, into her childhood and bring out the most important of these various fears which were incurred in these childish years. The woman says that at that time she became very frightened of a mouse; that is, the little animal ran out from under the sofa, across her legs and sent her into hysterics. The psychiatrist will then try to explain that this is a syndrome; in other words, her entire subconscious tense, the numerous fears and other obsessive forms of psychic happenings within her subconscious were based and primarily motivated by this mouse happening. But this analysis is not valid, and is quite likely to have very little if any effect upon this woman in solving her problem. This is because the psychiatrist or the psychologist did not know that this mouse episode had a continuity; the little mouse itself was only autosuggestive of various other happenings which had transpired in this woman's life and in diverse other lifetimes, going back perhaps many thousands of years. The mouse therefore represented lions, tigers, and sundry other ferocious carnivorous animals which had, in previous lifetimes, destroyed her, or they had killed and eaten her relatives, or in many ways, manners, and forms, had created very terrifying episodes in these former lifetimes.

The little mouse, for the moment, became the psychic representation of all these animals and it can be easily seen how this little mouse could therefore reimpose fear in the consciousness of the child to the point where she became hysterical. In future years in the life of this woman, different aspects of her life would be conversely intimidated by this fear aspect which has been reinstated within her consciousness; because now there was a direct subconscious continuity with all of these various other different animal experiences in past lifetimes.

All people today, universally speaking, have more or less of a fear of snakes. The fear of snakes is even

17

more rampant or generally accepted among people than diverse other types of deeply rooted subconscious fears. This is because snakes not only represent a certain destructive transpiring episode in previous lifetimes in different similar continuities, as with the woman and the mouse; inasmuch as the snakes could have bitten and poisoned many people, or that boa constrictors or pythons or other constrictive types of snakes could have killed these people; but even more important is the religious aspect.

In all past religions, universally speaking, the symbol of the serpent was the dominant spiritual symbol used by the priesthood in the various religious cultisms and in their numerous observances which were practiced by these sundry cults. Some of these observances or rituals were horrible beyond description, and no doubt left a great psychic fear within the psychic anatomy of most of the people who are presently living on the earth today and which largely accounts for their deeply rooted subconscious fear of the serpent.

So, you see, whatever it is in whatever aspect with which we are so concerned, there is a direct continuity with the past, whether it is in the more immediate present lifetime or that it continues back for thousands of years in hundreds of lifetimes, it makes little or no difference. The subconscious or inverted fear is there nevertheless and cannot be corrected until we uproot it and bring it out into the light of introspection and analyze it for what it is. In this analysis we therefore generate out of phase wave forms with the present tense which will largely cancel out the more dominant fear which is so subconsciously immersed. Yes, it can be said that no one is without these fears.

Almost all people will, at some time or another, cross their fingers or resort to various other little mental devices which can be considered superstitious in nature, but which are largely founded upon this same psychic inversion which carries them on back in different continuities into many previous lifetimes where these numerous expressive forms were much more largely used and more completely expressed as part of their daily lives than they are in the present tense. Crossing the fingers, for instance, is one of those little things which people used to relate them back into times when, as part of their religions in previous lifetimes, they put their fingers together because they believed this would in some way short circuit the energies which came to them from the astral worlds or that they would be able to short circuit or cancel out, so to speak, some of the obsessive astral entity wave forms which came to them; even though they did not understand energy as a wave form, the similarity of this expression nevertheless existed.

The Yogi, the Chinaman, and various other peoples of the Eastern worlds still use this same expression in their daily lives, and it is a common sight in the Orient to see people going about in their daily walks of life with their fingers crossed, because it is simply a way of life in which they have somehow subconsciously learned, as they believe, to protect themselves. However these devices have little or no value whatsoever, except in the general frame of reference that people believe in them.

In some more ultimate day of your evolution, you will arrive at that point where you can resolve all continuities and life expressions on a more general mental plane; that is, the mind becomes a functioning integral unit of expression, which can be used much more thoroughly and much more efficaciously than many of the numerous other implementations which you use in your present-day life expression. It will also be said that in that future day, the various obsessive energy wave forms which have stemmed into your present-day consciousness from out of the past, will be either largely or completely dissolved. They will have become known to you in the general sense that you can see they are the more primitive aspects of your life which developed the numerous symbologies which were used either superstitiously or in a cultistic manner.

In this respect, religion itself, whether Christian or otherwise, is just as obsessive as any other factor of relationship under which the present-day earth man lives; for religion is not scientifically related to the future in a sense that it can be actually resolved as something which will tangibly and realistically live in people's lives. It is only something which they vaguely hope for, sort of an Utopian existence which will relieve them from their present-day sense of care, worry, and other daily concerns.

Religion is also a direct continuity into past life-times in numerous other cultistic expressions which have similar forms or appearances of deistic expressions and subsequent symbologies in the various races of people who have inhabited this world. Almost all people living today have lived in these numerous past civilizations, such as Rome, Carthage, Egypt, Greece, the more ancient Chinese and Hindu cultures, and different other civilizations which have not even been unearthed or recorded in our present-day history and anthropology.

In all cases where we analyze these diverse expressive forms of life as we live them today, whether they are merely the subconscious automations such as breathing, peristalsis of the bowels, etc., or whether they are superstitious beliefs, they can all be universally resolved into the original and dominant principle of life, that is, they are merely like the TV transmitter forms or continuities of wave forms of expression which are reflected from the psychic anatomy.

When you study and begin to understand the diagrams and descriptions as they are given to you in your second lesson course, then you will possess the greatest secret of all; and one which is being so strenuously sought by the present-day men of science and medicine—how man lives and of what life really consists, in its various expressive forms and continuities in the world about you—merely resurgent energy wave forms which are beating in a never-ending, never-ceasing pulsation into your consciousness; energy wave forms which were actual experiences through which you lived in your past lifetimes. Today in this present life, they exist as vague unrelated or even superstitious expressions. They may exist as your religion, they may exist as various expressive forms of medicine or psychology; or they may just exist without any related reason which you may seek to find, unless you carry this continuity back into your many past lifetimes.

Therefore, in your day by day analysis of whatever you are, and why you are what you are, and why you act the way you do, you must always realize that these different expressions are merely continuities from these numerous past lifetimes in which you have lived through these experiences which are presently causing you some concern or in various other different attitudes and interplays of life expressions, that all of these forms do reside in your consciousness as of today. They will manifest and remanifest themselves in the many unrelated and seemingly intangible ways until you can thoroughly understand them and analyze them. On this basis then, you can say that they are obsessive. They will cause you to do many queer and seemingly unintelligent things which do not apparently have any purpose for their existence or their commission.

Even life itself, as it is lived by the physical man on this planet earth, will, in a sense, become a vast and unrelated delusion when we can see man living in

21

higher spiritual worlds without the body; we can only reasonably suppose or evaluate this condition when we take into our consciousness a great principle of life as it is expressed by the Infinite. That is, the Infinite is constantly becoming more infinite by regenerating Itself in ever-increasing numbers, manners, and forms of expression. This is done through the various interdimensional energy wave forms as have been so thoroughly explained to you in different texts. The usefulness and the purpose therefore, becomes clearly apparent out of all this chaos when this principle is understood; man is an evolutionary entity of intelligence re-expressing himself in whatever particular dimension to which he is so related at that particular time.

In this sense then, each individual carries either a smaller or a larger portion of the many different life expressions as he remanifests himself in his various life by life associations in different epochs of time. The continuities of these numerous expressive forms can therefore be correctly assumed to be obsessive in nature; they not only can form the destructive potentials of his life, inasmuch as they are seemingly unrelated to him in his present tense, but they can also form the most constructive part of his life.

In fact, when we look at the fear of death, it is, conversely speaking, the dominant and constructive obsession which keeps man in his evolutionary pattern upon the face of this planet from life to life into some future day, when he can begin to recognize the spiritual elements of this interdimensional principle which we have expressed to you.

Fear in itself, in whatever manner or form it is related to you, or to any person, is something which is not immediately or consciously related to the various aspects of daily life. However fear, while it is said to be a destructive or a coercive force, is not necessarily so but can actually form the libido or the driving force in every person's life, and will so continuously reassert itself until intelligence can begin to take its place and life can be continued on into the future in a more realistic manner and form without the necessary urgency of some or many dominant fears which are submerged in the subconscious.

The future psychology and psychiatry of the world as it concerns mankind, will, if it is to become constructive and valid in solving man's various mental and physical differences, have to be a much more extended psychosomatic medicine than presently exists. Instead of going back into the childish formative period of time in a person's life, the psychiatrist or the analyst will have to continue on back into many hundreds of lifetimes. The person involved will have to be given some sort of a correct summation of life as it is presently appearing in his surface everyday life; it is the general conflux of reassertion of many different kinds of life experiences through which he has previously passed. These various life forms are presently reasserting themselves as direct continuities of wave form expressions which stem from the psychic anatomy.

When these principles are thoroughly understood and the psychiatrist (or analyst) can practice this extended psychosomatic medicine, he will really and truly be casting out evil spirits. He will be doing what the witch doctor or the medicine man tried to do by dancing and shaking rattles; he will in effect be doing what Jesus did 2000 years ago when He cast out evil spirits from numerous people who came to Him. He will be actually giving a new lease on life to every person who comes to him.

The practice of witchcraft as it has been previously or even presently expressed is not condoned; it is unrealistic and does not involve all of the factors associated with various kinds of expressions, but it is also invalid on the basis it is only that which is transpiring in the more immediate present. Disease in itself, whether it is physical or mental is only the general conflux, as it were, of many different negative expressions from previous lifetimes which are manifesting themselves in the present circumstances of various parallaxes or junctions of these different negative expressions to the extent and degree that they can break down the physical anatomy and obstruct the natural mental functions of the individual.

These obsessive forms or obsessive expressions of life, do not necessarily always have to include such fixed pictures as they may reside in astral entities; they can be numerous daily life happenings in previous lifetimes of any individual, wherein he did live and re-express from day to day these various life continuities. The fact remains that so far as the future is concerned—and the future can be considered a cyclic pattern—anything which happened in the past does in this future become unrelated to it in a sense that we are concerned with certain positive and negative expressions in these cyclic manifestations.

While life could have been lived as an actual reality of the past and did not have any particular adverse effect upon the individual at that time, that same life superimposed in a subconscious way in the present could be very destructive to the individual, simply because it was out of phase or out of attunement, as it were, with the present; even though the individual may be living the same kind of a life, but in a re-expressed form or continuity makes no difference whatsoever. We are concerned here primarily with the expressive continuity of these life expressions as they reinsert themselves in cyclic forms. The subsequent differences as they manifest themselves as being adverse, are so in the sense that their polarities are changed to the present, or to some future lifetime which will be lived by this individual.

A more general abstraction could consist of viewing the Infinite in a more interdimensional manner, and as the Infinite is living and regenerating Itself, it cannot therefore be assumed that so far as our consciousness is concerned we could put our fingers on the Infinite at any time or place and get the same picture when we lifted our fingers and put them down in a different place. In effect, so far as our mentality is concerned, we are literally doing this very thing. We are lifting our fingers, so to speak, when we pass from this world, and when we are being reborn again into the physical world, we put our fingers down on the Infinite in respect to the fact that we are again assuming the direct continuity of the physical life.

However, during that interval, we shall say, when our fingers were lifted or that our mental consciousness was suspended from the earth life, the Infinite, in Its respect to us, changed completely; therefore when we tried to continue living the physical or earth life in a new reborn condition, we found that all of these many life expressions were, to a large degree, out of phase to the present. It was our problem then to take these various past lifetime experiences and to reform them or to reshape them into the present lifetime expression as a direct continuity of life.

In this respect we developed a new portion of the psychic anatomy, called by the psychologist, the subconscious, which forms a reconstructive entity to the various impounded infractions of different life experiences as they are lived in the present, and which, to some degree, must harmoniously attune themselves to many past life experiences, even though they are now, to some degree, and in some sense, out of attunement with the present despite the fact that the same continuities of life were lived in the past lifetimes. It can be easily seen that this is likely to create some kind of tension, or unrest, or strife with the individual.

If this condition is continued on into many lifetimes, it can be reasonably supposed this individual will amass, so to speak, a large number of various negative factors or psychic shocks from his past lives and these become very destructive (literally speaking) in his present lifetime.

When these confluxes are so harmonically attuned or joined together, they can give rise in the physical and mental consciousness of the individual to many different kinds of aberrations. The numerous illnesses, both in medicine and in psychology, which cannot be resolved by our present-day practitioners, and which are called by certain medical terms, can be very easily dissected on this basis; and as they are unwound, so to speak, like a ball of string, can be seen to be formed from these various lifetime continuities from preceding lives which have joined together in an unrelated fashion and manner in the present tense, and cannot be re-expressed by the individual in a normal life continuity.

This will be the basis of the medicine which will be practiced in some future time on the surface of the planet earth; when that time arrives, medical and psychological science will be much more completely serviceable than the present-day medicine and psychology which relates man only to the present. In that future day, too, we can resolve in a scientific and tangible manner, all of the numerous differences, both physical and mental, in any individual's life, not on the basis of some primitive elemental witchcraft, but in a purely scientific manner and form which will completely dissolve these various psychisms which are universally troubling mankind at the present.

Yes, we can even resolve the present cold war on the same basis; that our differences between this country and the great nation across the sea could easily be resolved when it is understood that this was a great parallax of many wars which have happened to mankind in the past. In the more purely esoterical

26

sense, these past wars were not resolved as constructive continuities in the expression of any man or any
nation, therefore they reside, so to speak, in the interdimensional form and manner as great negative confluxes. When these many wars were so joined together
in the present by the way, manner, and form in which
people live nowadays, they were harmonically attuned
to each other making one huge, great parallax or
joining of all of these various past wars, and which
now hangs like a great black cloud over the face of
the earth.

If mankind understood this principle he would be
able to very quickly and easily dissolve this great
karmic condition. For karma, which it truly is, and
as it must be truly seen, is the residual form of any
particular energy expression which is lived in some
former time and which reasserts itself in the present
in an unrelated manner to this present time. War
therefore is an obsession; it has obsessed individuals
and nations since the beginning of man's evolution
upon the surface of the earth. It will continue to do so
until mankind understands the Infinite, as a regenerative pattern of energy expressions which must always be related to each other on the basis of positive
and negative recurrences, and in such other scientific
aspects as have been so thoroughly explained in the
various texts of Unarius.

These things must always be so constructively
evaluated, not in the sense that they are purely materialistic values, but that the materialistic values as
they so appear are only the results of these interdimensional interplays of Infinite Consciousness as
they reassert themselves in this Infinite abstraction.
We cannot at any time resort to the more primitive
expressions as they exist in the world today. Science
has no reasonable explanation for the beginning of
anything, nor does it have a reasonable explanation
for its end; simply because science has not yet related

itself to the interdimensional factors.

The same conditions exist in the field of many religious forms as they exist on the surface of the earth; these things too, are all unrelated in themselves inasmuch as they do not include the necessary scientific factors and aspects of interdimensional consciousness as they are continuously expressed by the great Infinite Intelligence.

Look for the various obsessive forms of consciousness in your daily life and learn to cancel them out on the basis that these things are now unrelated, re-expressive forms appearing in your present-day life from out your many past lifetimes. They will cease to be obsessive and life will become a much more factual continuity of Infinite expression.

# CHAPTER 3

## A Destruction of Religious Fantasies

Almost everyone who has lived in contact with Western civilizations who, religiously speaking, professed Christianity, has heard certain familiar phrases or clichés which were uttered by the evangelistic expressionists of this religion; these phrases being such as "The Lord Jesus Christ" or "Accepting the Lord Jesus Christ as your personal Savior," etc. At the time of utterance there are several factors immediately apparent: the person who utters them does so in a manner and way which suggests to an observer, trained in certain psychological manifestations, that this person is traveling under a traumatic hypnotic trance which has been induced by a combination of strong psychic pressures, such as guilt complexes, fears, etc.

The untrained observer, however, does not and can not analyze the psychological position of this religious evangelist or adventist. In fact, he may be easily victimized and be also projected into the same trance-like hallucination by a combination of similar psychic rapports with previous religious contacts lived in other lives, all culminating in a conveniently expressed escape mechanism i.e., "Accepting the Lord Jesus Christ as your personal Savior." It has not occurred either to the evangelist or to his newly subjugated or intended victim, to completely and thoroughly analyze the religion which he so expresses, or rather that he is believing he is expressing. For there is, in truth, no similar parallel in his current expression and the gospel of life as taught by Jesus of Nazareth. Therefore, let us enter into a constructive historical analyses.

The phrase "Lord Jesus Christ," is obviously a merging of two personalities, brought about in long term usage by uninformed people. The noun, "lord," is a designation commonly used to signify an all powerful personality. In the case of the evangelist, the "lord" has a direct connotation and reference to the Old Testament Jehovah. Jehovah, in turn, is a more recent re-pronunciation of the designation Jahweh, an ancient Babylonian god, worshiped by Father Abraham; and which later (by Mohammed) became transposed into Allah. Therefore, "lord" is Jehovah, Jahweh, Allah, and he is also Ahura-Mazda, or Zoroaster, the more modern counterpart of Osiris in Egyptology. In all cases, however, and by whatever names designated, religious liturgies concerning these god configurations always contained certain basic parallels which are also being currently expressed in Christianity.

Paradoxically enough, the mission of Jesus was to destroy this god concept and to replace it with the Christ Principle, or the "Father within" each person, which was the personal development of abstract consciousness, attained through countless earth-life experiences as a *personal polarizing process of self* in each expression with a similar facsimile of experience posed in the Infinite. Knowledge of the experience could then remain, in essence, with the individual, which, when included with an infinite number of such polarized experiences, comprised and developed this higher Superconscious Christ Self and when it could be assumed that development reached a certain stage, could be the all-inclusive and dominant expressive personality with this person.

How then, save through ignorance, could the evangelist merge these two entirely different and opposite personalities—one a fictitious development of mystical ideologies, the other a realistic scientific development of an abstract personality actually endowed in some ultimate and with all of the god-like qualities and proclivities of the fictitious personality and with none of his temperamental vicissitudes.

In line with this historical analyses and in conjunction with psychological factors of personal development, it becomes quite obvious that Christianity is not a religion; neither can it fulfill any promises of personal salvation to any person. For, here again, the purpose of personal development is completely nullified in the "Christ Savior" position, adopted by the evangelist. The duped victim is now traveling in a twilight zone. Through his belief in salvation that Jesus died for his sins, or that he has been automatically relieved of these sins, through "belief" etc., he now has no personal moral responsibilities either to himself or to his fellow man.

In his make-believe world of fantasy and shadow, he is constantly confronted with two unrealistic opposites in his religion. The conflict between two opposite doctrines; the purported subjugation to damnation and hell as the price paid for a sinful life; yet, on the other hand, complete salvation by merely believing that he can be saved by "the Lord Jesus Christ." How then, could any sane human being rationalize a moral course of action in his daily life which would be utterly impossible to any person, save that he was temporarily, at least transported into a hypnotic trance-like condition which was sufficiently strong to blind him to the obvious differences in his religious fantasy?

The pages of history portray many strange and weird practices performed, individually and collectively, by races of people all basically interpreted as their religion. In fact, they are still continuously being re-expressed and readapted or merged into new adaptations or other religious forms.

Population wise, numerically speaking more than a billion people embrace a religion which has, as its predominant deification, the old Chaldean god, Jahweh, currently re-expressed as Jehovah and Allah, which also have other current similarities. Mohammed, and Jesus, the one and only prophet, indigenous to each religion which, in itself, presents a great contradiction; for unless Mohammed was Jesus incarnate (which he was not) the two religions would thus be proportionately contradictory.

There are more than 800 million Christians believing Jesus to be their personal savior; more than 600 million Mohammedans give Mohammed much the same position, and there are more than twice this combined number who place Buddha as their personal interpretation of a divine configuration with Brahma, who also is a parallel configuration of Jahweh; and Brahma, which likewise subdivides divinity into Shiva and Vishnu—the devil and Christ.

In the face of this great preponderant mass of evidence, certain personal realizations must be objectively realized. It cannot be rationalized, that because great populations believe in certain deistic configurations, they are necessarily true merely because of the number of believers. This signifies a much more important philosophical concept; that people of the earth, as a whole, are presently engaged in an evolutionary metamorphosis—that this same evolution has been going on for thousands of years. In this sense, the earth can be likened to a certain elemental grade in a modern grade school; small children coming into this grade, learn its curriculum and pass on into the next higher one, etc.

In the end we can visualize the earth man, past, present, and future, as involved in an elemental stage of his evolution. The many lives he lives on the earth can be likened to the many days he will live in his school classroom; and when, after a certain threshold of mental development is reached, he will graduate, so to speak, into one or more somewhat higher planets, where life is again resumed in the same evolutionary sequence, but in a somewhat more advanced technology.

To conclude then, certain constructive extractions can now be obtained from our analyses. As Emerson said, "Be yourself, imitation is suicide." Therefore, we also, as Truth seekers, constructively minded on our evolutionary pathway, must learn to detach ourselves from the herd and the blind, sheep-like attitude which often destroys sheep in their reaction to fear. After detaching ourselves, we must stand firmly upon the rock of personal and moral responsibility to the evolutionary principle of creation.

Upon this rock we must introspectively view the many and sundry dispensations of life, including the religion of our fellow man as merely his first approach to understanding the Infinite; in his various reactive interpretations of life, he has begun to form the first tenuous strands of projected thought which, like some climbing vine, he is trying to reach into the Infinite; trying to select various aspects of the Infinite as they so present themselves to him in his daily life. We will thus see that while the material or physical man as he so lives in his daily earth life, has not yet developed the more abstract mental conception, he is still vitally concerned with life as a reactive force which reaches through every daily dispensation.

He must therefore erect various compromising con-figurations, such as political and religious systems, which in turn, must again be subdivided into his own personal code of ethics. This then, is the world of today just as it has been for thousands of years. The same basic principles of material, physical reaction are just as predominant today as they ever were in any past historical epoch; and with all these num-erous reactionary elements, religion still occupies the same niche.

To the Truth seeker therefore, the strongest em-phasis must be placed upon personal moral integrity —not to be swayed by what seems to be masses of circumstantial evidence as they are generated en masse by populations. The supreme and ultimate goal of any human is personal emancipation from rote systems and the rhetorical minds which support them; for as these systems are constantly regenerated, so they pass; and with them the populations who liv-ed them and supported them.

If immortal life is to be attained by any human, it must be attained in a logical sequence of evolution which develops his mental capacity to such extensive proportions that he can live and function without dogma, creed, or rhetorical elements. He must live as a creative element or entity that functions re-con-structively with the Infinite. For this is indeed the way the Infinite Itself lives; the Infinite which not only created all forms and substances, but is constantly re-creating, and in this constant resurgence of re-crea-tion, is always the sum and total of all things.

It is clearly indicated in the idiom of our modern 20th century science, that no religion can be scien-tifically supported or proven. Biblical depictions are either archaeological history, or are fictitious and legendary in nature. Religion, therefore can practically be assumed as passé—it belongs more properly to the primitive aborigines who still roam the jungles.

As of today, science has opened the door to an entirely new dimension of understanding. Through the atom and associated fields of electronics, astrophysics, etc., mankind is, as a whole, approaching an entirely new concept, which can be referred to as the future religion of mankind.

Could it be prophetically assumed that in the passing thousands of years, our present day Christianity will reside in the museums, where it can be viewed by the visitor along with other antique objects as an amusing depiction of man's historical development? Amusing, yes, if it were not so tragic. To the countless millions who have died in the godless bigotry of their religion, to the countless other billions who have constantly been waylaid, thwarted, and plunged into miserable hells of physical and mental illnesses by religion, the superman of tomorrow who so views religion in antiquity, must do so with the moral lesson ever apparent.

Never again will he permit churches and temples to be erected to house the false gods of his supposition; he must ever be alert in his moral position to the Infinite; always constructively biased and minded, always independently expressing the Infinite into his daily life, and always finding a common brotherhood in the same expression with his fellow man.

# CHAPTER 4

## "Introspection"
## A Constant Challenge to Man

It is universally recognized by any philosophically minded individual, that our present day scientific technocracy and subsequent way of life present some obvious disparities. We have, in this technocracy, and through systems of communication, placed all races and nations of mankind in one great community, almost instantly accessible and a common property of all; yet instead of finding a companionable brotherhood, life in this earth community has now become a time of great stress and friction between various existing national factions, often resulting in bloodshed as seen in various revolutionary movements and a general holocaust is being prevented only by the thought of an all inclusive destruction.

Another apparent disparity is contained in the field of materia medica and associated psychology, and here again, while there apparently seems to be some knowledge of human anatomy and psychic dispositions, yet these various practitioners are daily confronted with an ever-increasing rising tide of insoluble conditions and enigmas. In the field of education, there are also enigmas and disparities which are constantly being increased and strengthened by the ever-growing additions of new knowledge.

In order to enter into a constructive evaluation of these seemingly great paradoxes, disparities, and enigmas, it is necessary to reduce all human factors of relationship into a common derivative which classifies all mankind in his various earth life dispensations as psychic; or more specifically, that he is—scientifically speaking—an electronic instrument, wherein the physical body assumes a robot-like position, expressing various physical reactions as part of the normal process of a vast number of vibrating wave forms which stem from a psychic anatomy and which, in this oscillating process, re-synthesizes in the wave form vortexes of the psychic anatomy, a counterpart of cell re-growth in the physical anatomy.

The concept of the psychic anatomy, its development through reincarnation or evolution, its growth and reformation in future lives, is a wide departure from the physical sciences as currently expressed in materia medica, and psychology. At this point the author wishes to make his position clear; he has no quarrel with science as science exists in an infinite conception. His issue is with the pedantic demigods of science who have, in their rhetorical dispositions, prevented the solution of the seemingly insoluble; they have curtailed on every front, every constructive endeavor to probe into the vast unknown nearby dimensions.

Heading the long list of these material minded demigods is Sigmund Freud, and perhaps no other person has contributed so much to the downfall of humanity. For in the presentation of a false and sterile psychology, he has attracted, in its contents, a horde of expressionists who are mentally insufficient to express themselves beyond the ironbound reaches of this pedantic demagoguery. The concept of life as postulated by Freud, has as its cornerstone—sex; and all human relationships must be interpreted as sexually motivated. This is extremely contradictory in the basic element of presentation, for as presented by Freud, sex is an instinct.

The concept that all newborn infants have a sterile mind smacks strongly of empiricism, postulated by Locke, the 16th century English philosopher; and here again it is defeated by the admission of one instinct. If the newborn infant has one instinct then, this automatically determines a continuation of instinct into its originating place.

Present-day psychology believes in the prenatal infant life, or that in the gestation period the fetus forms its first basic likes and dislikes or fears. This is also a contradiction to the Freudian instinct and also suggests and mandates a further continuation of the origin of reactionary reason, as expressed by the fetus; for if such a newly forming infant can react and form conclusions or basic fears within the womb, then, it must be concluded that there is some reasoning power.

It has also been determined by the encephalograph that all reasoning processes are actual wave form transmissions which are not part of the function or expression of the genes or chromosomes which started the growth of the infant. Therefore, reason was *not* inherited nor inducted by the infant. Also, it is well known that the infant is completely enclosed in a strong bag-like placenta, completely isolated, so far as nerve intercourse from the mother is concerned. Here too, reason could not be induced from the mother, and must be concluded that reason had its existence or origin in an adjacent dimension wherein this spiritual or psychic anatomy actually lived before the moment of conception.

Following this introspection that we have now arrived at the point where we can visualize a psychic anatomy or counterpart of a human living in an adjacent dimension this too, must be further concluded and investigated. The psychic anatomy cannot be considered spontaneous regeneration. It can be definitely proven that various precocities, proclivities, talents, gifts, etc., are not some mysterious handing out process by some god who favors a few; but are actual carry-overs, from former developmental phases which have been incurred in diverse life to life experiences and which can properly explain the true origin of precocities and (so-called) gifts.

It can also explain what an instinct really is; that there is a carry-over from life to life of a certain way of life, or a portion of life as is lived by every human. The newborn infant is therefore not relegated to merely one basic animal-like instinct which is necessary in procreation; nor can psychology be explained by any similar additions such as the gregarity, or herd instinct, which was added by Carl Jung.

Neither can the newborn infant be presupposed to have a completely sterile mind. At the moment of his birth, he has already formed definite likes and dislikes. The knowledge of prenatal life was well-known to the Chinese 6000 years ago and every Chinaman is automatically one year old at his birth. Even more important, the Chinaman also knows about reincarnation and how the people continue to live life after life as a normal sequence of evolution.

Strange indeed then it is, that our modern highly developed sciences have excluded these basic age-old scientific concepts and have relegated mankind into the misty world of spontaneous regeneration, which has neither fact nor reason for its existence; and is constantly being defeated in itself, not only by the pragmatically inclusive admission of even one instinct, but by the fruits which it has born in its administration.

For as science is a dominant influence in the world

39

of today, and in particular materia medica and psychology, thus science could turn the rising tide of confusion and despair; it could quiet the waters of international turmoil; it could solve all the enigmas; it could cure all incurable conditions; in short, it could point the evolution of mankind in the direction of the constructive, ever-progressive, Utopia, where man could advance as an earth individual who was so minded in the evolutionary factors of his life, that he was given the full import of his moral responsibility; that he knew all his thoughts and actions were creative effigies, either constructive or destructive, which would remain with him forever.

He would also be ever mindful that what he received from life would be a proportionate facsimile of the effort which he put into it, and all his sins and iniquities would be either directly or vicariously inherited by him from his past life-to-life dispensations as he impounded them in his psychic anatomy.

The future is infinite and presents a great challenge to any individual who can so visualize the Infinite; a challenge met in every action of everyday life, always matched in future life-to-life meetings of this great challenge. Nor can it be as St. George conquered the dragon. Life as the infinite challenge is never conquered—it is never concluded; each life presenting new vistas, new horizons which constantly tax the utmost mental and physical capabilities of any human so mindful of them.

So let us not become another Freud, a Jung, an Einstein, or a Newton; let us never lay down for our fellow man a circumscribed dimension; for the circumference of this circumscription will only include the limited dimension of the present horizon; and it will appeal only to eyes which can see a justification of their life within its circumference. Instead, let us be infinitely minded; we must always present within ourselves an unlimited horizon, never circumscribed. We must show to our fellow man the benefits of the unlimited introspection, by relaying into our lives the positive elements as they are so contained in the Infinite Perspectus, by manifesting them as the necessary physical impedimenta, the appurtenances and sustenances which are necessary for us to maintain progressive continuity into the future.

# CHAPTER 5

## Prayer vs. Frequency Attunement

It is granted by the author, that all past and present scientists, whose names grace the documents of history, have made definite contributions to man's general fund of knowledge in understanding the Infinite; yet because these concepts were not presented infinitely and as a small part of the whole, they had, as a consequence, an adverse or destructive effect. The contribution of Einstein in reducing mass and energy to a mathematical formula should have been the starting place of an interdimensional science; instead it became the atom bomb and eventually the present-day threat of nuclear warfare, so great in its danger, it is a deterrent to war; but nevertheless, existing as it does in the fear-ridden minds of the earth's population, it has sent thousands of humans into their back yards digging bomb shelters in some mad race for survival.

The mathematics of Newton became a focal point in various trials used by the courts of inquisition to send some poor unfortunate to his death at the stake or on the gallows; yet Newton's mathematics survived, becoming the basic understanding of physical law and motion and which is still preventing, to some extent, the escape of mankind into the free dimension of infinite introspection which has, as its expressionary element, neither a mathematical formula, nor an ecclesiastical dispensation.

Understanding the Infinite is an individual proposition acquired only in reliving the infinity of evolutionary expression. It is not reducible to a mathematical formula, neither can it be symbolized in deistic configurations; it is a more ultimate attainment compounded from infinite experiences, extractions of values, positive and negative, destructive or constructive, which blends the universal conception of Infinity in the landscape of the beholder, and as he so beholds, so he is.

Divergence of opinions, cloistered concepts, segregated races, profusion of pageantries, exuberances and depressions, are only the mania of a material world, for in the quiet of Infinite Perspectus any individual has, simultaneously, achieved the four seasons of reason. He is within and without, all dimensions, he is in conscious conformity with Infinity as a regenerative element in a subliminal creative expression which far transcends the vegetative life lived by the earth man.

Now that we have entered into the subject of prayer, and that the fat is in the fire, so to speak, let us continue on in our analysis into a more scientific interpretation. Up until this point we have generalized religion, its associated concepts, such as prayer as a contradiction to the science of life as taught by Jesus, and to present-day scientific knowledge.

Another way to understand prayer and its origin is to visualize it as one of the decadent forms of scientific expression which had their origin either in ancient civilizations, such as Lemuria and Atlantis, or in interplanetary expressions lived by more highly developed people. The ancient Lemurians taught the interdimensional concept of mind function, just as it is presented in our present-day Unarius. In fact, I am one of the original teachers. However, I am finding it almost as difficult today as it was 150,000 years ago, for in that time just as in the present, the aboriginal peoples of the earth were, and still are in a comparatively low state of evolution; excepting of course, those people who, in this present day, have gone through various progressive stages of development through the past ages which will enable them to fulfill and justify through preparation in Unarius.

The science of living must ultimately be resolved into a pure mind function, devoid of either impelling physical stimulus or subsequent physical reaction. On the mental plane, consciousness is an absolute integration of Infinite Consciousness which justifies all motions and apparent impedences as regenerative continuities of expression. Reaction, therefore, is never destructive, but is always seen as a regenerative remanifestation of its particular form.

Now, at this point, it must be understood this is a very scientific function which involves the mechanics of various oscillating polarities. In other words, the interchange of concept or form between various polarities is dynamically balanced as positive or negative, like a teeter-totter. The child who is temporarily up in the air is the positive, then as the board moves the cycle is reversed, then the other child assumes the positive position, remembering of course, that in the transference of concept from one pole to another, one must always be negative or lack what the other or positive pole possesses.

This can be seen as a two-way interchange of consciousness between higher dimensions of understanding and the lower dimensions which lack and need this understanding. This is the basic concept of positive regeneration from the higher Infinite into the lower more negative planes of expression. These lower forms are then inseminated, we shall say, with the higher concepts; then in turn these are remanifest into a still lower or outward physical plane and lower

44

negative polarities. The positive wave-form goes to polarize an abstract facsimile in the Higher Superconscious Self of the psychic anatomy where it again regenerates, as I have previously described. This is a never-ending psychic process.

At this point we will enter into another and equally important concept called psychokinetics. Obviously it should be most desirous for every person to not only incept or receive higher dimensional intelligence, but that he should learn to use and direct it constructively and in a greater quantity than could heretofore be done in the mere earth life transpositions.

The reality of this concept as it was taught in Lemuria to the aboriginal minds, became the basis for all past and present known forms of various kinds of magic, (black and white) necromancy, signs, portents, witchcraft, incantations, as well as the various ecclesiastical forms claimed to be performed by various priesthoods.

The casting out of evil spirits, or casting out an evil spell, are also part of the original Lemurian concepts which, through the childish minds of the earth people, degenerated into these various magical forms. In this sense, religion is just an outgrowth of these various mystical forces which are somehow vaguely recognized by all mankind and vastly different from the concept taught by the Lemurians who said, "Knowledge is power."

By knowing about the Infinite, any individual can become selective on the basis of frequency attunement. He can consciously accept or reject any or all parts of the Infinite which are constantly oscillating into the psychic anatomy; and on the basis of acceptance or rejection, he can attain a better and more fruitful life. Various wave forms which are not, at that moment of inception, constructive in nature, are not, therefore, contained in the psychic anatomy and do not remain with it; but oscillate through it just as a

45

radio wave can oscillate past your radio without being known or heard, unless you tune your radio to it.

The reverse situation is also quite true. Every person, physical or spiritual, is actually a broadcasting and receiving station. They are constantly radiating into the various dimensions the sum and total of everything which they are. This is done, just as is the TV transmission, on a basic sine wave frequency, and in this simple wave form, they are literally broadcasting into Infinity an exact replica or facsimile of everything that has ever happened to them which they have experienced or even thought about.

To the person who has trained himself to receive these messages and to tune into these various sine wave frequencies, every person becomes an open book. This fact, I have proven in countless thousands of past incidents where I have minutely described various daily happenings, objects, etc., to total strangers who knew of these things only unto themselves. This I am doing today and will continue to do so, and which is, incidentally, one of the demonstrative or dramatically provable aspects of the science which I am teaching.

Also, this science and the subsequent higher way of life can be acquired by anyone; furthermore the proper understanding and usage of this science, not only insures a more peaceful and productive life, but insures an eternal life lived in higher spiritual worlds where this science is lived by everyone, and not by a few visitors who come from these higher worlds to the earth world to demonstrate the reality of life.

Psychokinetics, in the broad frame of reference, includes such paranormal functions as astral projection, clairvoyance, clairaudience, etc. Understanding this science has enabled me to appear in different parts of the world, to people at moments of great stress. Some of these people have written their description of my appearance at that time; others have felt my presence. I am stating these facts, not because I wish to be deified or called a mystic; I wish to be known only as a brother to humanity who has come to the world at this propitious time to teach the higher extensions of scientific knowledge, which is a conclusion to the preparatory phase which I helped to teach 150,000 years ago.

The reason for this is because the aboriginal people of that time later reappeared in Atlantis in somewhat more highly developed lives. They who helped destroy Atlantis are reappearing in this present century as various scientists who are attempting to repay their debt and sin by rebuilding what they destroyed.

Others too, not destructively involved at that time are appearing as devotees or seekers and always find a climax to their search when they contact Unarius. Psychokinesis, then becomes the practical reality of life; a life lived in an existence which functions simultaneously and harmoniously with the Infinite—a regenerative principle of life that receives and re-creates what it has received. Therefore all is done in perfect conception and with the vastness of an Infinite and unlimited perspectus.

Throughout the various books and works of Unarius, I have taken great care to avoid the personal innuendo. I know too well the proclivity of human minds to deify the abstraction in a personal image; this somehow seems to temporarily absolve them— so they think—of the necessity of learning and assuming the moral responsibility of their lives. I have often said, "If I am ever deified, my cause is lost; and in losing my cause, those whom I have come to help are also lost in this deification." This was so with Jesus, with Buddha, with Mohammed, and with many others. For the true esoterical value of whatever they understood or taught was soon lost in the great preponderance of distortions and compromises which always arose in the minds of men, as a means to alleviate them from assuming the true responsibility of their lives as it was taught by such men as Jesus. For this must always be as it has always been, purely a personal relationship with the Infinite in which the Infinite is progressively understood, and becomes a part of the thought and action of every human.

# CHAPTER 6

## A Scientific Analysis of Prayer

Throughout various epistles of Unarius, great stress and emphasis has been placed upon learning a new way of life, a new way to think; and in line with these presentations, it has been constantly re-emphasized that the student should learn to desist from various age-old habits and practices and begin practicing his new-age future life technocracy.

Foremost among the age-old practices is that of prayer; and inasmuch as the new aspirant may be somewhat shocked by the sudden realization that prayer is most often quite useless, it is a subterfuge, an escape mechanism, or an obvious device wherein any prayerful supplicant is, in reality, talking himself into a passive state of mind. Some people may be so aroused in this new approach, that they may be inclined to try to vindicate their personal beliefs in prayer. They may assert that they have had prayers answered, or that they may know of many instances of others who have had prayers answered. They may also wonder and ask, "How are we going to get help?" or in some extreme cases certain individuals may be aroused to angry indignation. Realizing all the implications involved in presenting this new approach and new way of life, there must be a direct and conclusive answer, scientifically and logically presented, which will override the miasmic illusion; the illusion of mind under which the aspirant has heretofore been traveling.

Therefore, let us analyze this prayer situation, and find out if there is any truth in its generally practiced concept; or is there a better way? Entering very broadly in a philosophical stance, we must first assume that every human is a definite entity in the evolutionary scale which is a part and principle of the Infinite; and that this entity is, so far as the Infinite is concerned, presumably destined to evolve into higher states of consciousness. Therefore, it cannot be presumed, so far as the individual is concerned, that any position which he is now occupying in the scale of evolution can be considered the ultimate; for as long as consciousness, individually and collectively, assumed en masse, as a collective form and expression of life, and as these collective expressions are materialistic in nature, therefore, any and all of those individuals are functioning under a system of symbologies which, when incepted, instigate certain reactionary processes.

Conversely, with any individual or culture which lives purely within the concept of principle in action, in an interdimensional stance, and without reactionary stimulations or repercussions, but as an equalized oscillating function with the Infinite, then those more highly advanced functioning entities can be considered god-like, in the sense that they have passed beyond the dimension of symbology as it is lived on the planet earth. In other words, it can be correctly assumed—in fact, science as of this time and day directly admits as much—that in the great universes, there are conceivably, planets whereon people live, either in lower or higher forms of life. However, it cannot be assumed that these people, universally, either understand or know of the various religions which are a part of the earth life. These people too, all play their own role in the scale of evolution, and are as much a part of the Infinite Consciousness as the most devout Christian, even though they have not heard of Jesus or the so-called Christian way to salvation. They, like all other humans who have not heard of Christianity, are equally entitled to this progressive evolution. They, so far as the Infinite is concerned, are equally important; for the Infinite does not have a personal relationship on an emotional basis with humanity, either Christian or otherwise.

So far as the Infinite is concerned, people are somewhat like the cells or atoms in your body. It would be extremely difficult for you to separate these individual cells and atoms and enter into an emotional dispensation with them. Yet, as a whole they usually live and function perfectly without your direct conscious knowledge or direction. This situation is much more infinitely expressed with the Infinite; for the Infinite is not only the function and principle, the mentality, but is also the substance.

Therefore, when you pray, if you are praying to God, as you formerly supposed God to be, you are, in reality, trying to talk to all of the stars or suns, all the planetary systems with all their peoples, all the diverse forms of life, all the numerous resurgent dimensions of energy configurations, all the higher and more advanced intellects; yes, even all of those who inhabit the subastral worlds, (pits of hell).

Obviously, this is quite an irrational and asinine procedure; for your prayers or thoughts not being tangibly projected, either by form or substance, or by the correct knowledge as to whom you are praying, could obviously go astray. Moreover, as prayer is, in itself, always a negative approach, it is therefore negatively biased and can only harmonically attune itself to an infinite number of negative configurations.

How different is the more positive approach which can be used and is always correctly assumed, when any individual who possesses the proper knowledge and function of the Infinite, is therefore, with this knowledge, positively biased. He sees the plan, the purpose, and the completion of various cyclic transmissions in their respective expressions throughout the Infinite macrocosm; and in this realization, automatically assumes the correct positive bias and therefore can incept and receive into his daily life, a proportionate constructive expression.

To those who may say, "I have had prayers answered or seen them answered, etc.," let us examine if there is any basis for the assumption that prayer has been answered, especially in the manner ascribed to it. In common logistics, mathematicians have proven that according to the law of averages all things work out or transpire on the basis of 60 per cent. In other words, out of ten instances where prayer was thought to be answered, six of these would have occurred without prayer. This leaves only four which can be considered extraterrestrial in nature or that they may be called miraculous.

A miracle is only the transpiring of some tangible conscious objectivism without any known means or agencies. However, in pure science there are no unknown factors or agencies; every miracle must have certain basic reactive principles involved, even though these may not be known to those who witness the so-called miracle. Therefore, in pure science there are no miracles, and this is quite true in all instances. Yes, even the so-called miracles depicted in the New Testament have very scientific basic principles involved in their transmission and are therefore, really not a miracle at all, in the commonly accepted frame of reference.

Yes, and it can be considered that present day scientific knowledge has not yet extended into the extraterrestrial dimensions where those certain scientific principles are being constantly expressed. Consider then how do you expect your prayers to be answered if you do not know of the interdimensional, extraterrestrial principles which must be called into play before the miracle can be consummated. Again you are leaving much to blind chance; or, going on the assumption that here is some kind of a god personality, who, theoretically, can see and hear all things simultaneously, not only as things transpire on the earth, but in the Infinite Universe as well. This too, is an infantile supposition, and yet when the Infinite is properly understood, the Infinite does see and hear all things infinitely; not only as they are occurring, but without time. The Infinite is also seeing and hearing all the past and all the future.

This is done according to the principle of harmonic attunement as it involves the Infinite in all Its cyclic interplay. As you are, at any given time, individually speaking, only the sum and total of what you can conceive, how much more logical it would be, therefore, that, instead of blind prayer, you could conceive, to some extent, the Infinite in this broad extraction; and in this conception, you could visualize the more highly developed or progressive infinite evolution; and within this conception, you would re-express it into your daily life.

The comparison here is somewhat analogous to sitting behind the wheel of a car and praying for it to run and steer itself; whereas, the more intelligent approach is to obtain and use basic operating knowledge of how to drive. The same approach holds true with your future evolution. You must possess sufficient basic knowledge to direct your vehicle of life in a constructive and progressive evolution.

Therefore, so far as the remaining four seeming miracles were concerned, these remained miracles, because some unknown factor, element, or power, apparently performed a task which was beyond the normal capacity of any human expression. Here again a correct scientific analysis must be entered into.

Each instance may represent different conditions,

but in all cases these so-called miracles were the direct result of scientific principle in action and not because some supposed god-like or deistic being commanded it to be so. Even when the more advanced personalities, such as Jesus, aided or instigated what appeared to be a miracle, the principle in action was expressed in each case. Jesus always asked, "Believeth thou this?" referring to the faith or the possibility of conception with the individual involved. Then He stated, "Thy faith has made thee whole," or "By thy faith be it added unto thee," and in no instance did Jesus personally pray or enter into a miracle. When asked about miracles, Jesus said, "Of myself I do nothing, it is the Father within, which doeth all things."

Obviously, the Father is the principle in action, and this Father also had to "live" within every person; otherwise the miracle could not have occurred. It can be rightfully assumed at this point, that all people who had miraculous transformations, were preconditioned for this advent, not only in their present, everyday circumstances, and when they first heard of Jesus, but in the spiritual lives in between earth lives, they had witnessed spiritual healings and they had, in essence, their own personal spiritual healing before reincarnating into the earth life; to seek out such a person as Jesus who would automatically establish a spiritual rapport, which would, in turn, complete in a physical sense, the spiritual healing.

It must be remembered at this point, that the reconstructive physical process in which eyes were made whole or leprosy cured, happened at the time when complete psychic cancellation occurred in the psychic anatomy; thus being made whole, immediately reflected a strong and powerful perfect image into the physical anatomy, which rearranged automatically and molecularly, the conformity of the perfect psychic image, thus resulting in the perfectly healed physical anatomy.

In this sense then, time was merely separated from the individual healing transmission, for it could be reasonably assumed that all people involved in miraculous healings would be healed of their condition in any proper well-ordered progressive evolution. The value of a miracle, therefore, can be severely questioned, and could be reasonably supposed to be an invalid circumstance in such a normal progression. Many people who witness miracles become fanatically obsessed with an escape mechanism, or they may assume, in their fantasy, that they, too, are miracle workers. They may falsely assume their own personal miracle and in various fantasies, influence, coerce, dominate, and even proselytize more normal individuals into accepting their false fantasy.

In the erection of the Christian Church, this same fantasy has been largely entered into; not only in spiritual healing, but into any and all dominant factors of life. The hierarchy of the various Christian denominations all wield to some extent, this same fanatical power, which is, in actual reality, a crude and materialistic attempt to sublimate all earth life expressions into deistic configurations expressed and moderated by church systems.

In conclusion, therefore, miracles are not denied; their value, however, is questioned; especially when a miracle may occasionally occur in circumstances where those individuals so involved do not have a proper and constructive valence of evolutionary principle and Infinite Perspectus. So, if you must pray, pray then for the miracle of understanding; for understanding the Infinite will assure you the greatest of all miracles—eternal life; substantiated in the inclusion of not only everyday experiences, but the inclusion of the complete philosophy of creation and the function of its principle.

Almost needless to say, when your prayer has been

answered, and the miracle of understanding begins to manifest in your life, then prayer will proportionately be seen as your first elemental attempt to personally contact the great unknown which was, at that time in your past life, superimposed as some god image. You can also be quite sure that with the miracle of understanding, a proportionate amount of various terrestrial diseases and negations will cease to plague you, and as they vanish, the seeming need for prayerful supplication also vanishes, as it is replaced by a more intelligent approach to the evolutionary principle.

It would be wise, therefore, at this moment, to completely dedicate yourself to the new proposition of life—understanding the Infinite; to cease to rely on any pantheologies, deistic doctrines, symbolic expressions, prayerful attitudes, and after discarding them, earnestly seek the Kingdom of Heaven within; a kingdom which will never be found so long as you rely on the various pacifism's of your materialistic world.

# CHAPTER 7

## The Life of Jesus Explained

Any person who tries to constructively analyze the problems of human nature, is always impressed with a certain extreme perversity which any and all persons do, occasionally, express in their daily lives. This extreme perverse vicissitude of human nature can so dominate an individual that he will pursue an irrational course or an illogical reason, despite overwhelming persuasion for him to desist his irrational pursuance.

In general classifications, it can therefore be seen that of the 800-odd million Christians, people are largely pursuing the same irrational and illogical course in their professed Christianity despite overwhelming scientific and historical knowledge which completely invalidates this religion and reduces it to a null status. It is a reconformity of age-old paganistic expressions and doctrines which can be correctly assumed to be, in certain psychological stances, a life-robbing, demoralizing, coercive power which makes any adherent, not only morally irresponsible, but robs him of his personal right to think.

However, despite this great and overwhelming evidence against Christianity, this religion is, as of today, even stronger than it has ever been; partially because of the aforementioned perversities of human nature, and partially because of the extreme pressurization which demands the necessity of an escape mechanism, in lieu of a more constructive and intelligent approach to life and its problems. Therefore, among the ecclesiasts of this religious system, the priests are, perhaps, the strongest and most dominant expression; and incidentally, in their training in various seminary schools, these student priests are taught the true background and history of their religion which, for obvious reasons, must be suppressed and never brought to the unsuspecting mass of adherents who are always demanding that the priesthood preach and dispense religious concepts which are understandable to them.

There is also among classifications of ecclesiasts another group who call themselves Bible scholars and through the sense of false mysticism these various self-styled expressionists have surrounded themselves with the glamorous, rosy aura, and their supposition, that these glamour boys do not know of the true historical background; but they must know something of the scientific evidence which tends to destroy the illusion of their religion. However, a livelyhood must be made, and it is surprising to note the number of people who will don the cloak of some religious office, or expression in order to escape the necessity of working for a living; and in this office they will figuratively speaking, "sell their souls to the devil" for the express self-satisfying purpose of, not only wielding a coercive power over their fellow citizens, but manage to extract all the necessities and many of the luxuries of life in the process.

By far, the greatest single compromising effort to retain the strangle hold of the Christian religion is now being made; and in particular, certain new additives or concepts have been included to bolster up sagging religious dispensations which are beginning to melt under the hot light of personal scientific scrutiny. The latest and most recent concept among

58

the religions and Bible scholars is the new approach to that age-old unresolved problem; "who was Jesus?"

Up until quite recently it has remained that He was the "one and only begotten son," despite the story of the creation of Adam and Eve. Now, however, the self-styled Christian scholars have come up with a new routine, and it is now believed that Jesus was God incarnate. The presentation of the new lunacy will, at first, stun and shock the rational thinker and will temporarily leave him without a comprehensive reply. However, after mental equilibrium is restored, the complete and revolting asininity of this assertion becomes apparent, and immediately suggests certain great disparities and discrepancies; for this god incarnate theory, a god who was sufficiently intelligent to create planets and universes, all forms of visible and invisible life, had suddenly become very worried and very unintelligent about his position in the scale of universal concept and decided to appear among the earth people in order to proselytize them to his cause.

Vague as this cause may be, in this respect this incarnate would have the appearance of some political campaign, for the express purpose of reinstating God in his position in the Infinite. Even worse, however, God has, in this fallacy, been reduced to a position somewhat similar to an itinerant side show barker and magician who makes a precarious and somewhat nefarious living on the outskirts of civilization.

How could it be that a God, sufficiently intelligent to create heaven and earth, would be so reduced that he would have to incarnate and make a personal appearance? Could not this intelligent God be assumed to have, in his creation, a built-in method of communication with any and all forms of life, and especially with man? Could it not also be assumed that such an intelligent deification would have a master plan, whereby all mankind could, universally speaking, through a succession of earth lives, evolve into a higher spiritual life; a master plan which would correctly and scientifically answer all the seemingly unanswered equivalents in human indispositions?

In order to understand both the intelligent God and His Master Plan, and especially in understanding Jesus, let us enter into a correct and all-inclusive hypothesis of various factors involved. Every material earth man can be considered dual in nature; that is, he has a psychic anatomy and mind, and a physical anatomy and mind which is, in actuality, one and the same in respect to the fact that the physical and psychic anatomies and their respective minds are functioning harmoniously, in all aspects of life on the basis of the oscillating principle.

It is conceivable in the normal course of evolution that any individual can become spiritually quickened or alerted; that is through contacts made in the life in between lives lived in spiritual worlds, as well as in other ways, the individual becomes aware of the higher spiritual worlds and a better way of life. When this alerted state is reached, this individual then begins to incarnate, spiritually, into some of these somewhat more advanced spiritual worlds, such as are described in the books of Unarius, where he will study in some respective chosen field, a higher and more constructive expression of his vocation. He will then don the mantle of flesh in an earthly incarnation and bring into the world some form of the more advanced constructiveness of his particular vocation. Sometime in the more distant future, he will advance in his spiritual world life, to a point where he, temporarily at least, and for an indefinite period of time, will no longer have need for any further continuance of earth life incarnations.

In this state he has actually passed the point of necessity for an earth life; he is also most likely to be involved in a very concerted and specialized effort in the pursuance of more highly advanced knowledge and wisdom. In this state of consciousness, he is only vaguely conscious in memory of his former earth lives. Soon, however, he is confronted with the inevitable. Knowledge must be acquired in a certain ratio proportionate or equal with usage. He can not practice, so to speak, his newly acquired knowledge in even higher worlds than the one in which he is presently living. He must, obviously practice and use this knowledge in lower or earth worlds. In this respect he is also prompted by the mass of human misery which he vaguely remembers, and so he sets up a plan whereby he can, in a manner of speaking, incarnate into the material worlds. He does not do this by the usual method—rebirth into the physical body. He is spiritually advanced to the point where the physical body would be impossible to him; that is, he could not reasonably support a physical body in the usual psychic anatomy oscillating fashion, and so he uses an alternate method.

First, however, he must choose a time and place for his mission, for the time so chosen is usually selected to coincide with some extraterrestrial phenomenon. In the case of the higher overself or spiritual entity of Jesus, whom we will call Mr. X, this more highly advanced spiritual personality (Mr. X), chose His time of entry to coincide with an astronomical event which was the junction of Venus and Jupiter, and when these two planets were thus so apparently merged into one bright superstar, He would make His debut, so to speak, into the material world. The scene must also be set. The people of His country must, to some extent, be preconditioned for this advent and which, in the case of the people of Israel, was begun several hundred years in advance.

Through various prognosticators such as soothsayers etc., the people of Israel were told of this future advent; the Messiah who would come from Heaven to lead them from out the intemperance and misery of their times. And so the day of the advent approached when Mr. X would, in a sense, reincarnate as was stated before. He does not actually combine his whole psychic anatomy with that of the newly growing infant forming within the womb; instead he chooses an alternate method. An earth man who, for obvious reasons, advantageously connected through parenthood to various ecclesiastical dispensations currently in effect, is preparing to and about to incarnate in the usual manner, through the mother's womb which is so advantageously situated.

Mr. X then approaches this soon to incarnate earth man and presents this proposition to him; that he will only partially live his earth life, and in an alternate manner on such suitable occasions which will occur, the earth man, psychically speaking, will temporarily step aside while Mr. X uses the earth man's physical anatomy, while he renders various external physical acts or expresses certain teachings. This was the manner and way in which Jesus, or Mr. X, actually lived the life partially described in the New Testament; and while this life was being so lived, the earth man, who properly owned the physical anatomy, would on various occasions, step aside while Mr. X (or Jesus) performed the various miracles and gave the teachings. Then the earth man would return to his body and temporarily resume the more normal earth life.

At first this earth man whom we shall call Mr. A was very much impressed at what had been going on during his absence—of course those who witnessed the miracles and heard the teachings had no way of differentiating between Mr. X and Mr. A. To them he was one and the same person. Therefore, the various teachings and acts did come to the attention of Mr. A. He had also begun to be worshipped. Now this worshipful attitude could be quite easily shrugged off by

Mr. X, who thoroughly understood human nature. To Mr. A, however, the effect was different. Gradually, his ego began to swell; he began to feel a false sense of importance. Finally he began to think it was actually he and not Mr. X who was performing all the miracles and giving the teachings.

In usurping his false position he began to become arrogant. At first, the miracles had been performed with the admonition to go and not tell anyone that a miracle had been performed for them. Later on, however, as Mr. A so usurped his false position, he began to flaunt Mr. X's position and power in the faces of the priests and pharisees calling them hypocrites. He even went into the temple courtyard and chased out some of the mendicants who were peddling religious offerings. This quite naturally aroused the ire of those in religious power, as well as those who supported the religious effigy; and Mr. A was threatened with crucifixion.

By this time he had become fanatically immersed in his self-deification. He laughed at the threat and said, "If ye destroy this temple (body) I will raise it in three days," which was subsequently done in the crucifixion. Mr. X, even as Mr. A hung on the cross, was compassionate. He continued to have Mr. A pardoned and brought down from the cross before he was actually dead, and which was done by his close followers. Mr. A was then given a mock burial in the tomb, to satisfy the priests and rabbis; and in the tomb Mr. X entered and healed the grievous wounds of Mr. A's body and re-established him in health.

In this respect, as well as in all dispensations, Mr. X had been considerably aided by thousands of spiritual entities such as doctors, lawyers, and various literates who had, at the beginning of the plan, formed an alliance with Mr. X in his earth mission dispensation through Mr. A.

Now, as Mr. A was in the tomb and was so healed

by Mr. X, and His thousands of fellow workers, He did not desert Mr. A at that moment either. The guard in front of the tomb somehow did not notice that the stone was being rolled away by some close followers. He did not notice that Mr. A emerged from the tomb and walked away with His followers. And so as Mr. A walked away into the night, He was a thoroughly chastened and saddened man. He had learned His lesson. For the next forty days and nights He remained with His followers; He stayed in the background as much as possible, letting Mr. X take full control, and perhaps the greatest good of the entire mission was accomplished in that period.

Now it began to be noised about that Mr. A was still alive, so the priests started another witch-hunt to find Him, as well as other close followers and adherents. The priests were fully determined to stamp out this religious revolution, for as the whole mission of Mr. X had been to free the people of Israel from the despotic yolk of religious dispensations, the priests quite naturally would not feel happy as long as Mr. A or a single adherent remained alive in the country.

And so the exodus of Christian adherents began. They fled to all countries, principally Greece. Foremost among the Christian persecutors was a stooge called Saul—half Roman, half Jew. He was an official instrument of the inquisition. Several years after the crucifixion, he learned that Mr. A was living in Greece under an assumed name. So Saul, armed with a cortege, started for Greece with the avowed purpose of secretly exterminating Mr. A, along with other sundry Christians.

On the way to Greece, Saul suffered a sunstroke and in the intense mental agony of the condition, experienced a great hallucination. Like all people of this time, Saul was tremendously superstitious and in the moment of recovery from sunstroke a great psychism took place within his mind; he thought he

64

saw Mr. A appear to him and ask that memorable question, "Why, therefore, dost thou persecute me?" Perhaps it was really Mr. X who contrived this psychism in the moment of emotional distress. Be that as it may, however, Saul continued his journey to Greece, but a changed man. He also changed his name to Paul and began to lay the foundation for the first Christian Church.

The history of this first beginning has been historically recorded. Paul, who was illiterate, first contrived to proselytize various existing religions then in existence; and in order for him to make his new religion attractive, he was forced to adopt many religious observances, rituals, and various pantheisms. By that time, the effect of the sunstroke had begun to wear off, and Paul, to a large extent, again became Saul.

In the role of Dean Emeritus, Paul commanded two religious converts named Ireneous and Claustedeus, who were Greek scholars, to write the Testaments, the Biblical synoptic gospels called by their respective names. In each writing Paul was dissatisfied and commanded a fresh rewriting; the inclusion of various Mithraic rituals and observances were entered in the life descriptions of Mr. A and Mr. X. These, of course, were drawn from memory and were not written by those who were, at that time, accredited with their formation. The priests however, were always confronted with the obvious necessity of being at least partially truthful in their presentations.

During this formative period, Paul returned to Jerusalem for several purposes; to obtain fresh documentaries and to recover, if possible, some family wealth which he should have inherited. During his visit he was imprisoned by the priests for seven years, during which time he was severely persecuted by the head priest Ananias, who constantly sought his death. However, Paul regained his freedom and returned to Greece where he remained until the time of his death. This, then, is the true story of Jesus, and while credited with being the greatest man who ever lived, living the greatest life, is also the most thoroughly misunderstood.

Mr. X was the highly developed spiritual entity who transcended the earth man, Mr. A, and in this transcendent affiliation contrived to fulfill and justify the highest scientific principles of regeneration which Mr. X called the "Father Within." It was Mr. X who gave the teachings, who explained the "Kingdom Within"; the plan of Infinity encompassed as "In my Father's house and its many mansions." It was Mr. X who dramatically demonstrated to the world of that time, the conclusive evidence of a miracle, but which was, in reality, an extension of scientific principle beginning in the higher spiritual planes and terminating as a wondrous miraculous happening in the eyes of the earth man.

Yes, Mr. X and Mr. A are history; a badly warped, sadly distorted, and completely malpracticed history as it now presents a dominant element in the life of the present-day Christian; and sad it is to see the blind, sheep-like attitude of some 800 million people who follow the leader through the doorway of the pagan Christian Church to an unmarked, undetermined future, which becomes a vast graveyard filled with the bones of countless billions of spiritual hopes and aspirations for a better and more immortal future. And with these skeletons of hope and aspiration, the people themselves lie helplessly in an atrophied condition awaiting to hear the fancied sound of the trumpet which, they have been told, will bring them forth from this suspended state of animation, and where they believe they can begin a senseless, useless, spiritual life in some fancied heavenly city, lived without cause or purpose, or without reason for the sheer necessity of survival.

Yet even here the Christian is not sure or safe. In "Revelations" he is told that all these multitudes of people will be assembled in the judgment day before the gates of this heavenly city; and from the uncounted and countless billions of earth people only 144,000 will be selected as residents in this city; the rest to be destroyed, even though God had taken great pains, time, and trouble to rebuild the various innumerable physical anatomies of these people and restore the souls to these bodies, He would now breathe fire and destroy them all—save 144,000!

It is sincerely hoped that the presentation of this historical background, the inclusion of scientific principles, and a broad factual realistic philosophical approach will have, by now, given the reader sufficient knowledge and determination and sufficient power to spring the lock on his prison door, the lock of religious suppression and domination which has kept man imprisoned in his earth life—lo, these many thousands of years; and with the springing of this lock, just as Mr. A, powered by Mr. X, walked forth from the tomb of His material life and began His ascension into the higher spiritual realms; likewise, an ascension is the planned ultimate for every human who can conceive the Infinite God—God who is, not only the Creator, but is also the Re-creator and the Substance of His Creation.

# CHAPTER 8

## Armageddon—Giving Up The Past

Greetings dear ones: It is nice to share with you some of the quiet moments in which we can discuss that all-important personal question, your evolution —the various factors, ways, and means in which we can constantly attain a higher elevation of life. Tonight I should like to discuss a particular topic which I shall call the Battle of Armageddon. Now, I am sure that all of you have heard or read about this particular prophecy, which supposedly describes the forces of evil or darkness which have gathered, and opposing them are the forces of the higher Worlds of Light and the Angelic Kingdoms; and the great pitched battle which will take place between these forces, supposedly on the hillsides of the Holy Land.

Now, of course many of the old parables and prophecies which we read about in books like the Bible are quite difficult to decipher and interpret into their true meaning. Very often the prophets and various other people who first gave these prophecies, or those who repeated them afterwards, were prone to exaggerate, or perhaps they were carried away by the emotions of the moment. Actually, the Battle of Armageddon, as it is so described, will not ever occur in that particular manner or fashion; in fact there is a much deeper and greater meaning which can be interpreted by each of us, inasmuch as the Battle of

Armageddon will, in truth and in purpose, be fought individually by each person as he progresses along this pathway of evolution.

The forces of evil or darkness can be said to be always with us; these are the things of our past lives, the many lives which we have lived in the past. These represent all of the various emotional vicissitudes of which we have woven our little tapestry of life as we have lived these various past episodes. We have emotionalized in such particular portrayals of personal aptitudes which can be termed hate, jealousy, greed, anger, lust, and the other different dogmatic, critical, or nagging attitudes of life; yes, even the many insecurities which have vaguely distressed us, are all part of these old emotionalisms in which we have lived in the past. And so you see these phantom forces, which are supposedly gathered on the hills of Galilee, are really our own thoughts and emotions which we have impounded in our psychic anatomies in these various past lifetimes.

The same holds quite true for the future, and it is quite probable that it will be a long time before you are ever freed from them. Needless to say that until some indefinite time in the future arrives where you can more clearly equate and recognize these emotional vicissitudes on the surface of your consciousness, progress in a constructive evolutionary manner will be impeded. In fact, it could even be reversed, should these phantom horsemen from out of the past succeed in penetrating your consciousness to the extent that they can continuously strike blows against all of the constructive knowledge and evaluations which you have made up until this particular time.

It would be well to note that these phantom horsemen, as they use their different emotional swords or spears, can appear in your consciousness in a very subtle manner. You do not really recognize they are there, except until that time when you acquire a certain particular knack of learning to recognize them immediately, the moment they appear.

When you do so, and you can see they are the old emotional vicissitudes and the vices from the past, that you will no longer countenance them nor have anything to do with them, and by adopting some of the many more positive attitudes you will naturally adopt in the concourse of time in dealing with these things, you will see that they will vanish just as the mists of the morning vanish before the rising sun. In the future you will become more and more free of them, and your mental atmosphere will be consequently much clearer and less impeded by these obstructive and destructive forces.

This is indeed the true Battle of Armageddon. For, as you have approached that mystical land, such as was depicted in this prophetic description, the holy land of your own particular evolution, or as I have sometimes called it, the "threshold," when you are becoming consciously aware of the great spiritual worlds of Light, which are somewhat into your future, you will learn how to acquire a more satisfactory and suitable life by which you can live in these higher worlds.

This is all part of the stress, the turmoil, the questions, sometimes unanswered, sometimes answered wrongly, which you will constantly encounter in an endeavor to climb into these higher spiritual worlds. It will mean many lifetimes of this same turmoil and strife; various attempts to differentiate between the past, the present, and what should be concluded as a rational motion or solution to the problem at any particular given moment. As I have described them to you, the past of course represents these mystical, evil phantom riders which are also described in this parable.

This is the true Battle of Armageddon, one which every human must go through in his evolution before he can evolve into a higher state of consciousness and live in one of the spiritual worlds. In other words, it is a millennium—a time of death for the old lives which you have lived and a continuous effort to reinstate yourself in the higher or more progressive spiritual aptitudes. But whether you call your personal fight, your personal Battle of Armageddon, or the millennium, or just the battle of the old self, it is one which requires constant alertness. You must always remember that your life upon this material plane was primarily predicated upon these various emotional reflexes which mandated any particular reaction in your normal concourse of daily life. This is true, not only of the immediate or present physical life, but much more so as you re-created backwards, we shall say, into the more primitive beginnings of your evolution.

Overruling the host of various emotional complexes, which were the normal concourse of everyday life, was the great primitive law—survival, or survival of the fittest. The earth is normally a place of great stress and strife. This is so because in the eye of the Infinite Creator, all forms of life must be continuously sublimated in a more progressive manner, that out of the numerous plant and animal species which inhabit these terrestrial planets, there is always this continuous and never-ending evolution. This is all part of the way in which the Infinite Creator expresses Infinity; just as the great Infinite Creator is so expressing the progressive re-creative evolution in the higher spiritual worlds and in manners and forms which would be indeed difficult or perhaps impossible for you to conceive at this particular time; and we shall wisely leave these things where they belong—in your future.

Your problem is the present. It is also wise to remember that you will have no other moment in your life, either in the future or in any other manner and form which is not the present; for the present always determines the future. It also determines whether or not you will renege and go backwards into your past; for this can be done also, if you refuse to give up the power of the old self which has overruled your various motions through the past. For this material or temporal world has been, as I have said, so mandated as part of the particular regenerative spectrum. And so you see, dear ones, that each time one of these phantom horsemen gains access to your consciousness, he will, if given the opportunity, slash and hew away at the goodness or virtue which you have impounded in your psychic anatomy.

The trick, as I have said, is to immediately recognize these phantom horsemen or these old emotional vicissitudes, the moment they appear in consciousness. At this particular time when we feel the duress of the moment creeping in, if we become antagonistic, spiteful, hateful, resentful, critical, or any other of these various destructive emotional reflexes, then we must immediately, make sure as a counter measure to realize this is the old past, and take that all-important positive attitude toward them; they are the old past shadows of our former lives, they no longer hold power over us, we dismiss them. We must not let them have power over us in the moment of consciousness, and the longer they endure in our consciousness the more damage they can do us.

Perhaps I could point up this discussion by repeating the words of Jesus in the Holy Land 2000 years ago, when He said, "We must approach the Father as little children." In other words, this is a somewhat different angle to look at the way in which I have discussed this all-important question. The Father is, of course, the Infinite Creator, and as such, He is not involved with us in a personal manner. We are part of Him and He is secure in that particular bit of constructive information. However, you are not secure in your thoughts with Him; that is, your past life has necessitated the constant manipulation of various life factors in which you were involved at that particular moment, as was quite true in any particular lifetime.

However, approaching this threshold, this mystical land of Armageddon, or the Holy Hills of Galilee which is actually, of course, the threshold of your spiritual consciousness, then you begin to envision this great Infinite Creator. And vaguely in some way, you can within your own consciousness, be somewhat over-whelmed with the magnitude of it all. At that time, should you revert into your past, and use the various subterfuges which you have used in those past life-times, then, quite naturally, you will not get very far in your evolution into the future which the Infinite Creator has, in a sense, spread before you. For the Infinite Creator is your future. Or, we can say, if you tune yourself in, as is done in a similar manner with your radio, to the various wave lengths of energy which are stemming from out your past, then quite naturally in thought and consciousness, and in reality you will go back into the past. There is only one way to progress into the future; that is to constantly keep yourself attuned *to the future.* Of course, when I say constantly, I am using the one hundred per cent plus figure. Actually it is quite impossible for you at this time to use a one hundred per cent attunement with the future. This will have to become a way of life for you in some of the lifetimes which shall follow this present one.

For the moment this will be a continuous re-just-ification of all of these old past emotional vicissitudes with the Infinite future which lies ahead, and in the higher spiritual worlds you will not function in an emotional way; instead you will function in a much more logical and reasonable attitude of life, a logical attitude which merely means that you attune yourself, as I have said, in a radio-like manner with the vari-ous constructive evolutions which are ever function-

73

ing about you. In this manner you will accomplish two different dimensions of expression. You will be polarizing your own particular expression with the Infinite Creator, and also you will be polarizing a constructive psychokinetical expression into various less positive attitudes and ways of life which are still being lived by your fellow human beings on lower planes of expression.

This higher way of life is quite different from the emotional life which you have lived on the earth plane up until this time. It will take a tremendous amount of orientation of a constructive attitude. It will take a tremendous amount of sheer will and determination; it will require a tremendous amount of giving up, if I can put it that way. Actually, of course giving up is a blessing in disguise; for while you think it hurts or that it is painful for you to give up many of your pet emotional expressions, your various opinions, and things which you have held dear to you, up until this moment, in giving them up, the Infinite Creator can fill this void with a much greater and a much higher degree of expression. You will have new treasures, so to speak. You will find that your house of life is furnished in a much more harmonious way. The windows will be clean and bright. The doorways in and out will work well and be forever open to the visitors from the higher worlds; and they shall be forever shut to these dark phantoms which come from the past.

In this more serene and more complacent attitude, you will be able to reach out into the Infinite vastness of eternity which lies ahead. You will begin to rationally and consciously integrate the Infinite Creator into every thought and motion in your life. In this manner and form you will awaken to the beauty of the spiritual worlds which are ever about you. You will see the beautiful lights, the auras, the Luminous Visitors who come to see you in these moments. Your life will be filled with serenity and security which will

74

surpass all descriptions. These are not idle predictions or promises, but they have actually happened to many people who have taken this road; they are happening now to the various students of Unarius; many of them have already become illumined with the higher spiritual worlds and the people who live in them.

Life has gained much more luster, so much so that even the casual observer has noticed something unusual and different about them. These individuals cannot praise enough, the way they have taken; they can never cease to give enough thanks, nor be grateful enough for what has happened to them; for now truly their faces are turned to the East. They are facing their eternity. They are walking through the "no man's land of Armageddon" and approaching these higher spiritual worlds. Like "Jacob's Ladder" they stretch ever and anon; so many golden steps which will be taken by you in your future; steps which will ever lead you higher and into more luminous realms of Light and consciousness; worlds which defy description and the people who live in these worlds would be as living flames of Light. For this is the way of life—our evolution, our Battle of Armageddon; always learn to recognize the past, and if you are successful then you may be assured of eternal life in the Higher Kingdoms.

# CHAPTER 9

## Overcoming The Old Self

Greetings dear ones. Again it is the quiet hour, time for us to enter into a further discussion of our evolutionary pathway. In our previous discussion we entered into the conquest of the lower self, or as I called it, the Battle of Armageddon, that no man's land where we learn to slay, so to speak, the various dragons of the past, the phantom riders of hate, greed, malice, envy, selfishness, and other carnal lusts of human nature which have plagued us through our past life-times; yes, even to the present moment, and conceivably they shall plague us for a long time to come. Along with these insufferable monsters are other companions that keep them close company; diseases of various kinds, called incurable by our present-day doctors and scientists, but which always have their origin in the diverse emotional psychic shocks through which we have lived in these past lives and which have, through the malformed vortexes in our psychic anatomy, been perpetuated far beyond the life in which they were incurred.

The battle of the old self is one which can be approached from several different angles of introspection. We can approach it from a psychological stance; we can approach it from a purely scientific basis, or one of pure philosophy in which we can generally summate various indifferences in a more positive and compatible fashion.

Speaking of the conquest of the lower self, in a psychological stance, there are many and various equations, terminologies, and other nomenclatures which can be used and borrowed from our present-day psychological medicine. Such differences and equations, as they arise are justified by practicing psychologists or psychiatrists who are attempting to analyze the subconscious turmoils and strifes of any particular individual; they do so in an understanding which is purely third dimensional, and is superficial in a sense that it does not impound any of the more valuable perspectives which should be included in any psychiatric analyses. The psychiatrist, in his analyses of the patient, should be constantly aware of the fact that this person has lived many lifetimes; he has expressed both polarities of male and female in these previous lives; he has lived idiomatically and in such manner and form which was demanded of him by the community of people with whom he was surrounded.

The fact is that the subconscious differences, the incurable psychoses, or the physical diseases which plague humanity at this time will never be suitably solved or equated until therapeutic practices and analyses include these all-important perspectives of the individual's life.

They are also very important to you personally, and it is not entirely necessary nor is it wise to seek out psychiatric help if we are able to make a constructive start and evaluation in our self-analysis. Unfortunately however, to the average individual, or to you yourself personally who stand poised on the threshold of spiritual emancipation, it is still extremely difficult for you to objectively analyze these various emotional complexes which stem from the subconscious or from your past lifetimes.

It is first necessary to learn the sundry scientific

processes in which life is carried on by the individual; how thought, as a memory process is propagated and relived from one day to the next, from one life to the next; yes, and lived in the spiritual worlds in between earth lives. For such is consciousness; it is that Infinite part of the creative substance of thought which lives in an imperishable dimension, having nether time nor space in the generally accepted frame of reference which is understood by the earth man.

If we did not include these varied perspectives in our analysis we would indeed be lost; for the diverse ways in which life is lived, scientifically speaking, as oscillating wave forms of motion, which are so oscillating between countless dimensions, are lived partly in our psychic anatomy and reinstated in our surface consciousness.

However, for the time, I shall not delve too deeply in these more scientific and somewhat abstract principles. They are included in the various texts and lesson courses of Unarius and should remain the constructive study part of your life from now on; at least, until you are sufficiently indoctrinated in principle to understand the function of the Infinite. Scientifically speaking, we can say, in a broad sense, that each individual is an electronic instrument; something like the volt ohm-meter used by the technician in his analysis of varied electronic devices, such as a TV set. Your five senses represent the different scales of interpretation which are used by this technician as they are so constructed on his ohm-meter. Your sense of sight, smell, hearing, touch, and taste, are ways in which you differentiate the various wave forms into consciousness as they stem externally or as they are regenerated as nerve impulses. This has been part of your past evolution just as it is your present, and it will continue to be the function of your life into the infinite future.

The determinant qualities here are, of course, in their particular wave lengths and in which dimension they are so propagated and from which they are reflected. As our third dimension or our earth life is, conservatively speaking, one of the very lowest of the lower planes of expression, and is considered by many in the higher worlds, as one of the astral kingdoms, the earth world will then represent, to a large degree, wave forms and interpretations of oscillating motion which can be considered as omni-directional; that is, they start and they finish. In the fourth or adjoining dimension, these motions are always cyclic in nature and therefore, as the entity of consciousness is within themselves, they have neither time nor do they occupy space in a sense that they have a starting point or a finishing point.

As you have in the past, through the thousands of years, so interpreted life as a succession of wave form motions into your consciousness, you have thus impounded them in the next adjoining dimension in your respective psychic anatomies. There, they reside until you or some other external force can so cancel them out. In the eye of the Infinite Creator, it was so supremely conceived that man, as an individual entity of consciousness, so progressively inclined that he could in some future evolution of consciousness, become endowed with logic and reason to such an extent that he could be considered god-like in nature; to have power and dominion over all destructive and constructive forces, both in heaven and in hell.

In a sense of the word, to the earth man, Masters or Adepts of this nature were so considered and called gods. Therefore, the supreme prerogative of consciousness is that determinant in every individual's life which automatically relegates him as an individual being. The individuality of each person is therefore indestructible, or it should be considered such, and inviolate to the degree that we either as laymen, or as adepts, or masters, or even as gods, would not so contrive to change man from his willful ways; for life itself is predicated upon this master plan. In Infinite Consciousness are an infinite number of experiences; to learn of Infinite Consciousness therefore means to go through and realize the actuality of an infinite number of experiences. Actually this can never be accomplished; for Infinity Itself forbids us to circumscribe any dimension within itself. However life itself does, in the infinite sense, remanifest itself as a successive evolution of forms of consciousness which we resolve through emotional aptitudes as experiences.

In the future however, after a certain threshold has been past, consciousness can and does assume another proportion of introspection, and in this manner and form it will include as an attunement process, the sundry abstract proportions of Infinity as a constructive form of consciousness, rather than an emotional experience; thus polarizing various abstractions into constructive realities which are again projected and remanifest as positive polarities in less positive or more negative environments and surroundings.

In other words, when we ascend into higher realms, we in truth, become a radiating center of personal consciousness which becomes the mental manna for millions and millions of people who are yet to evolve to these higher planes of consciousness. This mental manna is the polarizing oscillation of energy which is a part of every life experience. They can be extracted from such experiences by any individual who would thus take the time and trouble to extract them. This is not necessarily a Pollyanna attitude, but reflects a constructive abstraction of the Infinite plan of evolution as an experience, either singular or plural, which will, in itself, remanifest itself infinitely and in an infinite number of ways until we have so mastered the Master plan.

So you see, dear ones, the constructive evolution which automatically destroys the past and lower self is not the simple metaphysical process which is sometimes outlined for us by the so-called purveyors of mystical sciences who drape themselves over the pulpits in our churches.

Science in itself, is the mandate necessary for us to open the door to the future. We will have to constructively understand evolution in a scientific manner. We will have to understand that the entity of intelligence is not impounded in some visual object which we consider mass; but always, objectivism, as it is in consciousness, in the similarity, or the facsimile of wave forms in their emotional impedences through our consciousness, determines and re-determines their own particular form in a regenerative manner which reconveys the picture of the present to us.

The science of this process is most adequately described in the lessons, and as I have said, it is a mandate if we wish to gain access into the higher spiritual worlds; we must learn to understand these principles, for our very lives in these higher worlds will depend upon how well we understand energy— the oscillating processes, the processes of attunement, polarization, and other such various attributes of energy wave forms. For in these higher worlds, we do not possess lungs to aerate our blood stream; instead we will aerate our consciousness and feed our bodies with an inflow of energy wave forms; and this inflow, our food, our very lives, will depend upon how well we can attune ourselves to the energy environment in which we find ourselves.

The astral underworlds are peopled by countless millions of souls who are living in the shadow of their past; they are re-manifesting life consciously only for the moment by these memories; by strongly and subconsciously reflecting into their consciousness at

81

the moment, the forms, the experiences in which they have previously lived. These however, are only temporary panaceas. They cannot be substantially endured, neither can they perpetuate the individual in his spiritual world to any indefinite length of time. Neither can he constructively evolve from these worlds by clinging to the shadows of the past; and so, as in the material worlds, you will also find that the conquest of the lower self is equally important in the spiritual worlds.

When we begin to live in these higher spiritual worlds as constructive oscillating entities of expression, when we begin to aerate our energy bodies, to feed them by the inflow of Radiant Energies to which we have attuned ourselves, then only we can say we are living a higher spiritual life. As part of that spiritual life, as we so attune ourselves to the inflow of Radiant Constructive Infinite Energy, so we will regenerate as part of our consciousness and our thought processes, reconstructed forms of this same energy which is flowing into us, and in this constructive thought process we will, in turn, re-radiate this consciousness into the lower planes of life.

Now, dear ones, how well this is accomplished will determine your future; how sincerely and perpetually you will dedicate yourselves to the never-ending quest for the higher life, will determine your evolution. You, and you alone, are responsible for it. No one else can do it for you; despite what you may have been told, your personal savior will be the consciousness which you attain in this higher way of life. You cannot be made fit to live in this kingdom of Heaven until you have reconstructed yourself.

This too, is part of the Master Plan which the Infinite Creator has laid out for all of us. It is the plan by which every individual, in himself, can become, in a sense, an Infinite Creator. For instead of sublimating experience into daily life expressions, he is

82

regenerating Infinite Consciousness into constructive evolutionary forms of consciousness.

The promise of the future is great. It cannot be interpreted in terms whereby we can gain benefit in a selfish manner. Our approach to our infinite evolution always must be made impersonally. Should we at any time wish to use any powers or knowledge which we may have gained, in a selfish manner and in a way in which we may attempt to glorify ourselves, then we and our cause are lost. We will descend to the pits of hell very quickly. This too, is the Biblical depiction of the tempting by Satan, and which is a constant strife and struggle for any and all who attain.

Never think for one moment that the sublime Utopia is ever attained. Life in any form, in any dimension, in any spiritual world, is lived as a constant equilibrium of effort and realization. The moment you lie down and rest upon your laurels, then truly you are lost; at least for the moment, and quite likely in that moment of weakness you will lose some of that hard fought for attainment. There are no alternatives, either you progress constructively into the higher dimensions, or you retrogress into the lower astral worlds and into eventual disintegration. Neither can you commit any kind of suicide, either physical or spiritual; for as a part and a participle of Infinite Consciousness, you must constantly regenerate life in one form or another. Energy cannot be destroyed, but always assumes another form.

# CHAPTER 10

## The Return of The
## Christ Consciousness

Everyone, I believe, is quite familiar with one of the more popular Christian ideosophies namely, "The Second Coming of Christ," and the generally believed popular version, as it has been depicted in pictures and in the various Christian dispensations, is that Jesus Christ will return to the earth riding on a flaming cloud surrounded by Heavenly Hosts; and in this advent the earth is supposedly cleansed by fire and the wicked are destroyed. There is also another, but less popular version of the destruction of the earth, as it is pictured in the Second Epistle of Peter, where, as Peter writes "The Lord returns as a thief in the night and the earth is destroyed and even the elements burn with a fervent heat."

Now, apparently there are two different versions of this same advent and which have, incidentally, caused some confusion among the numerous Christian practitioners and dispensators of Christianity. However, in these latter days, the Christian advocate has tried to side-step this apparent disparity and difference in issue, by proclaiming that Christ and God are one and the same. In this respect too, he enters into an entirely new world of confusing issues in the various relative dispensations of his Christian orthodoxy. It is not generally known but the same pictorial destruction has been quite frequently displayed in other religions of the world in more ancient times. For instance, a thousand years B.C. Zoroaster described the same advent, that Ahura-Mazda, or the father, and son Mithras, would cleanse the earth, that fire would flow like milk; and later the earth would be repopulated by those who were "good souls," fit for salvation.

In various other Biblical descriptions there are references too, to other parabolistic happenings which are not quite clearly defined in the language or in the translation of any of the present-day contemporaries of religious preachments. The reason for this condition is quite obvious and its explanation is also quite simple. It is because neither the layman, the practitioner, the ancient prophet, nor the other dispensators, knew of what the Infinite Cosmogony consisted, nor exactly how it came about that his particular psychism so transpired; whether it was Moses who, as he believed, saw the bush burning but was not consumed, or Elisha, or any of the other particular descriptive happenings in the Bible which were portrayed in such relevant terms referring to flames, burnings, etc., these were thoroughly misunderstood and therefore misinterpreted, not only by those who saw these visions, but also by those who followed afterward.

It is clearly indicated at this time we should enter into a complete presentation of just what actually occurs when such psychisms happen to certain people. First, these more ancient prophets, as well as some of the more modern contemporaries, who can be considered mediumistic or clairvoyant, or who possess that particular paranormal mind faculty, can, in certain moments, transcend the known physical five senses of the earth body and actually realize or see into the fourth dimensional or spiritual world about them. Likewise, if this person who is so clairvoyantly inclined and is having such a vision does not properly understand what is happening, and he does not understand the spiritual world which he is so viewing, he will, consequently, become very greatly confused; he will naturally misconstrue this happening as something of great portent and he will quite likely proclaim himself some sort of a prophet or a spiritual dispensator and succeed in leading thousands or even millions of poor innocent victims down the garden path.

In order for you to personally avoid these mistakes and to strip the so-called mystery from the mystical or spiritual world, it is quite necessary for you to understand of what this world consists. Jesus said, "In my Father's House are many mansions." Today we understand, through the findings of Einstein and other particular ways and means, that there are a great number of dimensions which are, to some extent, quite different from this third dimension or earth world in which we presently find ourselves. In the various teachings of Unarius these different spiritual worlds have been pictured to you in their true form; that mass, as it presents itself to you in the familiar scenes of the world about you, is no longer existent, simply because "physical" atoms are not in evidence in these worlds. Instead, these worlds are filled with beautiful, pulsating radiant-hued energies, and all forms, such as buildings, trees, or other such more familiar forms will naturally be composed of such more pure radiant energy forms.

If you could be clairvoyant for just a moment and see your physical body, you would see too, that it is not really solid as you believe, but it is actually a mass or sea of palpitating energy forms which the scientists call atoms; tiny solar systems of energies which are revolving within themselves and repeating their same timeless message. So far as the material world is concerned, this world is composed of these tiny atom forms which do not exist in this same form in the immediate fourth, fifth, or sixth dimensions. Therefore, if you see into these dimensions in any moment and become so transcended in your mind that the faculty of perception is therefore presented to you from the inner, let me say, you will see this immediate world as a radiant sea of energy and all familiar forms such as worlds, or trees, plants, or people, will be living radiant energy forms of these particular objects.

For instance, this same condition was quite true with Peter, who in a moment of transcendency, peered into the spiritual world and saw the earth revolving in its timeless sea of energy. In this radiant-hued condition he naturally believed the world to be burning, and when he came back from his moment of transcendency, he preached this false prophecy. For it is not conceivable that God would come as a thief in the night and burn the world, no more so than you would burn the hair from the top of your head, or a hand from your arm; simply because the world is a functioning unit of expression in the eye of the Infinite Creator. It is a world which has developed, through evolution, to form a platform or a certain dimension, a schoolhouse if you wish, wherein people can go through certain more elemental stages of their evolution.

The primitive concepts of placing one particular experience which has just transpired in relationship to another, or even into a general accumulation of such expressions with all such various pictorial happenings of supernatural prophecies, as the world being destroyed, or talking to God, etc., are merely psychisms in which these old prophets or leaders were momentarily transported into another or spiritual world. When Moses believed he saw the bush burning and talked with the Lord, it was merely that a certain astral entity appeared to him in his true form. The obvious purpose of this appearance was to completely enslave Moses, and the many thousands of Israelites; to convert them, shall we say, into a nation which was completely subjective to this astral entity who had not yet ascended into a more infinite perspectus in his understanding. There are many, many thousands of these same powerful astral entities who, on occasions, do appear to certain people and succeed in constructing some very different philosophies or religions in the world today.

The pages of history are written with these many different dispensations, and whether they concern men like Hitler or other such classical examples of history, such as Alexander the Great, Genghis Khan, or any of the other conquerors who set up small nations or civilizations within the confines of this earth world, these people were all, in themselves, being obsessed completely and dominated by these astral entities; and whether or not they so appeared as they did to Moses is irrelevant and of no consequence. The dominant force which drove these astral entities into the obsession of certain ruling entities was quite clear and evident. It is also conceivable that these various leaders were themselves reincarnated forms of these astral entities.

Now, you must not be dismayed by these revelations; you must realize that even in an evil dispensation, such as was expressed by Hitler, in the end, some great good was served. For this lesson made it possible for millions of other people, who followed after this terrible tragedy in human history, to make strenuous efforts to avoid a similar happening in the future. Our modern political systems, the United Nations, etc., are all most strenuously devoted to the task of avoiding repetition of such a destructive act. It must also be conceived that during the time of this great tragedy, when so many millions of people were seemingly struck down in various acts of war, that they were merely fulfilling their own particular place in evolution.

However, I must not stray from the true subject. Now we understand more properly what a psychic revelation really is, and how it can become a very badly misconstrued parable which will lead millions of people into diverse and sundry false concepts and retard their natural evolution of a more realistic approach of learning of the Infinite. It has been resolved, that prophecies or revelations, as a whole are merely psychisms wherein some individual, a self-styled prophet, if you will, has envisioned within his mind the energy world of the next dimension, the spiritual world, or as it is believed by the Christian, as Heaven. This leads us more directly into another one of those very popular fallacies which is most redundant in Christian circles to this very day.

This misconception is the "Second Coming of Christ" which was previously mentioned at the beginning of this text. The "Second Coming," like all other particular visions is, in a sense, a personal return of consciousness to each and every individual when he makes a certain junction of consciousness with these more immediate spiritual worlds. Buddha called this "Nirvana." What it actually means is that at some particular point in evolution, the individual gradually becomes more dominantly guided and motivated by the higher or Superconscious Self.

At such a time the individual can see within himself that the Superconscious Self is the all-motivating, the all-intelligent participle in Infinite expression as it concerns himself individually. To more fully explain this concept, we must refer to some of the different teachings of Unarius, and in particular to the lesson on the psychic anatomy. Knowledge of the psychic anatomy will clear up one of the age-old mysteries which has always confused, not only the religious dispensator of the past, but is also confusing the modern doctor of medicine and the psychiatrist.

In the ancient language of the East, such as the Aramaic, the psychic anatomy was called the "Christos" or the soul; and during the passage of time the Christian dispensations, the "Christos" or Christ, or the soul became personally integrated with Jesus; whereas in the true understanding of all human beings it can be immediately resolved that everyone has a psychic anatomy. As a matter of fact, no one could exist without it, for it is through the psychic anatomy that the various individual propensities are carried from one lifetime on through another; and it is the more ultimate concept of the Infinite Creator.

As you no doubt have noted in the lesson on the psychic anatomy (advanced lesson course), that it is subdivided into three different portions resolving itself into that which is called the Superconscious. The Superconscious is the Christos in a more pure sense of the word. While, as a whole, the psychic anatomy can be called the Christos or soul, yet, it will ultimately resolve in the future infinite incarnations that the individual can be more wholly the Superconscious Self. That is so, simply through the principle of constant regeneration, through various incarnations and in the millions of life experiences, a certain polarized element of each experience which can, through frequency relationship, affiliate itself with a small part of the Infinite Creator.

You must understand that this Infinite Creator is infinite in nature; that is, it can encompass distances and spaces which are beyond your concept. These distances and spaces are presently confusing the astronomer. Also, the Infinite can occupy in its entirety, a space which is even smaller than the nucleus of an atom. This is very difficult to conceive, but it is an actuality, if we can understand the Infinite as we should.

Therefore, as the individual progresses along the evolutionary pathway of life, and goes through the various experiences, these experiences will, in turn, polarize a certain small portion of the Infinite Creator in that dimension of the Superconsciousness which can pertain to the individual self. It is in this way that the individual can evolve into higher spiritual worlds and into future dimensions wherein he can become god-like in nature; simply because the infinite number of experiences which he has encountered in the lower worlds will now become an actual living reality, in the sense that he can see them, know about them, and know how to deal with them most properly; as well as realize their particular function and position with the Infinite Creator. Therefore, this individual can be assumed to be very god-like in nature; he can occupy many different worlds at the same time, in the sense that his consciousness is constantly oscillating with these worlds.

This individual can also be in direct contact in a clairvoyant manner with millions of individuals simultaneously, also for the same reason, through frequency attunement—much the same as the radio set functions—he is then oscillating with these millions of humans and with many other different forms of life. This is a very abstract concept but is actually the way to the more ultimate attainment of any individual who can progressively incarnate into the higher spiritual worlds. However, in such inter- mediate incarnations in the more relative spiritual worlds, immediately adjacent to the third dimension, the individual can be considered to have a more highly developed Christos or psychic anatomy; in the sense that the Superconscious has become the dom- inant part of the expressive motion of the psychic anatomy.

When this person has attained this particular point wherein the psychic anatomy as is presented by the Superconsciousness, does become the dominant, the guiding force in this individual's life—in fact it is the individual himself—then, this person can say that Christ has returned to him. He has made a junction, not only with the higher worlds, but he has also attained a junction as in "Nirvana" with the lower worlds in relationship to the many experiences which he has gone through in these lower material worlds.

It is at this point that the individual can truly say Christ has returned to the earth—the earth, as it is represented in those millions of experiences through which he has passed, and which, in their various energy formations, convey the exact transpositions of these diverse energy experiences—for you must remember that all things must be most properly resolved into energy formations, and that the meaning of all things is carried in the various justifications of these energy formations as they occur in oscillating patterns in your consciousness.

Therefore, to all intents and purposes, the junction of the higher self, as it maintains supremacy, becomes the complete guiding and motivating force in the relationship of the individual to the lower worlds, then this person can say that Christ has indeed returned to him; that he has made this proper junction so now the Superconscious is the true self. He is no longer confounded by the various idiosyncrasies, the emotional vicissitudes of the earth world, and the emotional consequences which he had formerly incurred in living through these numerous experiences. He is well on his way to becoming a god-like creature which I previously described; an entity which has been in fact, described in the Bible as one of the great Archangels such as Gabriel. Yes, even in the more advanced angelic forms which go far beyond the descriptions of Gabriel or any other angelic forms as they are so portrayed in Christian liturgy.

For indeed, the Infinite presents no place of demarcation, nor is there any cessation to anything. The Infinite, in Itself, is just that: a never-ending cyclic motion of integration, wherein the individual can never presuppose he will ever reach any ultimate destiny.

This is your challenge; this is the reason you were conceived; not because you were merely a creature of happenstance, born in the moment of physical passion; but rather that you are a participating element in the mind of the Infinite Creator. You are destined to become a god-like creature if you so wish; if you are willing to give up the false image of the material world and develop the consciousness of life in the higher spiritual worlds, where you will reside in such a world as a functioning integral unit of Infinite Consciousness.

# CHAPTER 11

## Debunking Various Religious Concepts

It is the avowed purpose of Unarius to debunk various religious aspects of life, and to strip sundry mysticisms from such confusing interpolations of religious expressions which may seemingly attempt to tear down, displace or perhaps destroy, certain time-hallowed and otherwise inviolate concepts which mankind has enjoyed since the beginning of history. While the destructive intent cannot be truly supported, yet there is a deliberate attempt to separate any individual who studies Unarius, from the generally accepted concept that the world, as it presents itself in the whole of human expressions, is the starting place. This is a universal practice among the varied races of mankind, either individually or collectively, to try to equate the entire Infinite Cosmogony on the basis of their own reactionary and emotionally involved world in which they are presently living.

The fallacy of this universal practice can be immediately seen if we look for one moment, either in the pages of history or into currently expressed dispensations of life about us; whether they concern the great struggle of two different ideologies, seen in the differences of communism and democracy; or whether they are expressed in various dispensations in the thousands of churches throughout the Christian world. Therefore, no attempt has been made, nor will one ever be made, to destroy or remove time-hallowed practices and concepts from among the many races of mankind who so practice them.

It is realized, not only by the moderator, but by those who express Unarius from the higher spiritual worlds, that the numerous expressions as they concern humanity in any community or society of life, are very necessary and relevant to them at that stage of their evolution. Our concern is centered upon the individual who has reached that certain threshold wherein he has already begun to discern the differences in his material way of life and the more advanced scientific concepts which may be pictured in the higher spiritual worlds.

Through the various lives lived in between earth lives and in other ways in which the individual has become conscious of the higher principles and ways of life, he becomes more and more dissatisfied with the emotional material world from whence he sprang. This is quite natural and is an ever-increasing consequence of evolution; for in understanding the dynamic principle of resurgent regeneration, by which the Infinite Creator functions, it is most mandatory that each individual successively progress in his understanding of the Infinite; that he must successively develop and interpolate into his life newer and more highly expressed forms of consciousness. These factors are already inborn, shall I say, in the most inner reaches of the various materialistic forms with which the earth man is surrounded.

All things possess a psychic anatomy which, in turn, contains the propounded energy wave forms so resurgently expressed by the Infinite Creator. These can always autosuggestively suggest to the individual the more ultimate creative resurgency behind the seemingly apparent disparities of the material world

—why the necessity of life; yes, and even life itself, for this factor too, remains, just as it always has been to the earth man, the most insolvable of all insolvables; that no scientist, no religious practitioner, no layman, no saint, and no adventist can give the correct interpretation of life, simply because the earth man universally has not yet progressed in his evolution to that point where he can accept the universal concept of the Infinite Creator.

To the earth man, God still remains an entity to be worshipped and to be otherwise compromised in a most child-like fashion and manner; and this same God, is apparently subjective to the lowest and most violent forms of emotional vicissitudes. In many and numerous ways the concept of present-day Christianity— as with all other religions, both present and past —has been constantly stressed or an attempt made to sublimate these various earth experiences into a more tangible reality of creation, which could explain the intangible of intangibles—life itself. But until such a concept of the Infinite Creator can be envisioned by the individual, no person can adequately describe either the reason or the way of life. Nor can he describe the purpose of this constant resurgent and seemingly purposeless continuity of various expressions which rise about him, in a constant and never-ending stream, the varied numerous expressions which seem to have no apparent reason nor do they have any function. They may be completely and absolutely intangible to him. There may be no reason at all for their existence. In fact, he can only plunge himself into the abysmal mire of self-hypnosis and resolve all these things in one fell swoop in the miasma of religion; that it is the nature of God to so express Himself, not only emotionally but that he must do so in ways which are intangible and incomprehensible to the earth man.

Such an ideosophy of life is incomprehensible and

can only be compromised when it is realized that as a whole, the earth man, either as the modern present-day twentieth century contemporary, or whether he is the average John Q. Citizen of a more ancient civilization; whether it is in Rome, Carthage, Egypt, or ancient Greece, man largely had the same imponderable and inconclusive mass of evidence of life about him; yet the solution was everywhere quite clearly as evident as was the apparency of these many different resurgent forms. For in the very nature of these numerous forms was carried the entire message of Infinity. The Infinite Creator could not, at any time, be supposed to be an entity separate and distinct from any particular expression as it concerned a dimension. God was not to be worshipped; rather, God was to be understood, not only as the Principle behind all life, but as life itself. This same God was the substance of all life as life expressed itself in the multitudinous forms of life expressions in which man found himself.

Therefore, the ever-apparent enigma of life, the imponderable but easily soluble solution to this imponderable is everywhere evident; so much so that it becomes the greatest of all paradoxes, and yet most easily understood by the individual who understands man as an evolutionary creature, that he cannot, at any time, supersede his mentality beyond the boundaries of any particular point in his evolution; because all apparencies as they concern form or the regeneration of form in diverse life aspects about him in the world, must always remain relative and tantamount to sundry past life expressions, as they concern these various interpolations of life and form about him. This is the basis of evolution, and most necessarily so, yet there must also be a positive bias; a great spiritual influence if you will call it so; a principle in which the Infinite Creator enters into the constant and ever-expanding consciousness and development

97

of every human. As each experience becomes a relegated factor and an integrated facsimile within the psychic anatomy of this individual, so does he begin his climb into the spiritual worlds; however, in the seeming disparities of the material world about him, this poses the never-ending challenge of his immediate environment; one in which he must always find a compromise or become psychotically mired in the miasma of his material world.

It is a common and well-known precept in modern psychology, as posed by the Freudian elements, that to present an unknown and intangible concept or element into the introspection or into the immediate environment of some human, is to arouse his antagonism. This is so because the ego is deflated; the sense of personal evaluation is somehow compromised and in such a compromising situation, the individual becomes irritated and may become violent should this more advanced concept be pressed against him. It is therefore within reason that we, who may possess some of the more advanced concepts of life, be ever mindful of those who are still elemental in their reasoning faculties; we must ever understand that their reasoning is always presupposed as a dominant element contained in the various reactionary forces in past experiences. Their mentality cannot at any time, supersede or go beyond the boundaries or horizons of their past world; that is, until such a time when the individual gradually becomes acclimated to a higher spiritual environment wherein he begins to be quickened by certain spiritual agencies and forces, he will then begin to see within himself the possibilities of the higher way of life.

There are no mysteries in the eye of the Infinite Creator. He is most expressive in all continuities and in all forms of life, either as they concern the material world or in dimensions which are far beyond the concept of the material mind. The Creator is not concerned at any time with hiding things from people. He has never at any time so presupposed any mysticism in the principle which made this constant and ever-regenerating principle so apparent and so immediately useful to every individual. When these facts become more or less known and to some extent practiced by the individual, he can then be said to become selective in the numerous presentations of the Infinite which come to him in the sense that the Infinite always presents the future in a new and never-ending succession of newer forms of experiences.

The selective process is not one which can be maintained on the emotional basis which mandated lifetime experiences. This selective process must become selective in an understanding and in a concept of the Infinite which determines the Infinite in all Its values, as well as in the Principle in which the Infinite motivates Itself in this never-ending, resurgent, and regenerating pattern of life. Consciousness and knowledge of the Infinite gives power of motion to the individual who so understands this Infinite. The common and more primitive or basic elements of metaphysics, as they are presupposed by certain practitioners on the earth today, are, in actuality, barbaric practices of psychokinetics which came from various practices of black magic, and witchcraft from out of past lifetimes.

There is no intelligent synonymy in the selective processes of life which should be related to these past agencies as they express themselves, either in religions, or in other such synonymous forms, which could be considered mystical or religious in nature. Only true knowledge of the Infinite gives the individual the power of selection, and in selection there is quite naturally a much higher state of evolution, a greater development of consciousness. As these developments of consciousness so transpire within the individual's mind, so do they encompass an ever-increasing number of interdimensional forms.

The ramifications of this ever-expanding conscious-ness are infinite in themselves, and will, as has been previously presented, create within the individual the effigy of the true God, the true expressive personal potential of the Infinite Creator, which is contained in the individual nuclei of intelligence. These various expressions as they will be so lived and expressed by that individual, are not emotional in nature; they do not encompass any system wherein the carnal law of the jungle can be satisfied. The individual will not seek a reward for his observance of some known humanitarian principle. Neither will he be able to assuage the various guilt complexes which will, in themselves, long since have been resolved in the new introspection of Infinite Perspectus.

How well it is then that we shall ever seek these widening horizons; that we shall always be fortified with the strength, the courage, and the conviction of knowing that the Infinite is the one and dominant concept in life. The Infinite Creator expresses Himself infinitely in all seen and unseen ways of life, to divert your course of life away from the churches, away from the political systems, and away from the customary manner and ways in which mankind lives as of this day or time, or in any other conceivable time; yes, and even to deny the truth of existence as it was believed to have been lived in times past. For indeed there is no truth in this or any other form of material life; simply because there has been that ever and never-ending attempt to evaluate the Infinite on the basis of the personal emotional experience, the earth plane life, the atmosphere of strife, tensions, turmoils, and animal-like instincts which are commonly lived by the earth man.

Man's attempts either individually or collectively, to eulogize himself into some form of divine concept are ridiculous. Until that time and place when the individual can, either individually or collectively, conceive within the dimension of his mind, the true Infinite Creator, the true principle of the Creator as He lives in that never-ending resurgent and regenerating pattern of life, until life is so lived with this principle ever in mind, then man is indeed a material creature, motivated primarily by the reward system, that life must be constantly placated on the basis of his own security, and his emotional values as they concern himself in the world about him. Primarily and universally as man practices life, he is concerned only that the world revolves about him; no other concepts, or no other ways of life are completely valid in themselves, except that he understands them, and he can be rewarded thusly, by them, in a sense, that he is so personally rewarded in that which he believes and that his beliefs are vindicated.

Pure philosophy cannot supplant a reasonable equation of life, no more so than any other specific agency or interpolation of various different mental levels which are expressed, either presently, or in historical configurations. As a whole, such philosophies, such numerous dispensations were merely adjunctive to any person who began his evolutionary climb, and at that particular moment philosophies or various dispensations were given as personal interpretations which were relevant only to the individual at that time. It is indeed unfortunate that such various expressions could be seized upon by exploiters at later times and contrived and refashioned or shaped into horrible monstrosities which dominated entire nations, created strifes, and wars, and in other ways so visited the races of mankind with great intemperances.

Yet true philosophies never have, nor shall they exist until they become inclusive in the ever-regenerating principle which concerns the Infinite Creator. For only in understanding such principle as it is so expressed by the Infinite Creator, can man begin to understand all of the common interpretations, the various vicissitudes, the material attitudes of the earth man. Also he can then begin to understand the possibilities of life beyond the grave and lived in a more tangible reality, than any which are presupposed by some religious faction. Yet it must not be supposed or presupposed at any given point that our immediate philosophy or understanding of life is supreme, or that it will remain insoluble; for such is the nature of the Infinite that if you wish to survive, then you must also impound within the horizon of your mental faculties an ever-increasing and a predominant horizon of infinite knowledge and an understanding of the Infinite.

So will pass the God-like deifications, the emotional intemperances of those gods who hurl thunder-bolts or who otherwise destroy, murder, and fornicate as they have done through the pages of history; either in the Bible or in other historical depictions which are, as of this day, held sacred and treasured in the hearts and minds of mankind. Yet, remain as they must, always merely historical accounts where man has descended into the vilest of all transpositions of life and then excused his vileness on the basis that he was either prompted, motivated by, or that this vileness was performed by the deity he worshipped.

God was never meant to be worshipped. Neither has God so indicated that He wished to be worshipped. God has always indicated that He was an integral part of everything that ever existed; and as an integral part, God quite naturally expected the expressive quotient of constructive evolution to be expressed, to be always expanded in the consciousness of any participating element or agent which was so contrived, or was a part of this Infinite Creative substance.

And so as we depart into the realms of Infinite Perspectus, let us not be dismayed by the cries of those who call us atheists, because we do not believe in their

102

God or in their ideologies; let us all remain steadfast
in our purpose—our faces turned to the Light of the
Infinite Creator.

# CHAPTER 12

## God and Mammon

Let us enter into some of the various factors and problems which confront the student of Unarius as he begins his climb from out the material worlds. We will begin with one of the classical utterances of Jesus, who said, and I quote, "Thou cannot serve God and, mammon too," or again, "To be in the world but not of it." In order to understand both the broader and more involved ramifications of God and mammon, we must first analyze what God and what mammon are, and note the differences in the ways people approach and live by these various concepts, thought patterns, and other psychological values in their numerous life interpretations. Mammon is a general classification of an Aramaic word which denotes the general material world, its various sins and iniquities, and the materialistic proclivities of all the people who are so strenuously involved in the material or earth worlds.

Conversely and in a somewhat different manner, God is, as presented by the Unariun concept, the scientific facsimile of all the visible and invisible worlds, the microcosm and the macrocosm. God is also the regenerative principle which activates all forms of regeneration which so appear, whether they are various atomic constituents of the material world, or whether they are the more highly developed life expressions as they are lived in the spiritual worlds. It can generally be agreed, so far as the material man is concerned in this immediate world, that he is largely a materialistic being; he is serving mammon; he is tremendously involved in the various materialistic earth life dispensations and the complexities which are involved in living these diverse expressions. He does not, to any degree, possess sufficient knowledge of the higher spiritual worlds; even though he may proclaim a religion, his religion is not, in a sense, a reality in comparison to the material world in which he is so living. Therefore, the material world does so remain dominant.

However, to any person who has so evolved to that point whereby he can conceive or envision within his mind the possibility of life lived beyond the material plane, this life can be reasonably supposed to be lived in a much more highly developed form of evolution; it is devoid of the various materialistic vicissitudes which beset the earth man, such as his wars and diseases; also the spiritual planes are places where life is lived in a more mental expression without the material forms. Now, should any individual arrive at this threshold of consciousness and find himself living in some material world such as the earth world, he is quite likely to be involved in divers and sundry karmic dispensations; karma in the sense of the word that he is quite likely to be in a condition of great mental turmoil or stress. Also he may be expressing outwardly through his physical body numerous physical diseases or conditions which do not yield to modern medical practice, for even the modern doctor does not have names for all these conditions.

Unfortunately, for any such individual so involved in this threshold, if he does not have sufficient guidance or an explanation for his various differences and difficulties, he is quite likely to be completely enmeshed in some of the countless diverse mental aberrations which beset so many thousands of people living in these times, just as these conditions have beset and enmeshed people in previous periods of time and in different civilizations. As there are no reasonable equations existing in the world today which can explain these differences, humanity, as a whole, must therefore look upon these various peoples as mentally or physically ill. If they are not so classified, they may express other forms of nonconformities such as peculiar, weird, spiritual, or religious practices. They may be involved in diverse physical or sexual perversions, but as a whole, these are people who are at the present time, to some degree, involved in certain psychic expressions which cannot be adequately explained either by the present-day psychologist, the practitioner, or the religious therapist. Nor can they be resolved in the pure concept of the individual himself, for he is so completely involved in these complexities that he is unable to recognize certain comparative values which may exist in the world about him.

As a student of Unarius, it is also quite likely that you are, to some degree, emotionally involved in various differences which may be quite apparent to you at this particular time. These may concern the differences in the attitudes of your many friends with whom you have associated in the years past. It may also concern you in the varied manners and ways in which you live, such as your eating habits and even the food itself. Clothing too, may present a problem from time to time, and as a whole, you may feel yourself resenting the many implications and the thought patterns which are involved with these various life dispensations. Clothing, food, friends, houses, and various other forms and patterns of life may become increasingly odious to you as you progress in your evolution.

You must always remember that as a student of Unarius, you are given the advantages of the diverse scientific interpretations which this science contains, together with the great aid and assistance from the spiritual worlds, in the manner and form in which these scientists, and doctors and teachers can project to you, their helpful energy dispensations; they do so tremendously aid you in canceling out sundry past life aberrations and help to rebuild your psychic anatomy.

In this sense you can visualize yourself as actually traveling through time and space at a vastly accelerated speed as if being fired from some huge cannon. You may in a few days, or in a few hours time, actually be rebuilt or reformed to a point which would normally take you many thousands of lifetimes to acquire in the ordinary reactionary manner you have been accustomed to until this time. Should such an occurrence happen to you and at any time you should be involved in a tremendous psychic upheaval wherein there may be literally thousands of years of earth lives removed, then the various negations involved in these experience quotients are so cancelled out in their negative proportions to you as they are so contained in your psychic anatomy. As this cancellation may so occur, you may become tremendously emotionally involved, at least for the moment, you may have a great sense of loss; you may feel that you have no friends in this world, and in essence this is literally so, for all of the former old earth forms with which you were previously involved, including your friends, have now passed on into another point of introspection. This situation is not to be feared, but rather it is to be welcomed, and each particular "working out"—whether it is small or whether it is large—should be a definite milestone which marks your evolution into the future.

If you dislike giving up your friends or the thought of so giving up these various earth life dispensations, you must remember that it is quite similar, in a sense, to the pattern of life you have already lived on the

107

earth. As a small child you lived in a childish world surrounded by other children with whom you played; these children have long since gone their way and would quite likely not mean very much to you, except that you can very faintly remember them. Even your brothers and sisters and your parents will have changed in their position to you, and you will feel quite different toward them than you did when you were a small child.

This all adds up to just one thing: you, like everyone else, are expressing a certain definite continuity in the sense of time, as the Infinite itself is so expressing, in the macrocosm and the microcosm, a constant and never-ending succession of regeneration of consciousness; so you, likewise, must do so in order to continue on in this evolutionary life process. Remember that various earth life interpretations, such as gregarity, and the ways in which people associate with others, are usually founded on inferior emotional values of life; that is, each person finds some reasonable facsimile of consciousness with his neighbor or with that person whom he calls his friend. When these numerous similarities of expression change, so friends pass from consciousness, it does not in a sense of the word mean that you lose a friend, for you should always envision within your mind that this continuity of life immediately brings other friends and other relationships into your consciousness.

Also through mental telepathy and in other ways in which the Infinite expresses Itself through every individual, you are always in constant continuity with every person you have ever known or with whom you have associated. That which friendship means to the earth man is a similarity of expression whereby he can evaluate, within the conscious earth life forms of his fellow men the similarities of his own earth life. It gives him sort of a feeling of security to realize there are other people who live just the same way he does and to some degree experience the same emotional complexes he experiences.

If, in the future, you find you are losing your appetite, that meat becomes obnoxious to you at times, that clothing feels rather tight and restricted, that the various life forms or patterns in the world about you seem to be heavy or useless, or they bore you, these are healthy signs and not to be feared as indications that you are becoming mentally aberrated. It merely means that in your sleep teaching you are already alerted and preconditioned to a much greater extent than you would normally have been. Also it means that you are making great progress, that is, if you supplant these various life experiences with the accumulation of another type of mental introspection or faculty which can be called more purely clairvoyance or paranormal. In other words you will have attuned yourself in a much higher degree to this great Infinite macrocosm and microcosm which is everywhere about you. You will see various life interpolations manifesting themselves as continuities of expression from the Infinite Consciousness.

These diverse and sundry introspections will give you a greater security and a greater knowledge of where you are going when you leave this physical flesh. You will know that life is, and can be, sustained in consciousness beyond the physical or material world; you will know too, that it is a progressive evolution, in direct ratio and proportion as to how well you can assimilate the various interdimensional factors which are so involved. And so you will learn to replace these diverse earth life values with much greater and more expanded concepts which will enable you to live life in the higher dimensions. Now of course, all people with whom you are, or have been, so concerned in this or any previous lifetime may not have been just friends or associates or even relatives. They may be another more highly developed form of expression which will, in the natural sequence of evolution, be carried into a much higher plane of life.

This is that which has been called, in Unarius, the polarity concept. No doubt you have seen various people in this earth life who expressed a considerable amount of polarity consciousness in the way in which they lived. A husband and wife could look alike physically, and also they could express such a great degree of harmony in their everyday lives that it seemed they were one and the same person. These people have developed, to some degree, a certain polarity between them. This polarity development means, that through various past lifetimes and in the many varied relationships, they have lived together as husband and wife, as father and son, daughter and mother, etc., and in the general exchange of life experiences between them, they have, as is the Principle of Infinite Regeneration, so accumulated the various values of these experiences from exactly opposite or diametrically opposed poles of consciousness.

Between themselves they would share the common attributes of so envisioning within their own minds what this experience is; but they would have arrived at this general consummation of experience quotients from two exactly different directions. This too, is all part of the infinite way God expresses Himself through every human being; just as in every other particular thing which you may see in the infinite macrocosm and microcosm, there are no two exact facsimiles at any given time or place, and also these divers and sundry forms are continuously changing.

So for these people who have so developed this polarity between themselves, we can expand this concept on up into the spiritual dimensions; and we can picture that when any two human beings can also interrelate themselves in the same polarity development with other human beings in the various multiples of four, eight, ten, twelve, etc., we can arrive in

110

some future spiritual dimension and see whole communities or whole planets populated by people who are expressing common polarities among themselves; we even go beyond this concept and see that the Infinite Mind of God Himself is composed of an Infinite number of minds who are so merged in polarity that they have become the universal expressive principle of life which manifests in these general continuities of expressions into all of the macrocosm and microcosm.

However, here too, we cannot assume any definite terminating point of Infinity, for Infinity immediately suggests an even greater interpolation of principle of expression and regeneration from further continuities of polarities as they are contained from one Infinite into another. However, to picture these concepts within the conscious mind, as they may be contained in such comparative values with which you are more familiar, is beyond the normal capabilities of the human mind. Your future, as it is so contained in the evolutionary principle, will present to you many seemingly abstruse differentiations and you should not, at any time, become emotionally involved with them to the point where they could waylay you from your evolutionary course.

You must always realize and remember that there is a logical and scientific way in which all things can be equated satisfactorily. So far as your present position in the earth world is concerned, you are evolving out of this world; you are not one of those humans who think this world is all there is, or that you are only here once and you're going to get the most out of it, etc., the famous last words of many humans who live today as they have lived from out of the past ages. As a consequence these people must return again and again to the earth worlds until they too, have that spiritual precognition which will enable them to gradually evolve from out these dimensions of the baser

111

material worlds, into the higher and more highly developed spiritual worlds.

Do not be confused at any time by what people may say to you, for one persons opinion does not change the face of Infinity. You are concerned with your own personal evolution, and in respect to the Infinite, this must be at all times progressive. It will also present to the Infinite, your own individual facsimile of experience and the interpretation of experience values which you obtain from your spiritual evolution. As these values change so must your philosophy of life; your science, as it is contained in the various expressions of Unarius, must be so adequately understood and used that it will enable you, at all times to most thoroughly compensate for the various differences which may seemingly confuse you for the moment. Friends, relatives, and even worlds will pass. This is the normal consequence of evolution. It is not to be feared, but it is to be looked forward to in anticipation; it is a challenge to your own mentality as to how well you can conceive within your mind the diverse factors which are involved in this progressive evolution. Should you fail to do so, you will revert back to the carnal primitive state of existence as it is lived in this world; even worse you may precipitate yourself into some of the hellish nightmares such as were pictured in Dante's Inferno.

So, do not be afraid to lose the present form of your earth world. It has enormous compensations in the way in which your future life will be lived; the many friends whom you will meet and live with in the higher spiritual worlds, the greater and ever-increasing horizons of mental introspection will be yours, when you have acquired the reasonable facsimile of mind equation; and you will be able to attune yourself to an even greater and ever-expanding Infinite Consciousness. This will be your challenge; how well you do this will be determined entirely by you. There is

112

no one who can do it for you, and there is no system, political, religious, or otherwise, which will even begin to adequately suffice, in a small way, any of the various evolutionary factors or their interpretations for you. This is what Jesus called, "Finding the Kingdom of Heaven which is within."

# CHAPTER 13

## Symbology—Idolatry

It has been philosophized that Truth is like a beautiful jewel of many facets, and it must be ever turned that fresh facets and new beauty may be presented to the beholder. In this respect then, let us turn our attention to another facet of this jewel of Truth and attempt, in the context of pure philosophy, to gain a more abstract reason for the various life evaluations which people are so concurrently expressing.

Universally speaking, this third dimensional or earth world can be said to be a world of symbology; that is, in the pure and simple philosophical stance, all things, all forms, and all derivatives of expressions derived from the various suggestions from these different forms, whether they are suggestive or auto-suggestive, reside purely in the dimension of symbology. The common interpretation of symbology in emotional values is contained in certain reciprocations of energy wave forms oscillating in the psychic anatomy. These interpretations were previously so continuously revitalized and rebuilt from previous life associations in these same common practices of symbologies. If you look about your world you will see that your house, your city, your community, and your nation are all, in a more pure abstraction, merely symbols; that is these forms exist as continuities of general expressions as

they were lived by you and others like you, throughout the past in numerous lifetimes; as energy wave
forms in collective conglomerate amassments, they
were thus continuously re-impinging themselves,
harmonically attuned into your consciousness.

Continuing further along the line in this retrospection, let us visualize that even the more common and
intangible elements of life are, in themselves, symbols;
even speech, the word forms, which are uttered in
various syllables, are autosuggestive in their nature.
That is, through previous familiar associations such
word forms were, through the dimension of reactionary, emotional experience, beginning to mean something in the form of consciousness as it was expressed in general continuities in your life. The furniture
which you use in your home, the pictures on the
walls, the numerous light waves which come to you
as they are reflected from these various objects; the
wave forms of sound which come to you, the sundry
sensations of taste, of feeling, etc., are all continuities
of wave forms previously associated with such similar
wave forms in past lifetime experiences.

Yes, even in numerous political systems, whether
they are called democratic, capitalistic, communistic,
imperialistic or whatever name you wish to give them,
as they express themselves, are not really, in essence,
of any importance to us other than upon the plane of
introspection when we can conceive them as again
expressive continuities from out of the past. As such,
these various and sundry symbologies are again
merely reliving themselves in a new expression or a
new form, and are compounded with the present tense
of time in different developments of environmental
situations; they can be said to be gradually developing,
or conversely retrogressing, or beginning to evolve in
certain stages of decadency.

History will depict that civilizations have risen and
civilizations have fallen, simply because these things

115

too, as they concern people, were also direct continuities in symbologies as they were expressed by the earth man in reliving certain resurgent or regenerative cycles of continuity of expression from the Infinite Consciousness. This too, was all part of this great concept of Infinity. The starting of evolution, as it has been pictured, the facsimilies, of the many varied life expressions impounded and amassed collectively, on the basis of harmonic frequency attunement into such energy configurations, have been described as psychic anatomies; and these anatomies are continuously re-expressing themselves into their original formative state or their original third dimensional world.

So likewise, the presentation of this more complete abstraction gives us a picture depicting in reality that all things are, in form and essence, purely spiritual in nature. The earth world, in numerous forms of expression, etc., merely gives more timely recurrences or re-expressions of the same continuities of expression from the previous cycles of life. Therefore, the earth man can be considered to be purely a creature of automation. His various libidos or drives are merely sustained forms of consciousness auto-suggestively or suggestively impinged in his consciousness to the extent that he can react to them.

Life itself, and the demand that life be lived is by far the greatest drive which is generally expressed by mankind today. Yet, mankind does not, as a whole, understand the reason this life should exist; neither does he know, in the more complete abstractions, the continuity of his life expressions as they are lived and relived from life to life or that they may be lived in higher spiritual worlds.

The point to be made at this particular time is this: as a creature of automation, man is, and must be continuously stimulated by the form of various expressive agencies which come to him from out of the

116

material world, forming the greatest part of the power motivating force in his life so far as his own personal experience is concerned. However, we cannot lose sight of another very important fact, that automation in the average human goes on successively from moment to moment, from year to year, and life to life, in many other ways which are strictly functions of Infinite Consciousness. That is the numerous energy forms and atomic constituents which are continuously regenerated in his physical body in various cell structures, and in many other physical functions are purely automations which are part of the general conglomerate amassment of wave form experiences lived from out the past and so recompounded in psychic anatomies lived and relived by different plant and animal species in the world today.

Now, at this point we must begin to look into the higher spiritual worlds and conceive within our minds the possibility that life, lived in the higher spiritual worlds, is not motivated by the automating devices of various different wave form impingements which may come to us on the basis of their emotional differences in previous life experiences. In other words, we may be able to assimilate or to take into consciousness, as they are being radiated in the general cosmogony, the sundry forms and expressions of life in a way and manner which is entirely unemotional in nature. That is, it does not present to us our own involvement in various life and death experiences from the past. Instead, it becomes a great harmony of expression as it is so universally and dynamically re-expressed from the Infinite Mind.

The implications of the concept are likewise infinite in nature, once having passed the threshold of conception wherein the individual mind becomes a functional entity of consciousness with the Infinite and is no longer emotionally involved with varied past conformations of continuities, then such a person,

117

who is so functioning in this more infinite manner and way, can be said to be God-like in nature. He has passed the dimension of emotional experience of his own personal involvement in such various continuities of expression which may have come to him from out of the past.

However, it must be remembered that, to such a person, concept must maintain a facsimile of consciousness in the more pure abstraction of sundry forms which may come to him; these too, can exist with him in a way and manner in which they can be continuously reattuned to his consciousness without the emotional quotient which was contained in his previous earth life dispensations. So far as the earth world is concerned and its expressive continuities, as they are symbolized in all forms of life about you, the divers and sundry and more objective realizations with these symbologies can be reclassified into such dimensions of introspection as various types of idolatry; that is, until any individual can and does have the faculty of independent thinking, as has been previously described, the ability to instantaneously and harmonically attune consciousness to the Infinite Mind without the ramifications of being emotionally involved from the past, he can be said to be a materialistic being. He is still subjective to the numerous systems of idolatries as they are composed out of the diverse symbolic forms which are always expressing themselves to him in the world about him.

Religion is a symbology, but true religion cannot be lived until the true inward nature of the higher dimensions is fully realized within consciousness. Religion must, therefore, always exist to the earth man as a symbology, wherein he can reasonably conceive that he will escape the diverse perditions of his earth world and be rescued by some deistic system. Idolatries, of course, take form and shape in many different ways. Bank accounts are built upon a common form of idolatry which is based upon the primitive urge to survive—survival without reason or without a reasonable equation of why life does exist. Likewise, if people are presented with the inevitable and inescapable fact that they too must exist, purely within the dimension of consciousness, without being emotionally involved and without the various concurrent systems of idolatries, they are immediately frustrated because their minds refuse to function independently from other experience quotients which have been so impounded in their psychic anatomies. They have not yet risen to that plane of consciousness wherein they are, in essence, an instrument which is capable of attuning itself independently and without emotionalism into the higher interdimensional interplays of harmonic relationship which exists throughout the Infinite Cosmogony.

Perhaps it should be pointed out that this is the problem of Unarius as it concerns itself with the various and numerous students upon the earth today; these people are taking their first step in the direction wherein their minds can be independently participating in such general energy configurations as are universally acceptable in the general scheme of Infinite Understanding. The problem here is basically and purely within the individual himself; as Jesus said, "Finding the Kingdom of Heaven within"; and finding this kingdom is not a proposition which can be acquired immediately. It will take many thousands of years and possibly much farther into the future than can be reasonably conceived within the individual before he attains a form of consciousness which is entirely independent of the environment in which he finds himself.

It is basically impossible for any earth man to think beyond the dimension of his own immediate surroundings as these concern him in the autosuggestive symbologies of his environment. A few people

119

have, to some extent, acquired a certain faculty which seems to attune them to some form of independence. These people are called mediums or clairvoyant in a sense that they may or may not be presenting, to some degree, certain unknown factors of spiritual dispensations to people with whom they are associating. This does not, in any sense, detract from our original thesis or the value of its content. The varied interplays of such psychisms as they concern the individual concept are, in themselves, purely automations of various wave form energies in which they were previously involved. Likewise, people who continue on into these various expressions may become lost unless they can find a suitable platform for equation.

We can best picture certain particular attainments of concept within our minds if we can visualize ourselves for one moment in the spiritual worlds without the knowledge of what these spiritual worlds are. At that moment consciousness is trying to assume or to re-establish itself in a thoroughly unfamiliar world which is not so autosuggestively inclined by symbology, simply because symbology does not reside in the higher spiritual worlds as is true in the more familiar earth worlds; therefore, the individual, as he now finds himself in the spiritual world, resorts to the common conscious or subconscious process. As he is purely a creature of energy and without a physical body, the psychic anatomy is, in itself, continuously oscillating in such various different earth life experiences as are more familiar or which are more strongly influential at that particular moment. The person can then be said to be living in a world of maya or illusion. He is relying purely upon his memory in a sense that these various psychic energy wave forms make the continuity of consciousness possible for him.

However, it is a false world and because these various energy wave forms which are so conveying such continuities of consciousness to him constantly must be recharged, and since he has no way of recharging them, save from the physical or the material surface of his life which is now no longer existent, these various energy wave forms which are so dominant and give him the memory pattern of his earth life, gradually begin to fade; that is unless he somehow can become parasitic and attach himself in the manner of attunement with some fellow earth man, whereby a certain proportion of this earth man's life will, to a degree, be reflected into or absorbed by the psychic entity of the person who has so attached himself to this individual. In that way, as an obsession, this disembodied entity can live for an indefinite length of time, or at least, until the earth man to whom he has attached himself, passes on into the spiritual world and likewise becomes an attachment to another earth man.

In the world about you, you will see literally millions of people and, as a matter of fact, practically every earth man has at least one or a number of these psychic attachments which are ever about him in every moment of his life. They are like little radios harmonically attuned to his various life experiences. They are reliving, to some extent, in a facsimile of consciousness, their various earth life experiences. Thus, at least temporarily, they seem to feel they are sustained or they are reliving these experiences, and until such a moment as they can again gain access into the material world through the womb, they will continue to do so.

This form of obsession is not entirely harmless, simply because most of these astral or spiritual entities, who have so become attached, may in themselves, be quite strong in their personalities; and they may, from time to time, try to impinge or assert themselves into the consciousness of their obsessed earth man. In this way the earth man can be said to

121

be obsessed. He is without reason for many of the acts which he does, in fact in moments of more complete obsession, he may even commit murder and other diverse crimes of violence, and be not entirely responsible for them; because in a particular moment of psychic emotionalism, the entity which was so attached to him took possession and controlled, in a sense, involuntarily coordinated muscular function to the point where the crime was committed.

At this point it becomes very apparent that you should be forewarned, and as you are forewarned and forearmed, you will be aware of the various dangers which come to you and which will be increasingly apparent as you progress into the spiritual worlds.

To be in the world and not of it will, in a sense, increase the consequences of the world about you, simply because these present a more complete opposite to that which you are generally trying to achieve within the consciousness of your own mind. The stresses and intemperances which were normally incepted by you in previous years or in past lifetimes now become some great crises or emotional disturbances. You become extra sensitive because you are more highly attuned and the implications of the earth life are vastly increased. Conversely you should have and use much more wisdom, much more introspection to counteract these great numbers of materialistic derelictions which have now become increasingly apparent to you.

The systems of idolatry and the life generally practiced in the symbolic form is quite useless to you in combating these various differences. Your philosophy should, by now, impound an entirely new dimension of introspection. In a sense then you can be said to be oscillating more infinitely. To lose one form of idolatry, as it is symbolized in your life, and to supplant it with another is quite useless. You cannot lose one form of religion, one form of life expression and supplant it with some other forms which, while they may seem to present differences, are really similar in principle. That is, they are merely autosuggestive symbologies with their more normally associated idolatries reasserting themselves in your own consciousness.

In the future then, try to always live in consciousness as it is so compounded by principle of regeneration. Expression as it is conceived in Infinite concept is most valuable to you and will give you a reasonable platform whereon you can reasonably equate all various differences in the world about you, and will help you to see how it is people practice their diverse symbologies and their attendant idolatries.

# CHAPTER 14

## Church Systems vs.
## Personal Responsibility

The dictionary defines religion as a code of ethics; however in a more generally accepted frame of reference, religion relates to the various interpretations of life which are considered spiritual in nature therefore religion assumes a certain transition of life or an interpolation of life values as they are concerned with various churches or deistic beliefs. It is also generally acknowledged, that at this time the Christian religion ranks among the greatest religions of the world; that is, numerically speaking, more than 800 million people profess in some manner or form to be Christian adherents. However, it is neither acknowledged nor conceded that the Christian religion is Christian in its interpretation. This can be historically proven and can also be seen to assume as its outward expression in varied church configurations, in deistic interpretations, as merely readaptations of old pagan beliefs or renditions in a more modern manner; but basically still remaining pagan in all various dispensations. This, in itself, presents an equally great paradox, for it is exactly opposite in all its content and rendition to the simple philosophical approach to life as was taught by the Nazarene, 2000 years ago.

To further study the life and the philosophy taught

by Jesus, it can easily be seen that such a direct philosophical approach would defeat the entire context
of Christianity as it is expressed in this present age.
The belief in the various configurations as they are
posed by present-day Christianity would, in effect—in
fact it does in all effect—render this simple philosophy of Jesus, completely ineffective and incapable
of operating in its effect with anyone who professes
Christianity and practices its various beliefs.

Conversely, the existence of any Christian church
or the entire context of Christianity, as a whole, would
completely pass from the earth, should the various
Christian adherents turn to the true philosophy of life
taught by Jesus. It can also be reasonably assumed
that the Christian religion would not have sprung into
existence and flourished during the past 2000 years,
unless it had somehow acquired certain elements
which can be considered, in a psychological vein, to
be coercive or mandatory in nature.

A case in point which demonstrates how well the
church edifice has taken mental responsibility completely away from the individual, was carried in a
recent story printed by a local newspaper. A woman
who was, at a particular moment, in a confessional,
drew a loaded revolver and threatened the priest with
his life, saying that he and other priests had not prayed for her and her family, sufficiently strong enough
to eliminate certain particular conditions which were
then in existence in her family life. This story immediately suggests many implications; that this woman,
along with some 500 million other Catholics, has
been taught, since birth, that the numerous interpolations of life should be considered strictly the
property of the church; that such munificent blessings which come to these various adherents are specifically handed out through the priesthood of the
church; also, that any and all people must approach
God or Jesus, through the priesthood. Moreover, it

suggests that the keys to heaven and hell are held by the sundry priests in the church; these keys will unlock the various different doors to any person allowing him to pass through.

How different is this great hypocrisy from the teaching which was taught 2000 years ago, by Jesus; the one who was purportedly to be the keystone or cornerstone in the structure of Christian beliefs. For Jesus taught the simple philosophy of life which mandated that every person must, individually, assume a personal and moral responsibility, not only to himself, but to the Creative Intelligence which engendered his existence. The keystone to the arch of understanding in this simple philosophy is posed in that teaching of Jesus, when He said, "Seek ye first the Kingdom of Heaven which is within, and all things shall be added unto you." Obviously, the Kingdom of Heaven is within, and not within some church as is posed by the priesthood. This is further verified by another utterance of Jesus when He spoke and said, "The Father and I are one and the same." This also clearly indicates that the Kingdom or the Father, which are synonymous, are personal property of every individual, and can be found within the confines of his own interpretation and from his concept of creation.

Obviously too, there seems to be some contradiction in a later quotation of Jesus when He was asked about performing miracles, and He spoke thusly, "Of myself I do nothing, but it is the Father within who doeth all things." While this may appear to be a contradiction, it is easily explained when it is understood; when Jesus spoke of the Higher or Superconscious Self—as it is explained in the teachings of Unarius— this Superconscious Self was an abstraction, synonymous to the Father. For in detracting from the personal noun content of the word "Father," Father became the Creative Intelligence which had, in effect, created the macrocosm and microcosm; and was, therefore, the inherent property of all substance both visible and invisible; and this "Father" was also a regenerative, progressive principle of evolution which propagated and fostered all forms of life, visible and invisible.

Therefore, here was the difference: When Jesus spoke in one manner and said, "The Father and I are one and the same," He spoke in the metaphor of the connection of the Superconscious Self with the Infinite Father. And when He spoke of Himself as, "Of myself I do nothing, but it is the Father within who doeth all things," meaning that the physical man did nothing; but it is the Father in conjunction with the Superconscious Self which was responsible for all the seeming miracles which were wrought by His interpretation of the Superconscious Self into various illnesses and psychic derelictions of people who came to him.

An even greater contradiction is carried in that utterance and instruction of Jesus, when He spoke thusly unto His followers and said, "Do not worship as does the heathen, nor in public places, neither in temples nor in synagogues, but retire into the closet of thine own self and seek out the Father within, that He may reward thee openly." How could it be then, that more than 800 million people who would profess Christianity, leave this all-important function of personal ethics, upon the shoulders of some priesthood; for should every one of these Christian adherents following the instructions of Jesus, start to retire into the secret closet of his own self and begin seeking out the Father within, it would soon be seen that the churches would pass from the face of the earth. And along with the passing of churches, would go the various other different heathen interpretations of life which are seen in the war-like attitudes of people against one another, the numerous parasitic attitudes, the demands that one ideology must be the ideology of all, the psychotic interpretations of life which so many individuals try to superimpose as the dominant interpretation of life upon thousands or millions of their fellow citizens.

It can be considered therefore, that any effect so far as the Christian is concerned in removing moral responsibility from the consciousness of the individual, or that the church has assumed this moral responsibility as its own interpretation or reference of life, people can, therefore, react toward one another as they see fit to do; that they may be sublimated into various reactionary differences, ultimately resolving all these varied sublimations by the right of intercession, as it is posed by the Christian Church.

How different this is from the simple direct philosophy of life as taught by Jesus; that we as individuals are, to ourselves, in reference to the Great Infinite Creative Intelligence, directly responsible for all thought and action in our daily lives. This does not resolve itself into dispensations which are rendered from some priesthood in the temple. It is the closet of our own inner selves. It is where we find the Father within who dwelleth in the Eternal Kingdom, for the substance, the understanding of the Father and the Infinite Kingdom, does in effect, become the substance of life. With knowledge comes usage, in a direct proportion and equilibrium which is manifest throughout an entire lifetime, and extends into any lifetime in which the individual can be reasonably assumed to reincarnate, to occupy various intermediate lives in spiritual worlds where he will again polarize certain quotients of Infinite Consciousness, which will be worked out and polarized with the Higher Superconscious Self. This is true reincarnation or evolution.

The development of the spiritual consciousness— the personal entity of spiritual consciousness—which is the inherent birthright of every human being, and which, as part of the regenerative principle of life, is instigated and propagated by Infinite Intelligence, and must ultimately function through all dimensions and transpositions of life, irrespective of color, race, creed, or belief. For the earth as a whole, as seen in conjunction with an infinite number of terrestrial planets throughout the great cosmic universe, is, in effect, the first of many stages of development through which man begins this evolutionary flight to a higher state of consciousness.

Church systems, as they exist today on this earth, are to some degree, necessary in the first primitive and elemental stages of man's development. However, they can never be conceived to be the more ultimate possibilities of concept which any individual can attain, should he pursue a constructive evolution. Infinity always poses the great challenge of infinite understanding, so that a person who is minded in a likewise fashion can always constructively expand his consciousness into horizons of understanding. How could it be that a Super Intelligence who was wise enough, sufficient unto himself through a regenerative principle of life to create planetary systems, galaxies, and even universes; yes, and universes beyond universes, be insufficiently intelligent to mandate the various transpositions of life into the priesthood of a few foundling priests, who had sufficiently coerced their fellow men into a false hypnotic belief in their supersedence of power over these poor souls, and mandated not only a somewhat more or less complete subjugation; but had also extracted from them a very affluent way of life. For these ministers, priests, monks, cardinals, popes, etc., all and sundry expressionists in these deistic configurations have set themselves up in power over their fellow men, knowing full well the hypocrisy of their position.

In this respect, at one time I was discussing the

129

various elements in the formation of the Christian religion with a minister, quite well known in this area. He professed that he knew, in fact was taught in the seminary, these sundry historical facts; but stated that the mother church did not allow him to teach or preach them to the congregation; but only in such aspects of life and their personal beliefs as would vindicate them in these respects. How great was the hypocrisy of this minister that he had not the inner fortitude to even contrive within his own mind, a vocal expression or giving voice to his own personal opinions on his religion; that he was mandated to give a strict circumference of interpretation in various deistic concepts, which were familiar to his congregation, to again reapply a certain salve or ointment to the sore spot of psychic pressure which everyone has in his transposition of life.

The great human complex which fosters the greatest reactionary content in all human transpositions and which can be psychologically termed an escape mechanism, is the sum total of all inequalities, all guilts, all presuppositions, and his overt acts toward humanity; so that the individual is pressurized into a great escape mechanism which finds its outlet and his greatest relief within the doors of his church, where again his minister will apply the opiate of religious salvation and salve to the sore spot of his psychic maladjustment.

Yes, I know these statements may sound startling, for when any individual suddenly realizes that he has now reached, and is passing over this threshold of conscious reality of himself, in retrospect with the Infinite, he is now suddenly confronted with an infinite existence which is not predicated upon the age-old escape mechanism, as it was deistically conceived with various pagan dispensations in past religions, but which is now realistically conceived as a personal element of personal moral responsibility, and his course and action determine the evolutionary principle of his existence. Man must now, in the future, and forever, be morally responsible for all acts and all thoughts as part of his consciousness. These would, in turn, become the substance of his future; not that he would be confronted with the inevitable judgment day and be judged by some false god; but that judgment would be rendered by himself, unto himself, by realizing in the more abstract precepts of consciousness, the difference between constructive and destructive evolution.

As these personal elements of life transpositions were so conceived and enacted by the individual, in the moment of their particular conception, they, in turn, become the material of his future. This was the way in which he found that he did truly seek and find the Kingdom within; that he had also found the regenerative principle of life which engendered all forms of consciousness, in personal reference to personal evolution, and the Father within, which gave the power of concept infinitely to each individual as he so conceived it within the dimension of his own life.

For in the future day when Infinity is so beheld and where moral responsibility is so predicated by an understanding of Infinity, then indeed the Father and I become one and the same. The Superconscious Self develops until it has become an entity of consciousness with the Infinite, into personal dimensions of reference in which it has endowed itself with certain regenerative and reconstructive processes derived from personal past experiences and mastery over these experiences in various material and spiritual worlds.

Nor is mastery to be misconstrued with such elements which can be considered egotistical in nature; for in mastery, function is attained infinitely, and according to the same lines of expression in which the universal Infinite so expresses Itself. For always in Infinity and with those who are so minded in evolution with Infinity, so must principle always be constantly reactivated, as the harmonic, regenerative, principle which functions and which makes life possible to them as a personal function.

How different then is this approach, this realization, and this life in the Infinite, from that of the savage barbarian who approaches some deistic configuration which he has contrived in his own mind. Or that he has so set up for himself the vision of priesthood in one of his fellow men, to whom he gives the power over him in his interpolation of his deistic manifestations in his daily life; or that he should continually, negatively, subjugate himself on bended knee, and pray to this false deification as a separate entity endowed with all human vicissitudes and temperaments; and if he is not constantly placated, if he is not so constantly compromised, if he is not so constantly sacrificed to, and given reminders of personal felicity, then could this god deification become angry, and refuse such munificent blessings to the wayward subject!

Such beliefs are indeed pagan in nature. They belong to the elemental mind of the savage barbarian who so contrived and conceived them. They do not belong in our modern new age in which mankind is supposedly functioning in more advanced dimensions of personal introspection, or that he is civilized; he is trying to abandon his warlike attitudes, he is trying to extend to his fellow man the concept of the golden rule.

So it must always be with each person who finds his pathway among the material worlds; should he wish to ascend to a higher life, should he be so spiritually quickened, and made aware of the possibility of a higher spiritual life; he will indeed have to find this way through the portals of his own consciousness. His interpretation of Infinite Consciousness into his daily life is not achieved through colleges, universities, nor in temples nor synagogues; neither in churches, nor in any other particular dispensations such as are found in the universal concept of material life; for these are, in turn, but their own relative personal aspects of interpretation which have been contrived from the barbaric past.

Educational Systems as they exist in the world today are, as a whole, merely historical; that is, there is nothing futuristic in any of these educational dispensations, save perhaps, a few very prophetic utterances which are only relative and indicative of some particular individual's more advanced perspective. There is nothing substantially proven in prophecy within the dimension of any person's life, and such prophetic beliefs reside purely on an esoterical plane in which the individual hopes someday may be partially realized.

How different then, is the dimension of understanding, which, when from within the consciousness of the individual, a substantial facsimile of the Infinite and Its regenerative principle can be compounded and seen to be actively working and participating in all forms and transpositions of life; to also give to the individual the highest and most substantial aspects of a future prognostication, in which he can envision the perpetual continuity of his life into ever-expanding horizons, into ever-increasing dimensions of relationships to his fellow men, wherein all principles of Infinite Creation will be fully vindicated.

The promise of the future as a prophetic utterance can never be presented as a singular happening in any individual life, predetermined as an act of consciousness; the future must always be envisioned as principle in action which, when combined with personal introspection, personal participation with this principle, can promise to the individual, the continuity of everlasting life. And so, if any person wishes to

133

attain the long-dreamed-of immortality, he cannot do so by presupposing intercession, or that someone has died for his wayward ways. Such beliefs must remain only in the infantile mind which presupposes salvation of life in the universal guilt complex of mankind.

The immortality of life is conceived in the idealism that participation is a natural consequence of understanding the principle of Infinite regeneration. So if you would seek the promise of eternal salvation, do not seek it in the manner and way of another man's life; do not seek it in his temple or church; do not seek it in his college, or his school; but seek it as Jesus said you must, within the secret closet of your own self, for within this secret closet there will come to you the thread of continuity of Infinite Intelligence; an Intelligence which will superimpose Itself into your daily life. It will give you a direct understanding into all forms of consciousness about you; there will be a direct connotation with this Infinite Principle in all things which you so manifest as part of this regenerative principle in action.

When you have begun to acquire this function of mind which links you with the Infinite Principle, then you are finding the Kingdom of Heaven. And as you see Principle in action, you will see the Father at work, the true Father which has engendered all forms of consciousness; the Father who, when working as the Creative Power of the Infinite, has contrived not only all the atoms in your body and their function, but in combination with all other atoms in the terrestrial macrocosm, and the planetary systems, the galaxies, the universes; yes even far beyond all this, the great spiritual worlds which stretch out in a never-ending series of progressive evolutions which you will make to them, should you so continuously, within yourself, strive to seek.

For again as Jesus said, "Seek and ye shall find, knock and the door shall be opened." So the power of personal emancipation lies within the dimension of everyone. It is within the secret closet of your own mind, it is not within the closet of another man; nor in his church. It is the way in which you will find within the secret closet, the way in which the Father can reward you openly.

For in this ever-expanding understanding, the continuity of life will be expressed, not as reactionary principle of old pagan deistic beliefs, but as an ever-expanding principle of continuity, of resurgent expression, of revitalizing, ever-changing, regenerating, life.

# CHAPTER 15

## Sufficient Unto Each Day
## The Evil Thereof

In various ecclesiastical dispensations which are Christian in nature, there are as in various other elements of life, a constant and repetitious uttering of different truisms and clichés. One of these truisms refers, specifically, to the life of Jesus of Nazareth; and this life is referred to as "the greatest life ever lived." No attempt will be made at this time to evaluate in an objective manner, the validity of this truism in respect to certain historical configurations.

The greatness of any man's life, in a manner of speaking assumed to be great, seems to be in a direct proportion to how well he has confused those who followed after him and tried to interpret the manner of his thinking. This was quite true with Socrates who confounded the people of Athens in his time and day, with the approach to thinking in an unlimited and unhampered dimension of introspection. The crusade of this thinking was later picked up by a student named Plato; others followed after, including Aristotle. Yet, even unto this day, the precepts of their basic philosophies and the manner in which they approached the interdimensional introspection has, to a large degree, been quite confusing to the various devotees who have followed after these expressionists;

136

and in contrast, with the confusion which they have generated, they have arrived at some greatness.

The same philosophy is true with the life of Jesus; a study of the various dispensations as they are contained in the New Testament, reveal an obvious fact; that Jesus taught in parables, obviously for the purpose which was quite well known to Him, to cause people to think their way out of a story, so to speak; and thereby derive the moral value of the parable. The same is quite true with Aesop, who compounded a series of diverse life depictions, each in itself, carrying the same moral lesson which applied to all human relationships. The value of such an approach to the deliverance of a psychological interpretation or some basic plane of moral reference should never be underrated; in fact, it should be considered as the best means to achieve certain ends when it concerns the dispensations of various teachings, which are somewhat either in opposition to, or in advance of generally accepted living practices.

In general, it can be considered that the most potent of all parables so uttered by Jesus in His time, and one which, incidentally, is the least understood and most neglected of all such parables, is the simple utterance "Sufficient unto each day, the evil thereof." Various different ways and means have been attempted, to try to explain this simple parable; all inadequate, and all insufficient; just as is the general approach to the varied parabolistically conceived concepts in the New Testament, which have been so sadly confused and misinterpreted in various ways and manners. To a large extent the value of the true Christian philosophy has been largely overridden in later and more subsequent developments by certain individuals in an attempt to establish a certain church dispensation of various philosophical configurations, and which were later misconstrued as religion. This was the basic task which Paul—who was formerly

Saul of Tarsus—took up in the beginning of the Christian church and its later developments into subsequent branches such as the Greek Orthodox and the Roman Catholic.

In these later developments, the true cause and purpose of Jesus' mission was largely lost; instead of the philosophical approach to his basic understanding of life, it was now completely overridden and distorted by false deification of the church concept. Indeed the very principle of self-emancipation from the dogma and rhetorical-like earth life, its creeds and its pedantic attitudes were, in themselves, the basic elements which over-rode and superimposed this false liturgy into the simple basic concept of Jesus.

The parable, "Sufficient unto each day, the evil thereof," while seemingly concerning some simple expressionary element of life was indeed much more than that, and in a general synthesis could be said to embrace the entire concept of a progressive evolution. For, in general, derivatives which could be extracted from this parable, anyone could see that the approach to a constructive and progressive evolution must be always predicated upon certain denominators of negative and positive relationships. It is in this sense, therefore, that we shall refer, in general, to certain existing scientific terms which relate, specifically, in the dimension of the electronic sciences as they are expressed in the world today.

The terms negative and positive relate to two polarities in the transmission of some electrical current which is traveling over any particular wire or through any given area at any time, such as in a radio transmission. The terms positive and negative also relate to the different or extreme ends of expression, or a complete reversal as it is concerned with the expression of its content, as an entity of expression. In this sense, we can likewise compare all equations of life in

138

a similar manner.

In retrospect with certain happenings of yesterday or in the year before—and assuming that we have extracted from these various experiences, certain comparative values of relationship with subsequent experience happenings—we can, therefore, equate past experiences into present, or more recent happenings on the basis of negative and positive polarities; or, that we have equated in retrospection, a certain difference of transposition as some past experience as it has, in a comparative sense, linked itself in a new value of relationship to the more immediate present, through subsequent experience happenings, even though these were, more or less, only remotely connected with the original happening. Therefore the past sequences of the former years, as progressive happenings were superimposed upon them, and can be considered basically as negative-positive experience quotients.

It is in this introspection and synthesis that we arrive at a much greater meaning to the parable, "Sufficient unto each day, the evil thereof"; for as these numerous infractions of introspection are thus compounded from out of the experience dimension of the past, in combination with more recent happenings; and considering that these are, in a sense, more positively biased, because of obtaining certain mastery proportions of these experiences, or that we have lived through them and gained something valuable from them; we have then, indeed, approached a realistic personal realization of the parable of Jesus when He said, "Sufficient unto each day, the evil thereof."

Continuing on, and expanding this concept into future evolutions, we can indeed form a very basic platform for properly understanding our progressive evolution into the future; not only as it concerns our more immediate future, in the years until that time when death separates us from our physical anatomy,

139

but also in diverse successive earth lives, or into any other lives which may be lived in higher spiritual dimensions. The position of negative to positive in respect to various experiences through which we have traveled is always the determinance, in its respective polarities, to our progressive evolution; when we can gain more in retrospection to where yesterday and its experiences have carried over as a positive manifestation or polarity of mastership, into our present dimension, or horizon of thinking, then we have indeed mastered more of this progressive spiritual, positive and negative—or negative and positive—equation, and therefore advanced our future.

Conversely, the same is true; while we should, in any event, be always so positively minded of the present in respect to the past, it is sometimes, sad to say, that many people take the opposite position and inversely proportion their past in a negative sequence. That is, if they have stolen an article in the past and they have gotten away with it, (so to speak) this seems to give them a positive position in their moral equation and they believe that in the future they can get away with something even larger and more extensive. This is conversely, the negative biasing of the negative past; and in this respect, the individual is sure to precipitate himself into a never-ending downward spiral, and only a direct miracle of strong personal faith and dedication can save him from the everlasting and never diminishing pits of hell.

So it is wise to see, that in the manner and life of a person, such as Jesus, in the supreme continuity of the Superconscious as an abstract proportion of the Infinite that even the most commonplace acts and utterances were those of great portent and meaning. Indeed, nothing, even in the most minute quantity could be neglected in this Man's life. It is sad to state that the subsequent years which He survived, were not perpetuated as a philosophical Light to guide people into a better way of life, but were expressed as merely a church configuration; that in this general deterioration of the understanding of His basic life philosophy there is, as of today, little semblance between the philosophy of Jesus and the dogmatic attitude of the church system which uses "Jesus," as its central configuration!

For as the philosophy of Jesus was compounded from the simple approach to life, through the doorway of concept, which every individual is developing in his evolution through time and space, and through the various terrestrial and spiritual worlds, this entity of consciousness is, in itself, the single cell of everlasting life which will ultimately resolve any such person with this cell into an ever-expanding program of eternal life.

How strange indeed, that this basic concept has been so sadly warped and distorted by the demigods of the church systems; how they have set themselves up on the pedestals to be worshiped, to be deified, or to be considered as the sole expressionary element in a supreme plan of consciousness, wherein the very principle of life was made possible through the intercession of consciousness—not through a priest, but through the doorway of personal experience in some particular life dispensation. For as the experience was so lived and gave unto this person living it, the ultimate answer to the configuration of some earth life dispensation, so could the more ultimate end be achieved; that in general and in subsequent and unlimited earth life experiences, the individual would have within his consciousness the general conformity, the general concept, of the universal Infinity.

This then, is one of the parables uttered by a man credited with having lived the greatest of all lives; yet to those who have studied His life and in comparison to existing forms and dispensations of this life, its existence as a religious symbol, is a complete reversal

141

to the doctrine of everlasting knowledge, and the acquisition of wisdom as a direct attribute in the continuous expression of everlasting life. The concept of salvation through intercession, or the remission of sins through intercession, becomes repulsive and defeats the purpose of this great life; defeats the entirety of its philosophy, robs the individual of personal integrity, and divests him of all moral responsibility, either to himself, his fellow man, or to his Infinite Creator. *For the life of Jesus and His philosophy was, in essence and in principle, the ever-expanding dimension of consciousness which, in itself, guaranteed Immortality as an entity of the Creative Consciousness or the Infinite Intelligence which had first sponsored Its beginnings in some terrestrial dimension.*

And so the enigma of Christianity remains, whether it is one of the greatest or the lesser of the world's religions; whether or not it is expressed in any of the current configurations or various denominations, these all have robbed the mission, the purpose of the life of Jesus, and despite their claims that He lived the greatest of all lives, He has, indeed, lived the greatest of all martyrdoms. For while He did (so history claims) in a physical world, die on the cross in the crucifixion; yet since that time He has daily been crucified in innumerable ways through various church dispensations. For the crucification of His ideology and His philosophy is the greatest of all human tragedies which has ever been written in the pages of history; one which has—in this day and time—brought mankind to the place where he is beginning to reap the whirlwinds of his indiscretions. He is beginning to harvest the fruit of his false and thwarted ideologies whereby he has sought to compensate the paganistic beliefs of the past, with the all-inclusive predominant philosophy of life which was taught in the parabolistic form and manner by

142

the Man of Nazareth.

Yes, great indeed has been the misconception of this Man; He did *not* teach to believe in Him, as a personal being, who would guarantee salvation; but to believe in the *Principle of personal salvation as a development of the Superconscious, or Christ Self, as a direct facsimile of the Infinite, Creative, Intelligence;* that you should be born into spirit before you could hope for eternal life; and that this rebirth was the development of consciousness which would extend into the Principle of Infinite Perspectus.

# CHAPTER 16

## Nothing Is Sacred or Holy

Every person who is sincerely dedicated in attaining a higher spiritual way of life, in achieving immortality, and living in the higher spiritual dimensions, should begin at once to learn of the Infinite Creator and to practice such knowledge; also, he should begin to strip from himself and remove all various materialistic, obsessive, intimidating concepts and thought forms which will remain with him in this material world. For as long as these different thought forms, which are coercive in nature, remain with him, they will surely bind him to the earth world and its way of life. These numerous configurations of intimidating agencies and thought forms can be anything from eating and sleeping, to different conformities of society, political systems, etc.; but above all else, his concepts of the religious systems under which he has been concurrently living, since the beginning of his evolution, must be re-evaluated.

In the words of the religionist himself, he must cleanse and purify his garments of all earthly taint before he can enter the kingdom of heaven. However, at this point we do depart from the context of religion; for any and all religions—whatever their names may be, and in whatever way they are known or practiced—do exist by the same coercive principle; that all adherents must resign themselves to more or

144

less complete dominion by the priesthood of these religions; all mental and moral justifications are, in the end, a result of the different configurations of deistic forces which are in effect at that particular moment. Therefore, the adherent, at least, so far as he is able to determine for himself, has been relieved of all moral responsibility and all personal integrity in justifying these different deistic systems which are called religion.

The way to a higher spiritual life is an interdimensional proposition, and predicated upon the individual presentation that every person must, through experience, and through other different personal factors of intelligent introspection, progress or evolve into these higher spiritual worlds as a matter of personal evolution. It cannot be done for him by the priesthood of a church or a temple; it cannot be done by some supposed deification. The individual himself, and he alone, can and must accomplish this supreme objectivism. To better serve the purpose of removing such obsessive and intimidating thought forms and other concepts from their position in the psychic anatomy, and the possibility that they are subconsciously or consciously exerting some influence in your daily life, we will again examine some of the more historical aspects or the beginnings of the Christian religion as it is posed in the Bible.

First however, we must destroy the illusion of sacredness or the belief that the Bible is a sacred and holy book. Actually there is nothing sacred nor holy in the entire Infinite Universe; nor in the entire Infinite macrocosm—save that our own personal and moral integrity should be held sacred and inviolate above all other things, and also our right to achieve immortal life through the doorway of our own personal integrity. The reference that the Bible is a sacred book is strictly hearsay and is not supported, either by fact or by any other means, despite the wide acclaim

145

among the ecclesiastical religionists who support their religion in this claim.

The Bible must be regarded as simply a compilation of fact and fiction, and it is largely legendary in nature; therefore, it can be reasonably supposed that these various protocols, which were related not only to community life, but also to religion in general, wherein the peoples of different nations were concerned with the development of this religion, had been handed down from father to son and from generation to generation.

In different epistles of Unarius we have presented various aspects of this historical background and explained how present-day Christianity is merged with numerous different cultisms and paganisms of the past; the derivations and extractions of these religions, were merged into the first Christian Church by Paul, at the beginning of the Christian era. Up until some two or three hundred years before the crucifixion, there is absolutely no evidence to substantiate any claim that there is a written record of the Jewish people; all such different histories have come down through the epochs of time as a matter of legend; that is, they have been stories told, retold, and recounted from generation to generation, and can be reasonably supposed to have a considerable amount of distortion and various other intimidating elements which have entered into the relating of these experiences; so at no time can they be reasonably supposed to be pure in nature and related to the actual transposition or happenings of those people. Moreover, those people were, in more ancient times, under the influence of various superstitions much more strongly than people are at the present time. They had no recourse to science, neither did they know of the diverse ways in which life could be manifest from the higher spiritual worlds, nor of the different agencies which were more scientifically related to mankind and his life on the planet earth.

Therefore, all religions were deistic in nature; they constructed their own effigies, worshipped them, and relegated the various dispensations of these gods through the priesthood of their churches. One of the prime deifications which has survived through time is Jahweh. Some 2500 years B.C., Jahweh, the old Babylonian god of Abraham, was worshipped by Abraham and formed the dominating figure, not only of Christianity, but also of the Moslem world and its readaptations of God known as Allah. However, the first five books of the Old Testament are basically intact in the Koran, just as they are in the Bible; and these were relayed down through the different epochs and phases of historical advents of the Jewish people in their final written form in the Old Testament.

Let us begin in Genesis to more or less scientifically scrutinize the Bible, to place it under a different light where, in the variances of this introspection, we can point out the most obvious flaws, discrepancies, and other false beliefs which have survived through the centuries. The Old Testament begins by saying that first there was darkness; then the Lord said, "Let there be light," and there was light. Now, this presents some obvious discrepancies, and a somewhat enigmatical position with the Creator who, up until that time when He said, "Let there be light," was apparently floating about suspended in space and total darkness, having neither purpose nor reason for His existence; yet such a powerful entity was able to instantaneously create light and after having created light, He then further points out the disparity of His position, that He was floating in space unattended and without any apparent rhyme or reason for being a God.

Now, after having created the earth, He found that it was complete in every respect, except for one thing —there were no people. So He created man, and in

147

this creation He apparently abandoned His previous hocus-pocus—abracadabra disposition and got down into creating more earth-like effigies such as taking mud from the river bank, and like some small child, constructed it into the figure of a man. Then He breathed the breath of life into it. This is a further distorted concept of that which we might reasonably expect from such an entity or a god who was powerful enough to create universes.

However, our depreciation of God is not complete unless we continue further into our discussion. It is said by the religionist and by the Christian that God created man in His own image; if this is true, then we can only say that the first and original concept of God, as being a Supreme Being, is not entirely whole and is subject to doubt and criticism. For all men are said to have a sexual mechanism, and if this is so and man is created in the image of God, then surely God had sexual parts. This is further substantiated by the fact that after having created Adam, God realized that Adam was alone, so He created woman; this He did by taking one of Adam's ribs; which further deviated from the usual hocus-pocus—abracadabra method by which He first had created the heavens and the earth.

It is not stated nor clearly defined in the Bible that woman was included in the supposition that she was also created in God's image; but this is usually taken for granted. Therefore, we can assume that as man and woman are now merged into two identities within God, that God was bisexual, or in other words, He was what is commonly known as a hermaphrodite. He was capable, not only of self insemination, but also He was capable of delivering a child. If this is true, then why should this same God so intimidate Mary, as is recorded in the New Testament, and enter into what is called immaculate conception; when God could have accomplished this same purpose individually and by Himself? Of course these various in-

148

timations in this creative process are false and ridiculous, and belong only to the infantile minds who can believe them in the fanaticism of their religion; they do not bear up under the strong light of logic or reason, and they have no place in anyone's personal religion.

Now, let us continue on into our discussion. Apparently, the place where Adam and Eve were stationed was in the Garden of Eden, an idealistic sort of a situation where they could wander around and do nothing but eat and sleep all day, and live, more or less, in a state of earthly bliss, which was very much like that which could be reasonably supposed to exist in heaven. There was no cause nor reason for Adam and Eve; they were here simply because God had created them so, shall we say, in a moment of experimentation or as an idle gesture. However, Adam and Eve, quickly found ways to relieve this monotony, and if it can be said to be so, there was a certain amount of hanky-panky which entered into the scene at this moment; this hanky-panky, it is said, was instituted by the serpent.

The serpent itself is one of those choice bits of Christian orthodoxy which is utterly false in nature; yet when they are stripped to the core, there is a tiny kernel of truth which shows that these different ideologies had their beginnings in a much more tangible and truthful relationship than they do so presently exist. The serpent is a representation of the sine wave which was taught in the Lemurian civilization so many thousands of years ago; yet the aboriginal earth man could not understand the sine wave and its implication in bringing any and all different earth life dispositions to him; all earth life forms of consciousness are the result of the varied sine wave transpositions. So, the serpent became the symbology of the sine wave because, as the little snake crawled through the grass, these primitive people saw the sine wave in

149

action; therefore, the snake became a symbology in relation to the various properties of the material world and its subsequent evil, which was always manifest in these different transpositions of earthly life.

The apple, in itself, was not really an apple; it was a pomegranate, and because it is composed almost entirely of seeds, was obviously the symbol of fertility. The implication here being that the earth world had, therefore, tempted Adam and Eve into some sort of a physical discrepancy, irrespective of the fact that they were quite obviously created for that specific purpose. In fact, the Bible does say, in at least one other place, that man should go forth and be fruitful and replenish the earth. Yet, at the time of the creation of Adam and Eve, this was not the thought which God apparently had in mind. And so when he found there was hanky-panky going on in the Garden of Eden, He became very angry and kicked Adam and Eve out of the Garden; so, they were forced to enter into the different phases of material life and work out their own destiny as best they could in their own way, irrespective of the divine guidance which they had had in the Garden of Eden.

If we go further along into this so-called holy book, we shall find numerous stories which have become choice and classical bits of literature in the ecclesiastical repertoire. These include such sundry depictions as Noah's Ark, Jonah, The Tower of Babel, the Walls of Jericho, Joshua, the sun standing still, the various exploits of Moses in the Exodus, and leading the Children of Israel into the Promised Land, etc. There are, of course, many others which cannot be mentioned at this time, but irrespective of what they are, if we examine them closely and strip them of their different distortions and fabrications, which they have acquired from telling and retelling through the generations of time, we will find that there is a perfectly natural or logical explanation to these tales, which completely strips them of any supernatural innuendo and relegates them into the more natural and normal phenomena of earth world happenings.

For instance, let us take the story of Moses leading the Children of Israel out of Egypt through the Red Sea; as you are familiar with this version: the Lord, at the command of Moses, parted the waters of the Red Sea, etc. However, this is not entirely true. If we examine the geography of the Red Sea, we will find that it is a long, narrow body of water which stretches almost directly east and west across the continents between Africa and Asia; therefore, it is extremely subjected to the differences in tides which are man-ifest by the phases of the moon. In the upper reaches of the Red Sea, where the entrance of the Suez Canal is located, there are vast tidelands; these are places where the high tides, which are sometimes twelve feet high, can sweep in over the land—which is a marshy, muddy place—and completely inundate it. At other times the tides will recede for many hours, during which time, the strong tropical sun will bake this mud and form a hard crust—something like thin ice—suf-ficient to support the weight of a person if he passes rather rapidly across the surface.

Now, Moses knew of this tideland, and the right time at which a crossing could be attempted; also, this wily old fox supposed the Pharaoh's armies would be chasing him at this same time. The Pharaoh was trying to recapture the Israelites because civil-izations like Egypt depended upon slave labor for the normal function of building and repairing various buildings, temples, etc. Therefore, the Pharaoh could ill afford to have thousands of Israelites escaping into some unknown place in a land where he would have no power nor control over them. So, Moses led the children of Israel across these tidelands at the proper time when there was the hardest crust and when the

151

armies of the Pharaoh, composed largely of horses and heavy chariots, attempted to follow, they broke through this crust, became hopelessly mired, and with the return of the tide, they were, of course, drowned.

Likewise, if we go back into more recent periods of Moses' life—which predated the Exodus—to the time when he supposedly inflicted the seven different plagues on the land of Egypt, by commanding God to so do, we will find that all of these seven plagues were quite normal and natural phenomena which had happened before this time and have happened many times since. These plagues, if you remember, were happenings or events which took place in the land of Egypt during the years in which Moses was trying to liberate the Israelites from the yoke of the Pharaoh. They comprised such things as the plagues of locusts, lice, rivers of blood, great darkness, the plague of frogs, and finally the death of the first born in Egyptian households which became the basis for the present Jewish Passover.

If you remember reading the history of Moses, you will find that when he and Aaron first went to the Pharaoh, Aaron cast down his rod and it became a serpent; however, this trick was well known by the Pharaoh and he was not impressed. He nodded to his priest to also cast down his rod, and it likewise became a serpent. Obviously there was a bit of hocus-pocus involved here, and a harmless serpent had been concealed in the clothing and released at the proper moment; a simple trick of magic which was known and practiced by many people at that time and present-day magicians have exceeded this bit of magic.

So having failed to impress the Pharaoh, Moses had to resort to other forms of chicanery. Having some knowledge of events which were about to happen, or which in various ways he was able to more or less predict, or anticipate, he would at the proper

152

moment, rush to the Pharaoh, tell him that his god was going to inflict a certain something on the land of Egypt, and when the circumstance arrived, he would point it out to the Pharaoh; after a series of these different happenings, the Pharaoh was evidently impressed enough to let Moses escape with the children of Israel into that famed land of milk and honey.

Let us examine a few of these peculiar advents which so impressed the Pharaoh, for instance the "Rivers of Blood." Today science knows there is a certain type of bacteria or algae which can be swept up into the upper reaches of the atmosphere; it is red in color and when it multiplies under the right conditions, will fall down into the clouds below; and when normal precipitation begins to occur, the rain sometimes is colored red with this bacteria. It is harmless and means nothing except that it is a phenomenon. Quite often mountain sides have been covered with this red snow; therefore, we can easily discount the "Rivers of Blood." Frogs too, have been known to have their cycles of appearance and disappearance in large numbers. Likewise, we all know of grasshopper plagues and lice too, follow a cyclic motion. The period of darkness over the land of Egypt could be easily explained as either an eclipse or an explosion of a volcano which threw great quantities of powdered ash into the higher reaches of the atmosphere; this could have hung over Egypt for some time and partially obliterated the sun.

So you see there is really nothing supernatural about any of these tales; likewise, any of the other stories in the Bible, which are so classically depicted in Sunday Schools, taught to children, and believed by adults, all, can be very simply and easily explained on the same basis. There was nothing supernatural in them at all. Moses was merely a charlatan who succeeded, just as many others did, in capitalizing on some natural phenomena or some fete of magic to

153

impress people into serving whatever purpose he had in mind.

So, if you would have eternal life in the higher worlds, begin at once to rid yourself of these false and idle concepts born from out the superstitions of the past, embellished with the aura of magical and worshipful sacredness and holiness; for these things are untrue, they will bind you to this earth world with chains stronger than of steel, if you continue to believe in them. They are strictly the property of the more elemental people who have come up through the pages of time to their present position in this earth world.

# CHAPTER 17

## Jesus' Mission,
## Debunking Religion

Let us continue on into the more recent part of the Bible which is called the New Testament. In our previous discussions we have entered into some of the more scientific factors involved in the so-called supernormal or supernatural appearances of various deifications which have formed the foundation of modern Christianity. In this respect, so far as that period of development in Christianity is concerned, that which might be called the more modern, Christian religion, originated by Paul, or Saul of Tarsus, contains more or less the same similarities, the same parallel in these diverse depictions which always imply the supernormal deification aspect of the religion. This is purposely done to enslave the various adherents to this religion in the same age-old mental and spiritual coercion which has always existed.

It is necessary that all religions have this particular hold on the various mental processes of the adherents; otherwise the religion would soon pass away and be nonexistent. Any religion exists because of the fact that it is dominantly subversive to those who believe in it. This does not necessarily imply that this religion is either factual or realistic; as a matter of

155

fact, no religion is such, but rather is entirely based upon such age-old superstitions and beliefs which have always concurrently existed among the peoples of the world. Throughout the New Testament, and considered in its entirety, we can say that it does graphically and astringently oppose the Old Testament; in fact, it was one of the last commandments of Jesus who said, "Ye have all heard of the laws of Moses," (referring to the ten commandments) "but I give you a commandment which is greater than all these."

In other words the entire mission and purpose of Jesus was to try to destroy the old illusions of this past religion, to destroy the concept of Jehovah, and the various supernatural phenomena which had embroiled the people of Israel for many thousands of years; to replace in the hearts and minds of these diverse and sundry peoples a new concept of life, which was predicated upon the realization of the individual's position with the Infinite Creator; in other words finding that kingdom of heaven within. Quite obviously, this mission and purpose did not suit either the Pharisees or the Rabbis in the temples, and it soon became necessary to liquidate Jesus; this was done in that very historical depiction on the hill of Calvary. However, even in the life, the various ways, manners, and forms in which Jesus attempted to explain the spiritual world, the creation and the purpose of man, this too, has been seriously deleted in subsequent historical portrayals, depictions, and expositions of existing Christian liturgies.

Today the situation is extremely complex, even though a concerted effort has been made to unite the sundry religious factions throughout the world, there is still the same dissension and strife existing among these diverse interdenominational credos who call themselves by various different names; all supposedly worship the same God or the same Jesus; all pro-

156

claim that through their particular doorway, salvation can be attained. Almost needless to say, should any of their adherents fully realize the intent and purpose of the mission of Jesus, this would automatically defeat the necessity for the existence of the church or the religion itself; churches and religions would rapidly pass from the face of the earth in direct ratio and proportion as to how well the general public, who proclaim themselves Christians, realize this all-important fact. For even in the New Testament one of the most vital and important preachments of Jesus, which still exists, is His admonition for people not to worship in public places, temples, or synagogues; but you should seek out the Father who is within the closet of your own secret self—that He may reward you openly.

One of the most popular and most concurrent misconceptions about the mission of Jesus is posed by the various priesthoods of religious dispensations and is contained in the principle of automatic salvation; that is, Jesus is said to have died for our sins. Now this is another one of those very purposeless and meaningless bits of nonsense which would lead us quickly into one of these blind alleys of reasoning, for the concept of salvation, as it is so posed in this exposé would automatically defeat the necessity or purpose for any human living his life upon the surface of this earth. It also defeats any of the previous suppositions in the Old Testament which would automatically relegate any sinner into the pits of hell after the commission of sin. Also any Christian adherent can quite naturally and logically toss off the burden of his own moral responsibility; he can be any kind of a hellion he wishes to be, and then in the last moment he calls out loudly to Jesus and will be saved. Therefore, it can be considered that religion, as it is posed in modern Christianity, is immoral in all respects and aspects in this divine intercession concept. This auto-

157

matically relieves any person of his own personal burden of assuming a position of moral responsibility, either to his community or to the Infinite Creator or his own personal deification of the Creator.

Here again, this leads up to one of the more classical misconceptions, posed by modern Christianity, the Judgment Day. Now this Judgment Day has existed in many other different religions throughout the world, just as the birth of Jesus was depicted more than five hundred years B.C., in the birth of Zoroaster and under identical conditions; so does the Judgment Day exist in various other ancient civilizations such as Egypt, as well as in the Zoroastrian concept. For here again was Osiris—as it is depicted on the walls and temples of ancient Egypt—who was the father of all, and overshadowed mother Isis who conceived Horus in Immaculate Conception; an exact parallel with this generally accepted belief is the origin and birth of Jesus. For Horus and Jesus, as well as Osiris with Isis, and Mary are all compatible and exactly parallel configurations.

We might interject one more small fallacy which is connected with the birth of Jesus, as it is written in the New Testament; there was a star in the East and the three wise men followed the star to the birthplace of Jesus, which was overshadowed by the star at that particular moment. Now, if this had occurred, these three wise men would have walked off into the Pacific Ocean; for the three wise men came from India, or at least from the land of Persia, and they would have had to walk west, and the star would have hung in the West and not in the East as it is depicted in the Bible! I am mentioning this obvious fact to show you conclusively, how it is that people will accept anything that is given to them in the guise of religion, and swallow it hook, line, and sinker, without the slightest attempt to analyze its surface values, as to its true intent, purpose or origin.

158

Getting back to the Judgment Day, and as it is depicted in Revelations, God will somehow or other resurrect and reconstitute all people in their physical bodies. When this particular bit of fallacy was first originated in the primitive minds of the believers long ago, they did not have any concurrently existing statistics on present-day populations; they could not realize that God would have to resurrect perhaps several hundred billions of people and line them up against the wall of the Holy City—so to speak—and then choose only 144,OOO people out of this vast multitude; the rest would be shot down by some kind of a celestial firing squad because they were sinners and not fit to live in this beautiful reconstructed Holy City.

Some religionists have attempted to shrug off this seemingly improbable presentation; they will say, just as it was said in the time of Zoroaster, that the world will be cleansed by fire; after the cleansing people will be returned to the earth where they will live in a land of milk and honey, and there will be no sin or evil. Here again is one of those very fantastic suppositions which defeats, in all intent and purpose, the very necessity of life itself. We could well imagine what would happen when billions of people repopulated the earth without any of their old values whereby they sustained life upon the planet earth. We must remember that the various drives which form the power behind all motion, as it is supported in our present-day civilization, just as it has been supported throughout the past ages, are compounded from the many infractions of positive and negative expressions which are called good and evil. If we do not have evil and everything is good, then there is no necessity for anything; the drive is all gone. There is no reason to do anything else except to lie back upon a pink cloud and float sublimely through space and time to some unfathomable end.

However, this idealistic picture does present a very

definite escape mechanism to any person who is pressurized, so to speak, by the various complexities of the life he is living; for it must be assumed that if this person is neither intelligent nor logically biased enough to inquire into the intent or purpose, or to otherwise analyze that with which he is being presented, then he will fall victim to these diverse obvious religious devices. So he is taught from the cradle to the grave, he is held in the stranglehold of this false religious supposition, he will continue on, from life to life, embroiled in these same false suppositions until he realizes the fallacy of the entire situation and begins to recognize the true purpose, the true creation, and the true concept of Infinity, as it is posed in the teachings of Unarius.

Back in the sixteen hundreds, in the Middle Ages of Europe, there lived a man in the land of Holland, a Dutchman by the name of Spinoza. This man has, incidentally, written many pages of philosophical portrayals which have existed in their entirety and content down into modern times and have been one of the sundry elements of philosophical explorations which have been pursued by various students in the universities of this time. Spinoza stated at one time that the Bible was filled with lies, derelictions, depictions of lust, murder, etc., and parts of it were not even fit to be read. For this very drastic statement, Spinoza had to flee for his life; for in those days, the courts of inquisition flourished and the streets were often the scenes of divers and sundry sacrifices in the form of the so-called religious heretic who dared to set forth some doctrine which was contrary to the beliefs of the Holy Roman Empire.

Burnings, hangings, and other different types of killings were a daily occurrence in that age and time. However, we are not entirely freed from these numerous courts of inquisition, and the ways and manners in which they constantly re-manifest themselves in

160

our more modern and recent periods of time, although the constitution is predicated upon certain basic freedoms, such as the freedom of religion, the stern and austere religionists always find ways and means to punish these various different people who dare to go beyond the confines of this restricted and rhetorical dogmatic religion. Typical of the more recent attempts to institute a court of inquisition was portrayed in that classical example of the Scopes trial in Tennessee, when a certain college professor attempted to teach his students that the human body was a product of evolution and could be traced, in its continuity, back into the more primitive forms of earth life; these linked and re-linked the different species in somewhat of a regular evolutionary continuity as it was explained by Darwin.

Perhaps neither Scopes nor the religionist took the time or trouble to separate the entity of spiritual being from the physical body which manifested itself upon the surface of the earth. Inasmuch as these two entities are entirely separate—evolution and religion are both seriously in error. These factors should be thoroughly understood by anyone who attempts to solve the riddle of evolution for himself, that under any and all circumstances the entity of consciousness must be sustained in a certain vehicle. This vehicle is the dimension in which it is propagated; for the wave forms which are manifested in the transmission of life must always be synonymous in nature, and convey the direct relationship with the past and the present.

Therefore, in the development of any human entity or human being, we must include these very important and dominant factors; that the psychic anatomy has, in its consciousness, developed the vehicle of the human body as a suitable place wherein various transmissions of life are lived in the atmosphere which originally instigated the formation of this body in its evolutionary pattern. However in this case, just

161

as in all other diverse types of analyses, we must always shift the focus of attention or the originating place, from the third dimension to the fourth or adjacent spiritual dimensions which are, to all intent and purpose, the true originating point and source of all appearances of life as they exist; not only on this planet earth, but also on all planets and solar systems in the great Infinite Cosmogony which comprise, not only our own universe, but countless other universes scattered throughout space.

Yes, and even the spiritual beings, who live in the higher worlds, can look upward and see the same continuity of evolution; that the presupposition of form or vehicle as it is lived in any of these spiritual worlds is an attribute of expression which comes from an even higher spiritual world and so the continuity continues on upward into places of origin and ways and manners of expression which are entirely beyond the comprehension of a third dimensional mind. This is all part of that scientific presentation which is contained in the lesson courses of Unarius. There is only one ultimate purpose which has been conceived and which is necessarily mandated in the evolutionary conformities in which man finds himself; that is, in the natural progressive continuity of evolution man must always—from time to time, in these re-manifestations of cyclic forms, which might be called personal epochs of any individual, or collective society of humans—abandon his individual precepts of creation, of the numerous religious forms, of various social structures, and other various conformities with which he has so surrounded himself, and which he is obeying in the impulse of the moment as a radiated form which constantly re-establishes his continuity with the past.

In order to live in the higher spiritual worlds man must abandon these forms, for progression is mandated by the inclusion of an ever-increasing and larger number of precepts of consciousness. These involve worlds which are beyond the comprehension of the physical or third dimensional mind; and any person who wishes to live immortally and beyond this third dimension, or, in other words, to be saved, to live in a heavenly kingdom, must do so on the basis that he can—not only in his future evolutions reasonably begin to include these higher worlds as an actual reality of consciousness, he must also include all manners, ways, means, and forms of living in these higher worlds, just as he is doing in his present so-called civilized world; just as this same person has done—if we trace the history of this individual back on through the ages of time to the place he began to form the first entity of consciousness which was sustained from life to life as his personal ego.

This is why the presentation of the Bible, when we consider all of these facts which have been explained to you, is, then indeed, one of the greatest fallacies of all time. It is one of the greatest unsupported suppositions which has enslaved countless millions of people for almost 2000 years; and it is quite likely to continue to do so for thousands of years into the future, or at least as long as people so continue to reincarnate and are held in the vice-like grip of these superstitious and supernatural suppositions from the time of birth until the time of death. Or should we reasonably suppose that, in the evolution of time, mankind could universally adopt a more intelligent introspection of life as it concerned him in the generalities of his existence?

However, such an occurrence is not likely to happen, inasmuch as the earth represents, to some degree, certain grades of development very much like the primary grades in an elementary everyday school. People come to the material world as a development from the various constituents of animal-like forms which have previously existed in the evolution of reincarnation of form into the physical world. The combination of these sundry entities as they are solidified, so to speak, in one common psychic anatomy does begin to expand the consciousness of this particular psychic anatomy, so that it can re-express itself into the material world, in a much more complex fashion. This is man. For man does, not only express certain continuities of animal forms, inasmuch as he procreates in exactly the same manner and form as do the beasts of the field and forest; but also he does, in many other aspects of his life, exhibit the same animal-like attributes as the animals of the field and forest.

Yet, with all this he has also managed to include, in his various different life transpositions, a certain recognition of higher or deistic forces; this means that he has started that separating process which will, in some future time and place, reasonably develop his intelligence to live beyond the animal kingdom which is represented by the earth world. Therefore, the earth does, as a whole, serve in the synonymy of creation as a grade school. People who live this earth life in the succession of numerous evolutions or reincarnations are, in effect, passing through the various primary grades of the school; and when they have passed through them and attained the consciousness necessary for them to live in the higher spiritual worlds, quite naturally they do not return except on the presupposition that they can help others who have not yet advanced in their evolution to a point where they too, can escape from these material worlds.

However, it should be noted that should any of these higher or more advanced personalities return, they are only interested in people who have gained within themselves, a certain precognition, that it is possible to live in higher spiritual worlds, minus the physical body.

Unarius, as a proposition of life, does not interest

164

people who are completely steeped or immersed in the physical third dimensional world. The meaning and purpose of life, as we explain it to you, has no reasonable foundation of supposition; simply because these people have not yet developed to the point where they can intelligently include, as a matter of oscillating wave forms within their psychic anatomy, the necessary precognition which will intelligently pose them with the possibility of life hereafter lived realistically. Any suppositions of an existing life after death to the materialist must therefore exist as a rather vague unrealistic supposition which has held him more or less under the thumb of the various existing religions throughout the world.

Therefore, continue to seek the Kingdom of Heaven which is within, for this, in the practical reality of concept, as it includes the necessary justifications within your own consciousness, will be the manner, way, and means in which you can truly escape from the material worlds. If you are satisfied with this world however, there is no purpose or use for you to continue on into the possible explorations of a realistic life into the future. This exploration and this way of life is important only to those people who have realized it within their own consciousness; not as a presupposition or an escape mechanism but as a practical reality and one which includes all of the most vital and important elements in a progressive evolution. Therefore, all Biblical translations must be tossed into the wastebasket where they so rightfully belong; for they cannot be included as realistic or factual interpretations of what might or could happen in the future. They are merely vague innuendoes which were presupposed by primitive minds who had neither reason, logic, nor science to explain them otherwise. And so the Bible will remain the greatest paradox of all times, because, not only of the unreality as it is posed within itself, but it holds people in slavery.

# CHAPTER 18

## Even The Fall of a Sparrow is Noted

One of the classical utterances of Jesus which is often bandied about and severely misinterpreted is one in which He said, "Even the sparrow which falls by the wayside is noted." This quotation is one which can well point up the various and obvious interpretations among the Christians as to just what God is; and in reference to this quotation, as well as other extractions which are made from the New Testament, the Christian religionist always comes up with some rather vague explanations as to what God really is. He may picture God as the Supreme Being, something like a white-robed Santa Claus of gigantic size, who sits upon a white throne somewhere off in the skies, and in some mysterious way has a mind which can instantaneously discern all that is going on, not only on planet earth, but in the countless millions of solar systems throughout great numbers of galaxies and universes.

Of course this particular ideosophy is utterly ridiculous and infantile; there is neither scientific reason nor logic to support such a fantastic supposition. However, in this present day age of science, we can reasonably equate what the Infinite Intelligence or God really is, and form a comprehensive idea within

166

our own minds as to the complete entity of the Supreme Being if it can be called an entity—which it is not. As this God is the Creator of Heaven and earth, He must therefore be logically assumed to be an infinitely scientific sort of proposition; that is, a mind which could reasonably construct atoms, build up solar systems, and suns; as well as to construct the spiritual worlds, both astral, and sub-astral, etc.

This therefore precludes any scientific supposition which has its roots steeped in some age-old mysticism; instead, we must go directly into the archives of existing scientific dispensations to find the origin and the correct concept of God or the Supreme Being, the Infinite Intelligence, etc. In this scientific analysis, we can also find our particular position and function in this Mind of the Infinite Creator; also how it is that this Infinite Mind could discern and conceive all things instantaneously.

Therefore, let us first take our position and our function in this Infinite scheme of creation. Every person has what might be called a definite plane rate vibration; that is, through the various mental and physical processes in which you are presently living, there is one basic cyclic form or manifestation of energy, within which there oscillates a large number of secondary or numerous subdivisions of such energy formations which are all basically attuned to this original oscillating frequency. This base plane vibration or cycle is oscillating in the next adjacent or fourth dimension. It forms the basic part of what has been commonly referred to in occultism as the aura; and people who are sufficiently sensitive or clairvoyantly inclined and who can see an aura, always say that it is composed of many different colors; color of course being a rather loose interpretation as to these various levels of reference which are used by these sensitives who can so discern auras.

Now let us say just for convenience that you are

167

oscillating on a base plane frequency rate of one million megacycles. A megacycle is one million cycles; therefore you would be oscillating or functioning on this base plane rate of one trillion cycles per second. This speed is of course incomprehensible to your mind; however, we are using it as I said, for convenience. Now, to search through all of the diverse peoples of the world and find those who also oscillated at the same frequency, it is quite likely that you would not find very many, if any; and those people whom you did find so oscillated at this base plane rate would or would not necessarily be connected to you in respect that their entire psychic anatomy was also vibrating with you.

In other words throughout the various secondary subdivisions of energy wave forms, which are oscillating in conjunction with your base plane frequency rate, you would find that these sundry individuals had certain strong differences of various rates of vibration, which would in themselves portray the differences in the life experiences which were impounded in the numerous psychic anatomies. For all people traveling in their evolutionary pathway, even though they pass through similar experiences, always interpret these diverse experiences of life somewhat differently, in respect to their comparative values on the basis of frequency relationships with other past experiences and so on ad infinitum.

Now you might say that there were probably very few people harmonically attuned to you, what then? However we must go into a very much higher concept and one which will involve considerable mathematical calculation; so for simplicity sake we will adhere to round figures. Taking your base plane frequency rate and using the multiple or the subtraction of the number two, which is a close approximation of the fundamental law of harmonics, we can then multiply or subtract your basic frequency and arrive at a very

168

much larger number of people who would be harmonically attuned to you on this first fundamental frequency.

Proceeding in this same mathematical subtraction and multiplication, we could extend these secondary third, fourth, fifth, sixth, and so on, multiples of this harmonic system into many thousands and thus we would include every person living upon the face of the earth who was either closely or remotely attuned to us on the basis of harmonic frequency relationship. Now, extending this same mathematical calculus on one step further, and remembering at the same time that these vibrations always exist in the next adjacent or fourth dimension which is timeless and spaceless space—so to speak—which means that as it is now acceded by science and by other learned men and women of the world, there are literally hundreds of millions of earth planets similar to our own scattered throughout the great universe and in other universes which can be reasonably inhabited by people very much like ourselves.

On this basis then, and remembering our harmonic law, we can associate or harmonically attune ourselves with all of these countless hundreds of millions of planetary systems throughout the universe on which there are countless billions of people living very much the same as we do in terrestrial or earth-like conditions. When you can conceive the vast and staggering proportions of this calculus, then you can easily see how it is, that we are in this respect connected to every human being, not only on the surface of the earth, but throughout the vast and limitless cosmogony.

However, we have not completed this particular point with our calculus; we have not yet suitably equated how it is that the Infinite Intelligence, or God, can conceive everything instantaneously. We must proceed one step further and remember always the

169

very positive concept of Unarius, that the Infinite God is not only the sum and substance of all things, but is the active regenerative principle which is constantly sustaining and recreating new forms; not only sustaining old forms as they exist in the atomic constituents, which comprise the planet earth, solar system and our visible universe; but also that which is going on into the various higher spiritual worlds and associated planetary systems, as well as into the astral and subastral worlds and their many different configurations and planetary systems.

Remembering that an atom is a solar system of energy, and is sustained from the next adjacent dimension; we can look into our physical bodies and see that these physical bodies are comprised from some sixteen elements. An element is simply an atom which has a different number of positive or negative charges of energy in respect to similarities in the nucleus of the atom itself. This gives it that which the scientist calls its atomic weight. There are sixteen different kinds of atoms in your body. These range from calcium, potassium, oxygen, hydrogen, nitrogen, iron, sulphur, etc., to the entire number of sixteen; each one with its own particular atomic weight and consequently, just as you have in the auric sense, each one of these tiny atoms has its own base plane frequency rate in which it oscillates. These, in turn, just as we have equated your own mental position, are oscillating into the adjacent fourth dimension on the same basis of harmonic relationships, and in this way they are connected and interconnected with all other atomic forms.

Likewise, through this same system of harmonic interplay, we can extend these connections on into an infinite distance, so to speak, in the cosmogony. In fact, we can trace the energy source of all atoms through this harmonic system of energy transferences clear into the very heart of the celestial kingdoms, or

170

possibly the originating source of energy itself. Therefore you can now see that all atoms are connected on
the basis of harmonic relationship. All humans are
connected on the basis of harmonic relationship.
We can also extend this same calculus to include all
fauna and flora which exist in these planetary systems; that is, all of the animals of the forests and the
fields, the birds, fishes, the plant life, as well as all of
the innumerable forms of the invisible. The macrocosm, and the microcosm which is not visible to you
can be so included in this same interplay of this same
harmonic relationship. At this point we can easily see
how it is that this vast macrocosm and microcosm
are really one and the same thing, on the basis of this
harmonic relationship.

As it has been so previously described, the motivating force behind all of this is that constant and
never-ending interplay of regeneration, which not only
sustains all of these forms, but also is continuously
regenerating new forms; this is God, the Infinite Intelligence. It is the sum and total of all things visible
and invisible. When the complete concept of this tremendously enlarged macrocosm and microcosm can
be somewhat equated within the dimension of your
mind, then it can easily be seen how God can note
the fall of the sparrow by the wayside and He can also
simultaneously feel, sense, hear, or otherwise be entirely conscious of every other thing which is happening, not only in these visible astral or solar systems
in which you may find yourself, such as the planet
earth, but in the vast invisible microcosm which you
will yet visit in your future evolutions into time and
space.

In fact, you will never arrive at any point in this
evolution where you will see a cessation of this interplay of harmonic principle. Once you have established the principles of this calculus within your mind
and see this regenerative principle always in action,

171

then you will truly possess the secret of life and a correct concept of what God is, and what constitutes God. This concept will not, quite naturally, be the same as that which you formerly had when you went to Sunday School as a small child and heard someone say words to the effect that God was some mysterious being living in the sky.

Instead you will have a correct and scientific concept within your own mind of what the Infinite Intelligence or God really is; on this basis, you will be enabled to further continue in your evolutionary course by adding the various other necessary additives and constituents of concept which you will find along the way. These things will, all in turn, recreate your psychic anatomy into such suitable vortexes or conformations of energy wave forms which can suitably live in the environment of the higher spiritual worlds, where you do not eat food, you do not drink liquids, nor do you breathe air, but you are sustained by your knowledge of the Infinite; because this knowledge does, in its ratio and proportion of knowledge enable you to breathe, I shall say, or to attain your sustenance directly from the Infinite source of the God Source Itself through the same process of spiritual osmosis as you are now, in a sense, manifesting physically in the interplay of various chemical reactions within your physical body.

This then, is the correct interpretation of God; a scientific, logical, and realistic interpretation which, in itself, relegates such present-day existing beliefs into the dimension from which they originally sprang; that is, in the barbaric past which indulged itself in the infantile deifications of God forces which existed as manifestations of the elemental and unknown forces of the world. Today in this scientific age, there is no logic or reason for these beliefs to exist. Even school children have a vast wealth of scientific knowledge at their disposal; knowledge which could in a brief moment destroy these age-old pagan beliefs upon which present-day religion is founded.

Therefore as you go about your daily tasks, and in such rote systems in which you presently find yourself involved, try to keep this concept of the Infinite Creator within your mind at all times. And whenever such moments of convenience so occur, re-establish these principles of calculus even more firmly, by visualizing that in all things, in all consequences, and in all appearances, behind these seemingly physical manifestations there is that all-important regenerative principle of the Infinite God, functioning in the same immutable manner in which it has always functioned. It shall never cease, and it will constantly sustain all forms of which you are conscious, and in which you have placed yourself in attunement. It will also regenerate within your consciousness and automatically suggest and re-suggest new conformations as the width and breadth of your mental horizon expands.

This is the way to eternal life; for eternal life cannot be sustained indefinitely from the material worlds. There is a definite mark of demarcation, one in which the physical man is served to a certain point; beyond this lies the vast and great unknown; unknown to you (earthmen) at least, these many, many mansions of which Jesus spoke. The spiritual macrocosm, if you wish, also is a part of that great Infinite Regenerative Intelligence which will sustain you on through the countless eons of time.

# CHAPTER 19

## Equality is Nonexistent

It is universally recognized that these are indeed perilous times which involve great differences, not only between nations of the world, but racial differences among nations themselves. With this thought in mind, perhaps it would be well to pass a few moments of discussion on these various attitudes which are rampant in the world today, so that we may develop a more secure philosophy within the tenets of our own minds; also, in this extension of sundry abstractions, we may gain a more comprehensive evaluation of the Infinite as a whole.

If we were to look at certain current statistics or scan the various headlines in newspapers, we would say, in reading these diverse and sundry descriptions of life as they are lived throughout the world today, that civilizations, or races as a whole, are at this present time, falling flat on their faces; we are in an age of rapidly accelerating decadency. In fact we could say that in every common expression of daily life, we would find some example or some particular display of decadency, which would seemingly motivate us or propel the world into some abysmal reaches or into eventual destruction.

The cold war with Russia as a conflict between ideologies is a typical case; also, we could point out different existences as they manifest in numerous racial groups throughout the world; the African Negro, or the Negro as he is so living in our American cities as an Americanized or naturally born American citizen, the differences in races and in the various expressions of people as a whole, which are largely the product of their evolution, the singular attribute that every human mind must constantly maintain its ability to single out, for the moment, and extract from the emotional experience its value, and compound this experience with other such extractions as they have been lived in previous experiences and that the whole compound being lived from life to life will conceivably, in a progressive manner of evolution, so elevate this particular person to a much broader understanding of the Infinite as a whole. This could naturally occur if this individual does not become unbalanced in various negative valences and become enmeshed in the carnal consequences of various undischarged psychic conditions.

Perhaps of all the many idealisms perpetuated by mankind, in his general anthropology from generation to generation or from civilization to civilization, we should consider such idealisms as are contained in the Constitution of the United States; some of these idealisms, while they may seem to be very worthy, could be, in the more extreme extensions, a misunderstood or misapplied knowledge of the Infinite and actually become destructive in nature. For instance, let us take the idealism as it is postulated in the Constitution or the Declaration of Independence; that all men are created equal. While it may seem that this is one of the most worthy idealisms, it has been historically proven to be one of these destructive idealisms; inasmuch as it is universally practiced among the various peoples of the United States, they have differentiated according to their own individual propensities and their own mentality that which constituted the equality of mankind and in particular how it affected them personally.

Actually, equality, in any sense of the word, is a mirage; it is a nonexistent and presupposed element which has always been in the consciousness of mankind and, in itself, relegates the thinking processes of man into other diverse interrelated expressions which, to some extent, do have a similarity with equality. We can say that the old law of Moses, "an eye for an eye and a tooth for a tooth," was a way in which equality was so expressed in a reactionary manner and form. Yes, even the Golden Rule given by Jesus, "Do unto others as you would have them do unto you," is merely another system of equality. While it may seem to be a great idealism, yet, as it assumes certain derivatives of personal consciousness among sundry individuals who try to use it as a basis for their own personal motivations and reactions, this Golden Rule, just as all other systems of equalities, leads into tremendous stresses and many other destructive mental and material practices.

A much better method to use in equalizing the various differences in life is to sublimate them into an interdimensional consciousness; to actually relegate them into the expression of Principle itself. The proposition of equality has given rise to many conflicts, not only of a personal nature, but also, in effect, it was the means of instigating the disastrous Civil War. Today racial groups in this country are posed in antagonistic attitudes toward each other, simply because they are presupposing equalities on a material or a life basis. They do not understand the principles of equality as they are posed in Infinite Consciousness. To better understand how principle is sustained in all equalities, we must look into the Infinite Consciousness Itself to see how we can obtain a better derivation of what equality should really consist.

In order to do this we will again revert to the cardinal principle of the Infinite Creator, that this Infinite

176

Creator or Intelligence is not only the sum and total of all things visible and invisible, but it is the activating regenerating principle which is constantly maintaining these diverse forms in interdimensional manners and ways. The Infinite, therefore, cannot be misconstrued at any time to be an individual or a being. Therefore, He is not inclined in various emotional values of life. He is not emotionally concerned with any one or a number of configurations which comprise Infinity, simply because Infinity is, in Itself, a part of all of these various particular interdimensional manifestations and forms. The Infinite, in a sense, can be correctly assumed to be all-powerful, all-wise, and immortal in all things.

So far as the relationship of each individual is concerned toward the Creator, each is, by necessity of his existence, and by his position on the scale of evolution emotionally connected with the Infinite Creator. Mankind universally, and as a whole, now so living upon the surface of this earth, is emotional in nature. No man, in the past or present, could be completely absolved of all the emotional values as they concern the earth life. Therefore, it is imperative that we at once transfer the point of focus, as it were, from the position of equality as one is equal to another, to the place where it most properly belongs— equality exists only with the Infinite Creator.

Mankind, as a whole and as he so lives today, is not a created individual; he is a product of evolution. He is a compounded number of values which have survived the idiom of the personal ego from one particular lifetime to the next. In the various different experiences of these numerous lifetimes, he has lived by the basic elements of philosophy as they have surrounded him in his material world. These were reactionary in nature and the very drive or libido, which sustained him in these various lifetimes, was propagated and necessitated by a system of comparisons with his fellow man. This system of comparisons or equalities has given rise to many of the baser criminal propensities which have been expressed so universally among mankind.

To be equal to your neighbor, to be as wealthy as someone else, to have the opulence in clothing, and sundry other different displays in the material life, has led many individuals into various devious pathways of life, to become criminals and various other typical kinds of mental and physical inebriates. The principle of equality should be universally understood and expressed among mankind, as a way and a method in which all expressions of life can be equalized in the eye or mind of the Infinite Creator, as a certain proposition of regeneration in various experience life forms which are motivated by the cardinal principle which equalizes all things; that is, regeneration: the living from one experience to the next, from one day to another—should be lived in the sense that we understand properly the values of creation, and this creation is constantly expressing itself universally about us.

Equality will be achieved in any person in his mental perspectus when he can conceive this universality of equality as it is being universally expressed by the Infinite Creator. He will, however, inversely be plunged into the pits of despair and helplessness, if he tries to equate this general principle of regeneration and equality into the proposition that he is equal to his neighbor. He should realize at all times that the inequalities as they are expressed by every human being are, in themselves, direct attributes which can be said to be expressive attributes of the Infinite Creator as they are lived through every individual. We could well imagine the chaos which would exist in the world if everyone looked alike, dressed alike, and had the same interpretation of values as did all other people. To say the least, such a world would indeed be a monotonous place in which to live. In fact, the proposition of equality, as it exists in the Constitution, automatically defeats itself in the supposition or the presentation of this equality. That is, the equalities in the freedom of speech, worship, and various different expressionary forms of life, as they are all varied and diverse and possess no equalities in themselves, would automatically defeat the proposition of equality as it was expressed individually or collectively by mankind.

Therefore, to generally conclude such suppositions would be to immediately supplant this vicious practice of mental logistics, which attempts to equalize one person with another, with a more realistic approach and understanding of life and the connection of every individual to the Infinite Creator. We, as individuals, must, in the concourse of evolution and as we live from life to life, be reasonably able to arrive at some more ultimate destination with a great achievement in relationship to our mental perspectus. That is, we will be interdimensionally minded and a functioning unit of Infinity as we are connected to the Infinite Creator Itself. In this respect too, Infinity is maintained and no two such highly developed or evolved personalities could be considered, by any stretch of imagination, to be exactly the same. They would all express individually the same individual propensities and various other different attributes of infinity as the Infinite was capable of expressing Itself; none of these highly developed personalities would ever attempt to equalize himself on the common basis of divers values which the earth man has set up for himself.

Even our monetary systems, our numerous social structures, and our moral codes, written or unwritten, are merely attempts to equalize mankind. That is the reason all people today are lawbreakers. Every person in our United States is living under a system of laws which is extremely complex, and it is estimated that there are at least eight to ten thousand laws which are constantly, in effect, governing every individual at any moment of his life. It is, therefore, theoretically or practically impossible to conclude a days work or a twenty-four hour period of life which does not involve breaking at least one or more of these laws. While these evaluations may seem to be a bit tenuous, yet they exist nevertheless, and it is merely one more way of proving the entire fallacy of equality.

The Infinite Creator, in its infinite number of ways of expression in the constructive and reconstructive evolutions of interdimensional interplays, does so continuously defeat this proposition of equality, and if we wish to become infinitely minded, we should destroy at once this fallacious misinterpretation of one of the most carnal laws to which man has ever subjected himself. Equality is merely one more way in which the material man is attempting to sustain, from day to day, or from life to life, the various earth values he has found and impounded into his psychic anatomy and which can be generally summarized as his ego; they are the diverse differences in his makeup as he expresses himself in the community of people in which he lives.

It is fortunate indeed that the Infinite Creator could foresee these various weaknesses in the mental attitudes and philosophies of mankind as he evolved in his upward path in evolutions; in foreseeing that in the more primitive pages of man's progression, equality would be one of the sustaining drives in his material world. The Infinite Creator, likewise, made it physically and mentally impossible to ever achieve such equalities; in fact, the more strongly this false concept was pursued, the more this individual who was so pursuing this fallacious interpolation would become submerged in the sundry fallacies of interpretation. It would ultimately resolve in the mental processes of his mind, that he should abandon this attitude and seek out something more realistic by which he could equate the great number of factors of his daily life. So as you live your daily life, in whatever particular niche or expression you so presently find yourself, do not attempt to evaluate the various values of your particular expression with those of your neighbor.

You should in all manners and forms, equate these diverse appearances as the different relative factors of your own evolutionary expression as it was so compounded with the various abstractions of the Infinite Intelligence which has made all things possible for you. The fact that the Infinite is, in Itself, Infinite, will, at some time or other in your future, make Its insistent demand that you should become more and more infinitely minded; and as you progress into the Infinite and become so minded, you will find that the common comparative values such as are found in different earth life equalities have passed, and you will develop a new system of mental logistics which will more basically interpret the various values of life in which you find yourself.

Therefore, in concluding this discussion, we can say, that should the Negro—who is presently involved in the sundry conflicts of segregation, as they are being expressed at this time—understand his true position in evolution and the values which could be obtained in that evolution, and also that his neighbor, the white man, could, in a similar manner and form, equate the variant values of progressive evolution, racial differences would cease to exist. The white man and the Negro would be on a compatible basis; their life differences would be completely dissolved, and a new concept or a new integration of life could be resolved from the understanding of the sundry true values of interdimensional expression which we have

181

just discussed.

Also, it could be reasonably assumed that, if the nations of the world and the various millions of people which comprise these nations could so universally understand this same infinite proposition, then political systems which stress the differences in ideologies would also be dissolved, and nations as a whole, could consequently resolve themselves into a universal brotherhood of expression in which a symphony of form and motion could be established; one in which all people could realize individually and collectively the universal expression of the Infinite Creator.

However, if this could or would ever come about, or be included in some future age, then the necessity of this earth world and the carnal state of consciousness in which people are presently involved, would pass. We could say that even the necessity of evolution itself would cease to exist; or that the values of various infinities or expressions would be needless; in fact, creation itself would be needless. Our whole concept of creation must involve, not only the higher forms and aspects as they are universally propagated, but we must also include them in the great number of the more primitive expressions which are, by necessity, the starting places in evolution. In this respect we can at least say that the lower dimensions are, to some degree, equal to those which we might call spiritual worlds in their *purpose* and in their intent in the expression of the Infinite.

However, let us not digress again into this equality concept, for equality must always be universally resolved as a way in which the Infinite Itself is expressing Itself in the equalities of diverse differences in polarities as they pass from one expressive form to the next. Man has not yet, universally speaking, so far as the earth world is concerned, progressed his mental attainment to the point where such equalities can be

182

superimposed in any general synthesis of life. He always automatically instigates strong stresses and frictions within the mental horizon of every individual who so attempts to equalize them on the basis of various earth life dispensations.

# CHAPTER 20

## Armageddon Fought Individually

In this discussion I am going to depart from my usual procedure of acquainting you with some of the more abstract principles of progressive evolution and enter into a more personal dimension of introspection, or one which can be considered as a detrimental influential aspect. You have all heard of the Battle of Armageddon, either as it was historically depicted by Nostradamus in his prophetic poems, or as it was Biblically prophesied. However, the Battle of Armageddon is not some advent which is to be fought in some future time between certain good and evil forces. The Battle of Armageddon has been going on for some years; as a matter of fact, throughout the past histories of the world, it has been fought in different epochs of time; such as in ancient Lemuria, more than 100,000 years ago, and at later dates in civilizations, such as Atlantis some 15,000 years ago, and on down to the present time. But wherever we find various civilizations and these confluxus of migratory peoples, as they have swarmed upon the surface of the earth, we have found them fighting, to an extent, the Battle of Armageddon. This is not merely a parable which exists as an advent but is an actual conflict between the astral worlds and those people who have, to some degree, succeeded in placing their feet firmly upon the evolutionary pathway in a progressive manner which will lead them into higher spiritual worlds.

The conflict between good and evil has been historically portrayed in many different times, and the advent of the Armageddon has been prophesied in different civilizations. Zoroaster predicted the Battle of Armageddon in his particular spiritual dispensation, just as Buddha also described the personal conflict in attaining Nirvana or the spiritual junction of consciousness with the higher dimensions of life. It was Jesus however, who carried the greatest impact and message in personal attainment and the way in which this attainment could be achieved by any individual. He also very dramatically demonstrated His own personal Battle of Armageddon and the victorious assault of the dark forces who succeeded in destroying His physical body; and actually, through their conniving cleverness, succeeded in turning His message of life and hope into one of the most dogmatic and rhetorical religious movements the world has ever seen.

In order to better conceive what this great astral conflict is all about, and how it is carried on, let us create within our minds a certain picture. If we think for a moment, we can see, in a sense, certain radio or TV waves are streaming through the room. There may be several thousand of these different wave forms all carrying definite impulses which can be translated by a radio or a TV, into the sound of the voice and carry the message; or they can also carry a picture. Let us enlarge this concept to include an interdimensional aspect; that is, we can now picture around us thousands of different kinds of worlds or planes of consciousness. These people are all compatible in these various planes; and as they so have

185

established intercourse or communication between themselves in some similar respect to that which is being carried on in the material world about you they are harmonically attuned to each other on the basis that their different mental concepts are similar in nature.

Now, some of these planes or worlds will extend on upward, so to speak, to a point where they become nothing more to our inward vision than a great and beautiful sea of light wherein people are living, much the same as they are Biblically depicted, as archangels or various other very highly developed personalities in bodies of pure radiant pulsating energy of the most intense quality.

Conversely, if we look the other way, we shall see other planes extending on downward, so to speak, and as they decrease, they become less and less intense with light, to the point where they seem totally obliterated in darkness. This is a manner in which we have created this picture within our own minds; for in truth, the people who inhabit and populate these numerous lower planes, have in a sense, shut out the light from their consciousness. They have become self-centered and selfish; they believe the whole world revolves around the immediate periphery of their own mental horizon. They have continuously re-inflated their egos with all the various platitudes of self-deification, and thus they have shut themselves out from the inflow of life-giving light which should normally come to them and make a more progressive evolution possible. For you must conceive within your own minds that your physical body may be, to an extent, nourished by food; but the greatest part of the nourishment comes from within the interdimensions in which the psychic anatomy lives, and is reflected outwardly into the physical body as the life-giving property of that particular influx of interdimensional energy.

Should you, in a psychic manner, succeed in partially tuning yourself out from that inflow of energy, then you will consequently suffer; and should you succeed in tuning yourself out from the higher forms of radiant, life-giving energy which comes from the higher dimensions, then you will also become spiritually atrophied. You will become selfish and self-centered. You will become dissatisfied with your life. With this great pinching off process and dissatisfaction, you will inversely try to look about the world in which you are living and place the fault, or blame for your condition upon other people and the way in which they live. You will see great friction in political systems; you will also see great cause for distress in every way, manner, and form of life. This will be done, not because you can see better worlds above you, but because you have pinched yourself off and you are not making a constructive analytical analysis of your own position.

This is the way in which the people of the astral worlds, and especially the subastral worlds live. You are all very familiar with the neighborhood busybody, the person, who goes about, whenever opportunity presents itself, and sets up a whispering campaign; or he may be destructively minded and try to influence some person against another. They may, in various other manners and forms, try to exert their influence in whatever opportunity so presents itself. In fact, they are a real menace to the community in which they live. Some of these meddlers can be found in other places, such as in churches or in temples; they can be ministers or priests; they also can be political figures. But wherever they are, we are going to find persons who are trying in a very subconscious and subversive way to influence people, one against another, or trying to bring the world to their way of thinking, or to place the blame for some irrational conduct of life upon some unsuspecting and totally innocent people. In short, these are the "love me, love my dog" people; and the astral underworlds are peopled with these busybodies, these meddlers who are trying to influence, subversively speaking, people who are not within the immediate jurisdiction of their evil influence.

Now, if you can picture in your mind that throughout the room—or for that matter, in any place or in any way in which you may be involved in your various and daily life transpositions—there are at any particular moment, a great number of these astral worlds in direct contact with the mental thought processes which are going on in your mind. This is done through harmonic attunement with the diverse and sundry configurations of earth life dispensations in which you are participating. These attunements are subconsciously made even though you are not aware of them; in this sense you are, to an extent, wide open to the many influences which these subversive astral forces can project against you in a psychokinetical fashion. You must also realize that these astral worlds have different civic organizations and governmental systems; they have leaders or overlords; they have whatever particular kind of configuration you would like to picture within your mind as various ruling politicos or deifications of these underworlds. These are people who have, to an extent, succeeded, in their selfish way, in creating a dimension for themselves and have attracted other, but somewhat weaker minds, to the banner of their subversive way of life.

In this way they can maintain, for the time being at least, a certain form of life even though they are gradually pinching themselves off, and facing eventual destruction in the very lowest of all astral underworlds which are peopled by the demons. Yet, these people are, in a sense, desperate. They realize they have erred, that they have gone wrong, and, to an extent, in this desperation they also become inclined

188

to grasp at straws; to carry any and all people who come within their reach, to the same impending doom which is their lot if they continue on in their own particular selfish dominion of consciousness. Therefore, as you go about the various tasks in your daily life, the little menial dispensations which are necessary, to a degree, for you to complete your cycle of earth life, these various astral underworld influences will come to you in varied and numerous ways. This is so because at that moment and time when you became more completely dedicated to advance yourself, you also automatically set in motion, the entire sum and total of these numerous different subastral worlds in a combined and concerted effort to prevent you from attaining an upward and progressive evolution.

Moreover, as you began to advance in this upward evolution, the attunement of your own particular personal psychic anatomy also became attuned to the higher dimensions of life through which you were traveling. In this manner the contrast between the radiant qualities of your own particular psychic anatomy—as it is so expressed in the sum and total of knowledge which you had accumulated in these higher dimensions of understanding—also became a greater contrast to the darkened grayness of the astral worlds, and the psychic anatomies of the people who live in these worlds. By this contrast, the greater became their effort to sublimate you in all your efforts, to bring you down to their level; to hold you within their grasp. For within the psychotic reaches of these minds, there is a complete obsessive quality which demands that no one can be superior to them in their particular way of life. In this sense, they are completely irrational; they are blinded to the better and more benign influences which could be theirs. They have a concerted and concentrated program, within their own minds and within the organizations in which they participate, to subjugate and to hold any person who comes within the reach of their influence.

It must also be borne in mind that in these various first stage progressions which you are making at this particular time, you are very vulnerable to these various subastral influences. You have, up until this particular moment, developed a psychic anatomy from the many different life transpositions in material worlds similar to the earth world or a part of the earth world. In this respect, your psychic anatomy is your old self; as the old self is still very strongly a part of you, through harmonic attunements in these various earth life dispensations and associations, these subastral world people can very strongly influence you in a manner and form which is particularly difficult to determine at any given moment. This is so because of the obvious fact, that the old self as a part of you, is oscillating in consciousness with you; therefore, you cannot objectively rationalize what the particular emotion or reaction is at that particular moment; either it is a part of the old world, and an influential dominant character of the astral underworlds, or you are minded so to speak, from the higher planes of Light in their inspirational qualities in the more reasonable and analytical phases of mental development which they are trying to help you develop.

This is where you can become your own worst enemy; should you at any time fail to discriminate between the higher planes of Light and the subastral, subversive influences which are dominating you from your old past—through the lower self which you have developed in the past—and if you should fail to discriminate in a manner and form, with a completely objective introspection, and continuously fail to realize the nature of your position, or how these various worlds are influencing you in your numerous acts of life, then you will indeed become one of these subastral forces.

Fortunately however, there is a sure-fire way to discriminate in all of your various acts of consciousness, how you can actually determine, at any moment, whether it is an old past lifetime, subversive influence coming to you from out of the past and from the astral worlds, or whether you are being constructively minded. This sure-fire method of discrimination is very simple and very effective when it is properly used. This is to simply realize at all times that nothing, absolutely nothing in the world about you, or in your environment is actually caused by you. The moral responsibility of all your own thoughts and your actions *are* actually *you*. You must not, at any time, blame any person, the world, or the political system for what seems to be some negative happening. Any dissension or strife which arises within your consciousness should be determined as products of your own concept; they are your own personal property. In short, they are your own old self, trying to rear its ugly head above the slime and mire of the past world where it grew and made life possible for you in those more primitive stages of your evolution; it is trying to rear its head into your present. It is trying to influence and subvert you from a progressive evolution.

Also, in these various dissatisfactions and mental tensions which arise in your mind and consciousness, you may try to use different devices or escape mechanisms; you will attempt in diverse and numerous ways to expurgate these various tensions and strifes, not as something which may personally involve you or incriminate you with the consciousness that it is your own personal conduct; but always these devices will seem to assume some form wherein you can discharge them upon other people or upon other conditions. In this respect prayer is one of the obvious devices used by hundreds of millions of people;

they are trying to blame their God in His varied dispensations for their own personal acts of consciousness, for their own personal conduct; they blame God for this and that. They say God is punishing them for their sins, or they may even pray to God to have Him show their neighbors the way of their particular method of thinking or way of life. In short, through prayer, God becomes the scapegoat and is an obvious device used by hundreds of millions of people to somehow discharge these various different psychic derelictions in which they are involved.

There are many other ways in which people try to discharge these numerous differences in psychic pressures which are generated in contrast to their old way of life into the present tense. Some particular devices are the political systems in which their country is presently involved, the various different aspects of community life, etc. Of course it goes without saying, the greatest psychopath of them all, who is trying to discharge these sundry psychic derelictions, is the Evangelist; the person who goes about with his own personal crusade to try to convince everybody in the way of his own religious concepts. Some of these Evangelists have grown to world-wide fame and are known throughout the world; they have succeeded in presenting to hundreds of thousands of people, the same hypnotic escape mechanisms which they seem to find when, temporarily, at least, they escape the reality of their mental position by believing that some fancied God has relieved them of their sins and the way in which they have lived their past lives.

By whatever manner or form you find these varied different psychological devices—if I can use the term—wherever you find them, and people using them, you will find the astral underworld forces at work; for each one of these various psychic devices are tools, sometimes expertly used by the minions of the underworlds. The messengers go about and place these tools in the hands of unsuspecting earth people and help to tear down their own particular mental temple of understanding which they have been building through the numerous stages of earth life reincarnations.

The problem with any individual who wishes to aspire to a higher dimension of understanding—if he wishes to become one of the members of the higher worlds of Light, where life is lived in quite a different fashion than on some material worlds—that is for this aspirant to realize it is within the pure dimension of understanding Infinity, objectively, that he will be able to make this progressive evolution.

At no time must he use any obvious devices for using the Infinite to advance himself in the dimension of a personal relationship. The Infinite is infinite, and can be made infinitely possible to any human only on the basis that the Infinite is objectively realized without the implication of personal, dogmatic, rhetorical influences which are always carried over by every human, from out of his past. In other words, the freedom of thought or concept, as it must be carried on in the higher dimensions is purely a product of infinite understanding. It is quite different from the former selfish attitudes which people expressed in the lower planes of life, which were directly a byproduct or a carry over from the more primitive stages of their evolution, and in such earth lives where the law of the jungle—survival of the fittest—was the mandatory element of daily life. Actually, people figuratively and literally, in many different ways, fought a daily life and death battle; not only with the various beasts of the jungle, but later on other killers came to take the place of these shadowy forms; numerous diseases, different levels of life where the common values of the economies of life were so expressed in obtaining the daily necessities of life from the soil, or the manufacturing of various products into usable articles for their fellow men were also part of this battle.

193

These are all, by necessity, ways and manners in which people have lived on the planet earth; they are also, in a competitive way, the ever-expressive principle of survival of the fittest. For every person today is in actual competitive combat with his neighbor on the basis of actual survival. This is commonly referred to as the "rat race"; it is well known that if any person lies down on the job, so to speak, he can be run over by the trampling hordes of his fellow men. He is forced by the sheer necessity of life to stand up and participate in his daily struggle for survival. As it was quoted before, this survival is another manifestation of the old primitive law of the jungle, survival of the fittest; and it is an incumbent law which always is found in any earth life dispensation.

For in the spiritual worlds where life is lived in a different fashion, there is a complete departure from these older and more primitive expressions of life. As the concept of understanding with any particular entity, who occupies these higher dimensions, is concerned infinitely, then in such a manner, he is harmonically attuned to the vast interdimensional inflow of supreme intelligent, reconstructive, re-creative power which is ever surging and resurging about him; and in this harmonic attunement, it becomes the substance of his life; it is his food and drink; it is the way in which his psychic anatomy is, not only sustained but is also, to some extent, progressively re-attuned to even higher forms and higher inflows of this Infinite Consciousness.

Likewise, in a manner and form, this higher and more highly developed entity, is also reciprocating, or he is radiating as a positive polarity into dimensions which are somewhat in a lower state of consciousness than his own. He does this in the sense that he has passed through these various planes of life, and has still retained, in a sense, the polarized knowledge of these planes in which he has lived. In this manner he

194

can, therefore, use the inflow of this higher Infinite Power and reshape it or reform it, so to speak, and relay it in the radiant process into the lower dimensions. It now becomes reharmonically attuned to those who are living in the lower dimensions through the knowledge of this higher entity who has lived in them. This outward radiated force or power from this entity then becomes the inspirational food and drink of any people, say, who can be harmonically attuned to the inflow of this higher state of consciousness and to the one who is relaying the power of the Infinite into their own immediate perspectus of life. It is in this manner and form that millions of earth people constantly find, within themselves, this great resurgent power which gives them the necessary impetus to carry forward. It gives them the inspiration, the inward faith and knowledge, to some extent, to carry on, despite a continuous succession of adversities. They can even find, in the agonies of their death beds, a higher inspirational value, which will nullify the negation of that particular experience.

Yes, and there are those from the higher worlds who will actually reincarnate into the physical life body, so that they can become a polarity to these higher developed personalities with whom they associate. In this sense a more direct rapport is attained with various different denizens of the earth, so that a greater proportion of power, intelligence, inspiration, etc., can be conveyed directly to them. This becomes the magic alchemy of life to many of these people who are so contacted; they find the miracles happening to them, just as they happened in the Holy Land 2000 years ago. Yet, primarily all people who are thus so contacted, and feel the inflow of this radiant, vitalizing, life giving, intelligent energy are actually, to a degree, quite strongly preconditioned for this advent. They have been alerted through diverse and sundry past life dispositions and associations through in between world concourses with various different higher dimensional configurations of life, to a point where they can mentally conceive the possibility within themselves of a better and higher way of life.

When these people have thus attained this mental perspectus, then the reincarnate entity from the higher plane of life can find a rapport; he can, through harmonic attunement, connect himself with the varied psychic subconscious or even conscious thought processes of any one of the preconditioned people so that he is a substation, and relays directly to them, a much greater degree of the inflow of this constructive Infinite interdimensional energy. It will re-assume itself and appear in the surface, life in diverse miraculous transpositions and various different adjustments which always occur when this particular junction and function has been attained. This is the opposite side of the picture which I had previously described to you.

The benign influence from the higher dimensions can be yours if you are so consciously aware of the processes involved in these transpositions. Conversely, if you are relaying the influence and the cancerous malignant effect of the lower astral worlds into your daily life, in the form of jealousies, hatreds, or other different attitudes of life; or if you may be attempting to circumscribe the dimension or the way in which other people live; yes, you may even know of or understand a higher way of life, yet much of this knowledge will be subverted should you be insistent to your fellow man that he subscribe to your way of thinking. At no time in our personal evolution should we feel a dominant urge to convert our fellow men to our way of thinking. We must always realize within the infinite reaches of the great Creative Intelligence that every human has found his own particular niche in life at that particular moment; he is a product of evolution, just as we are; and his particular point of evolution is just as valuable to him in the karmic lessons of life as the one in which we are involved. Should he, at any time, come to us with the understanding within himself, that we can give him something and share with him a higher quality or expression of life, then we can do so; but only on the basis that it is acceptable to him, and with his understanding that there is a better way of life and we can help him attain this better way.

Likewise, we should never misuse those who come to us from the higher planes of life; we should not try in any way to demand from them; we should not expect them to work miracles for us which would automatically nullify our own personal integrity, the power which we should exercise, within the dominion of our own lives, and rationally integrate all various forms of life as a product of our own consciousness and our own voluntary effort. It is quite useless to assume that any person would reach a higher plane of life by simply being levitated to it. The higher way is always attained in a direct proportion to our understanding of this higher life and the effort we use to attain it.

Let us not be diverted through various and sundry aspects of life which come to us and which may be the direct influence in some different kind of a psychic rapport with some of the subversive astral underworld forces and influences. They are ever at work; they never lose an opportunity to subvert you from your course of constructive evolution; they will warp, distort, confuse and misalign at every given opportunity. You will be constantly put to task within the confines of your own mind to keep your world well-ordered and straight; you must always keep the forward and upward progressive evolution within the dimension of your own consciousness, and you will refuse to be deviated from it.

You will also immediately rationalize that all of these various different malignant influences which come to you are products of dissention, borne from out of the astral underworlds and from your association with them as a progressive entity in some past lifetime. Quite conversely, the position which you may now, or shall in the future occupy, will present exactly the same problem in your progressive evolution. This is, in itself, Infinity and you can never conclude any particular point in your evolution where you can say that the lion is lying down with the lamb as it was parabolistically portrayed in Revelations. For in progressive evolution, the lion is always just outside the door: the lion of the past, in its carnivorous aspects, will destroy you should you let it again come into your daily life.

In other words, the lion is, in essence, the sum and total of your past, your many different lifetimes upon the earth and their innumerable experience quotients. Conversely the lamb represents the infinite future, white and unblemished in itself, it is still uncontaminated and untarnished by the realization of personal influences. Compatibility with the lion and the lamb, in any figurative sense, is only an assumption which begins when we can arrive at some conciliatory point, in our personal life evaluations, where we can completely compromise the past with the future, and place within the concept of our own minds, the complete compatibility of evolution as it exists in Infinite Consciousness. When we have arrived in our evolution at this point of compatibility in an infinite sense, we can truly say that the lion is lying down with the lamb, and they will remain in a passive state of consciousness with our future until such times as we may become falsely enamored with the past.

We may inadvertently contaminate our present position with the Infinite with various different, negative past transpositions. We may wrongly interpret or give them the incorrect bias or position in our introspection. When this foible of human consciousness has thus occurred, we can assume that we are in a more dominant attunement with the past. In that position the lion will then arise from his passive state of existence beside the lamb, and he will devour the lamb; or in other words, with this symbolic act of configuration, he has cancelled our chances, or our position to a progressive evolution, by devouring the concept of that future Infinite within the confines of the past. Thus he has also, in a sense, devoured the unfortunate person who has allowed himself to be victimized by becoming re-attuned with his past in this more dominant subversive personality expression.

This is the true translation of the parable of the lion and the lamb, and unless any person has a proper knowledge of the Infinite, a way of rationalizing the numerous values in an integration of consciousness, the symbology of this parable—like many other similar configurations in parabolistic form which are contained in the Bible—will lose its meaning. All parables in the Bible can thus be more accurately transposed when a broader and more fundamental knowledge of the Infinite is obtained. The description which I have just enumerated to you also becomes, in a sense, the translation of the parable of the Garden of Eden.

For here again, the compatability with present consciousness in any individual, as it is correctly biased with some knowledge of the Infinite, can be presumed to be a more pure state of spiritual consciousness. However, should this consciousness be contaminated with the serpent of the past, then it becomes a temptation. The tree which bears the "fruit of life" is, in essence, the sum and total of the past as the person has so realized it; and again reverting to the past, he is, in a figurative sense, plucking the apple from the tree; or that the serpent, the symbology of the past inequalities and differences of the material world, hands the apple to him, makes absolutely no difference whatsoever, for the temptation has occurred and the individual has succumbed to the temptation which arose from the past. Therefore, the passive spiritual state of consciousness, represented by the Garden of Eden, passes away, and he is thrown back into the derelict past with all its various sins and iniquities and a constant submergence of self into a never ending successive degenerating spiral into oblivion.

The meanings of various parables within the Old and New Testaments, as they are portrayed, have not been sufficient in themselves; they have been incorrectly interpreted by the masses of humanity who picked up these varied symbolic forms, and contrived within the dimension of their own minds, to distort them into configurations which conformed to their own limited horizon of thinking. The interpretation is thus never carried into the infinite dimension in which the original parabolistic form was so contrived and so conceived. This is, in essence, the same tenure which has been followed in the construction of any religious edifice and particularly in Christianity. For here again the liturgy of this religion, as it is supported by the various priesthoods and other exponents, who are, in themselves, elements of expression of Christianity, has thus contrived to build this into a rote system, tremendously dogmatic and extremely rhetorical to the extent, that survival is continually mandated by these expressionists. Their influence often reaches into the innermost secret recesses of personal life expressions, and in some churches, even dominates the sexual associations of various families.

The net results of such subjugating influences, which are felt through these religious systems, are immediately apparent to any person who is even basically trained in certain psychological elements. As a person is robbed of the power to think, or he is robbed of the power to act, irrespective of whether this action is evil or good, then the person can be considered to be well on his way to complete atrophy. If you held your arm in an absolutely immobile position for an indefinite period of time, the joints in the arm would fuse together, the muscles would become very flaccid, and they would not have any power within themselves to manipulate the various cord structures or bone segments of the arm; in other words, your arm would become a dangling appendage on your anatomy.

The same is true of your mind; and in any respect in whatever dimension of function in the process of oscillating infinitely through the psychic anatomy, where this process becomes even partially suspended, then we have the possibility of the beginning of a cancerous atrophy, which will, if given opportunity, spread throughout the entire structure of the psychic anatomy. The person then becomes more or less of an inert blob of energy substance which floats in the plasma of the universal expression, or we can say, he has reverted back to the place wherein a certain metamorphosis will take place, and this universal supply and substance will again regenerate this degenerated form and substance into something constructive in a normal and well balanced scale of progressive evolution.

This is the cycle of the accession and recession which is always immediately apparent in any position in any person's life. It cannot for one moment be conceived—in fact the thought is intolerable—that we could reach any fancied position in our spiritual evolution into the higher worlds where we could retire, so to speak, and lying back on a pink cloud playing a harp, float in utter complete happiness and oblivion through eternity. Such a completely passive state of existence would nullify, not only the objectivism of evolution itself, in the development of an entity of consciousness (which could be conceived as infinite in its expression), but so having arrived at the point where such an expression in an infinite capacity was about to be realized then this person would irrationally retire on the presumption, that now he had completed his work, and he would naturally be expected to atrophy completely. Having thus started the downward trail of evolution he would, as an entity of consciousness, reach that more ultimate point in the downward progression where the facsimile of individual expression was completely absent; and he would revert back to the common point of supply and the regenerative point of substance in the scale of infinite evolution.

At this point we must not contrive within ourselves to enter into the more abstract derivations which are automatically suggested by the presentation of this concept. The beginning, or terminating point in any evolutionary concept is practically nonexistent; that is, in infinite conception nothing is incomplete in itself, but functions perfectly in principle; therefore there is no terminating point nor is there any beginning point in Infinite Consciousness. Infinite Consciousness has survived, and always should be pictured in the individual consciousness as a constant survival, a never-ending and a never-beginning survival of Infinite Consciousness which supersedes far in advance of any concept or tenet of human consciousness that can presuppose the starting or ending point in any evolutionary cycle.

Therefore, the individual must remain content, for the present at least, with this particular concept of Infinity. Infinity must wait, so to speak, as far as you are concerned, until that day and age when you can conceive Infinity in a somewhat more expanded position. Even in that future day however, do not presume that you will find a terminating point; neither will there be a beginning; for a beginning and an ending are synonymous in all respects, and one must be present in order for the other to manifest. The function of the Infinite is completely abstract in all expressions, and therefore, remains as a completeness in cyclic form which is manifest in its entirety in interdimensional function. It can never be separated from itself; it cannot be placed in any particular position but resides infinitely throughout Infinity.

In this respect the Infinite is infinitely wise; and in knowing, It must conceive evolution as a cyclic form, propagated and supported by the inner dimension of inner consciousness as having a starting point in any particular concept or realization as it concerns an individual entity of consciousness, such as a human being. Here, the scale of evolution, so far as humanity is concerned, is a collective integration of various different infinite form substances which are more or less amassed, so to speak, through the process of evolution, by the principle of harmonic attunement, which in turn, has been re-created as a negative polarity in the environment of some particular material world dispensation.

Here the principle of positive and negative polarity is of the utmost importance; while the facsimile of a certain negative appearance in life is always inversely supported from within by a similar infinite or psychic polarization as a positive element, the transmission of these two different polarities, as they are more directly concerned within the attunement of their own particular expressive elements always, in turn, re-catalyze or polarize various other different additive concepts within the mental horizon of the human, as these are concerned within the confines of his psychic anatomy. In this respect, therefore, it must be thoroughly understood, by the aspirant to a higher way of life, that every act of consciousness, if fulfilled in a physical follow-up is, in effect, a universal part of the whole; it is attuned harmonically to every other different cyclic manifestation in the entire infinite macrocosm, as such, an attunement through these many harmonic planes of interception, the person, in turn, at any given point in his evolution, can be considered to be a person of infinite proportions.

He has within the dimension of his mind the complete and abstract power of reaching out into the Infinite, and aligning himself, harmonically speaking, with any particular transposition of life. He can manifest anything he wishes in his life; however when a person reaches this state of consciousness the material life has reached a point of complete abeyance and is completely superseded by the principle of Infinity Itself as a reconstructive element. This individual then, can be presumed to have passed that point where any particular manifestation of spiritual consciousness will integrate as personal adjutants in his own way of life; or they can be presumed to be demonstrative values used to impress his fellow men with the greatness of his understanding. They are not used to waylay the past insecurities and various different elements of the past life which can be largely considered as an escape mechanism, presupposed into the present and in the future.

Any individual thus harmonically attuned with the Infinite is, in all effect, an element which is reciprocating infinitely. Within the dimension of consciousness of his mind, he is completely aware of the Infinite in all its most abstract ramifications. He is completely aware of its constant, never-ending, resurgence which it constantly recreates within itself, the utmost in all abstract forms of consciousness. This person can also intelligently rationalize that each earth man, as he starts his evolutionary climb, is thus so confronted with the Infinite; but having a singular mind as a point of transposition in the immediate present as a third dimensional time element, he therefore can be selective only at the moment and in relation to the environmental pressures with which he is so surrounded.

In this way the individual begins his ascension or climb into a more advanced and Infinite perspectus. In this climb it can also be presumed, in the various cyclic transmissions of numerous earth lives, which are innumerable in number, that he must become selective; first he becomes selective on the basis of the immediate apparencies which are engendered by the aforementioned environmental pressures.

Then, the earth person's progression advances to a point—and it must be remembered here, that the principle of Infinite expression is always progressive in nature—where he, so traveling into Infinity, must always be consciously minded of this progression, and it can be presumed that he has reached, and begun to pass over a certain threshold—this threshold is his spiritual consciousness—to the point where he has grown, or expanded the dimension of his own particular perspectus of life to begin to include diverse and sundry deistic elements; or he has acknowledged, in more or less material aspects, that there are, within the dimension of his mind, certain particular facilities, or manifestations which cannot be compromised and cannot be explained in ordinary material stances.

Thus this person has reached his threshold of spiritual consciousness; he again reaches, so to speak, into Infinity, and in reaching comes out with some of the more pure and uncontaminated realizations of the Infinite which must be reshaped within the mental horizon of his own mind. These realizations must conform with the different ideologies, the various configurations with which he is familiar. His mystical effigies of God, or the diverse gods with which he is associated, always must contain the various temperamental and emotional vicissitudes of his own nature. In this respect mankind, up until the present time at least, and universally speaking—so far as the earth man is concerned—has not reached that plateau of understanding wherein he has completely separated the entity of the Infinite in his consciousness from these sundry emotional vicissitudes.

There are, in all religious factors, still certain dispensations of emotional values which are mandated, to a large degree, by the very existence of the church system itself. For should any person reach and pass the threshold where he becomes more completely introspective into Infinity, then church systems are no longer necessary in the mental horizon of his own daily life. He has now reached that place where he can interweave, in his daily life, various interdimensional facsimiles which are more completely abstract in nature, and he has taken into himself more of the infinite manner of expression.

When this has occurred to the individual, he becomes completely passive to the old past; he does not, within the dimension of his mind, participate in the earthly activities, as they are presented to him in his daily associations, in the sense of the word that they are, as to other people, the dominant libido or drive in his daily life. The necessity of life itself, as it is lived by the physical man, mandates a complete subjugation to this physical life. However, to the person who has thus become infinitely minded, the physical life assumes its more proper relationship to the Infinite; it is merely another plateau in which any earth man can be presumed to have a certain interlocking relationship with the Infinite, as it is relocated within the dimension of his own physical life. At this point then, the infinitely minded person can be presumed to be in that position Jesus spoke of when He said, "Being in the world, but not of it." It was very true with Jesus, just as it has been with any and all individuals who have reincarnated into the world and yet have not been one of the citizens of this world in the pure sense.

Any person who is infinitely minded and has assumed the mantle of flesh in a reincarnation for the object purpose of re-expressing Infinity to his fellow man, has naturally assumed some of the inevitable consequences which are always attendant to such a reincarnation. For, by now this infinitely minded person is so much more positively biased in his respect to the Infinite, that the existence in a material world demands the greatest amount of various different jurisprudences; it demands a direct and continual daily usage of all of his knowledge to sustain his life in the physical body upon the earth. This is quite different from the physical life lived in general by the earth man who is, in essence supported by a psychic anatomy which is compounded from divers physical drives. For with the spiritually advanced person, his drive has now been superseded by an Infinite knowledge, and his function in an environment which is foreign to a spiritually advanced person must be supported by a direct knowledge of all processes involved in sustaining life as a continuity of expression, in a scientific form and manner; and as he represents the positive polarity which very easily can be discharged to the material world, it remains a problem with him to compromise various continuities of expression in his relationship to his fellow man.

This is what Jesus meant when the woman with the issue touched His robe and He said, "Who touched me, for I felt the virtue leave me?" In that moment of touching His garment, this woman automatically discharged certain stored up energy—which Jesus had in His more immediate psychic aura—into the constructive rehabilitation process of her physical anatomy. It was in this manner and respect that Jesus was very often forced to refrain from intercourse with His fellow man and flee to the mountains where, in absolute tranquility and silence, He could again reach into the Infinite and recharge the numerous psychic structures and the different physical auras; so that He could, and would return to His earth life and continue His mission.

No, Jesus did not pray when He was in these mountain solitudes; in fact, if a complete accurate biography of Jesus were available, it would reveal that Jesus did not pray at any time; neither at the time of commission of miracles, nor in His abstinence from the society of His fellow man when He was in the vastness of the mountain seclusions. The process of mental integration which Jesus used and which superseded and supplanted the earth man's form of prayer was a conscious, constant, continuity of expression with the Infinite. In this respect, prayer was entirely superficial; in fact prayer would have been completely detrimental to a person who had reached that mental plane in life where he could conceive the Infinite as a relative function within the dimension or circumference of his own mentality, that it could be used as a dynamic principle of reconstruction in the evolution of his fellow man.

So, the various picturizations of Jesus, in which it is supposed that He prayed, or that He conversed, in a sense of the word, in a prayerful attitude with the Father, are entirely fictitious. They are merely the distortions which have been, either accidentally or intentionally, included in the numerous translations of the scriptures as they were first compounded from the memory contents of many different people who had survived the witch hunt after the crucifixion. In this respect the principle of continuity of expression with the Infinite into daily life, becomes a predominant principle of life to any person who has passed on beyond the precincts of the material world. In this state of consciousness any person docs not need to pray. He has arrived at a place where the *Infinite* is the *dynamic activating principle* of his life; in this respect then, his chief problem is to keep his conscious or physical mind in a more passive position to the more highly developed Superconscious, which he has thus developed through the various countless ages of life lived in numerous environmental conditions.

Any person who has reached this position in his life is also mindful of various other different principles and positions of compatibility, at which he must arrive, and these must be compromised in the mind of the earth man. To the earth man, who sees the personality reincarnate of some advanced spiritual being, such as Jesus, the age-old escape mechanism becomes completely dominant; he approaches this reincarnate personality, whom he calls a master, and on bended knee asks to be relieved of various physical and mental conditions. This is in direct opposition to the mental position of the perspectus which this spiritually advanced person is occupying. He knows full well the value of personal integrity which should and must be developed through the dimension of personal experience, the mastery, in effect, that this person, in going through the experience, gains the more infinite ramifications of the infinite experience, as it is concerned within the finite dimension of his own material consciousness.

The personal integrity of any person is not advanced, in fact, it is retarded if any mental or physical condition is miraculously removed from him. He is retarded in his natural progressive evolution, simply because the age-old escape mechanism has now been strengthened; he will, in the future, when he reincurs the old physical remanifestations of strife in his physical or mental perspectus, again try to seek some master or some deistic configuration which he hopes will relieve him. His search, should he not find this person, will be unending and of course fruitless; for as his search continues, so does he plunge himself more deeply in the abysmal reaches of the subconscious and subastral worlds, where fact is distorted into fancy and reality into fiction; so the more highly developed spiritual entity is confronted with a problem. He must enter into a certain compromising situation with the principles of progressive evolution. He must arrive at some very delicately balanced point of equilibrium where sufficient amounts of Infinite Power can be projected into this poor earth man's consciousness so that he will have the necessary incentive, the desire to continue in his search for a higher way of life; or that he might be inspired to seek out the correct solution to any and all of his present physical enigmas.

Needless to say, that at the point where this jurisprudence must be entered into, the advanced spiritual personality is taxed almost to the limits of his mental perspectus. For he is compassionately moved by the suffering of his fellow earth man; yet he knows that to give him more than just the right amount of the various esoterical or spiritual values in personal demonstrations of healing, etc., would be to rob this person of the incentive or drive to acquire a better way of life. For a miracle, in itself, must be more than a miracle, in a sense that it simply heals a condition; it must also give a great impetus, a great drive to this person to acquire a higher and better way of life. The mere manifestation of a miracle in a person's life should also be a catalyzing agent which would help to reconform various existing psychic malformations; to discharge any one or numerous psychic shocks which have been impounded within the psychic anatomy from past physical dispensations.

This then, is the way in which the Infinite again relives in one or more of the numerous forms of earth life dispensations which concern the earth man. The return of the savior, the Messianic content of any religion, should not be conceived within a church system, as an actual advent where Jesus, as the Master on the right hand side of the throne of some great white-robed Santa Claus, called Jehovah, descends upon a burned out earth to again re-establish, in some manner or form, the atomic constituents of a physical body and to bring out of the pits of hell, the various and associated personalities who are to reinhabit these reconformed physical anatomies.

Such a supposition is infantile. It has been born from out of the reaches of a primitive subconscious mind of a person who tried to arrive at divers and sundry deistic configurations and their dispensations through the elemental and emotional values of his own life. The true course of life is evolutionary in nature; it is progressive; it must either continue onward and upward, or it must continue downward. At no time will there be a point where a person can be presumed to be coasting, or to remain in some suspended state of animation. For the attributes within every wave form, as it is manifest, and as it is part of the Infinite Intelligence, must again regenerate; always it must be harmonically attuned. It always must be a part of the whole; it has no beginning; it has no terminating point; it remains constantly an ever-changing, resurgent, manifestation of the Infinite in action.

In this respect every person who is so minded for a better life, must appropriately understand these dynamic principles of infinite function and action. It cannot be otherwise. There are no intercessors, save in the concept within the consciousness of each individual, as he seeks out the Kingdom of Heaven which is within the concept of his own mind.

211

# CHAPTER 21

## Born Again of Spirit—Defined

Let us again take one of the more popular and well-known Biblical portrayals of the life of Jesus and try to clear up some of the mysticism, the miasma, and other various mental derelictions which concern the more ultimate truths in these diverse expressions which were uttered by the Nazarene. Jesus said to Nicodemus, "Except ye be born of the spirit, ye cannot enter the kingdom of Heaven," and Nicodemus wondered and asked, "How can it be that we are again born from the womb?" and Jesus said, "Nay, ye are not born of the flesh, but ye are born of the spirit."

This particular philosophical utterance has been the cause of much concern among the Christian adherents in different translations from which they have attempted to evaluate a very complete abstraction of the evolutionary principle in which all individuals are so vitally concerned. This is the emancipation or the freedom of the individual from the various carnal earth world existences and their numerous reactionary experiences—to supplant all of this past evolutionary reactionaryism with a more fundamental and basic concept of life which is lived in spiritual worlds, more highly developed than the material worlds, and minus the different emotional and reactionary methods of life which have, up until this time, supported all human beings.

If we look into the various evangelical elements which have attempted to dispensate, or to otherwise moderate this teaching to their different adherents, we will indeed find strange and rather obnoxious practices. The minister or the priest will succeed, through a very vehement display of oratory, in arousing his congregation into a hypnotic frenzy; and in this released hypnotic frenzy, inhibitions will vanish, the various adherents will hit the sawdust trail, as it is called; they will roll around in the aisles, sit on the mourner's bench, howl, scream, and froth at the mouth. After this horrible display has ended, they will happily go home believing they have been born again of the spirit, and have received Christ, or the Lord, etc. From that day on, at least for sometime into the future, they are quite likely to go about the world in a rather unrealistic position. They are still mesmerized or hypnotically projected from the reality of their existence; they are constantly attempting to reverify or resubstantiate this false position in their varied attitudes of life.

The proposition of being born into the spirit is indeed a far different process than that which has been preached by the evangelist, or by other different ecclesiastical dispensations. Being "born into the spirit," in reality, means that we continue on into the higher spiritual worlds over a period of many hundreds or even thousands of lifetimes, or many hundreds of thousands of years, earth time, in different elements and phases of living wherein we succeed in extracting the various values of experiences and interweaving these concepts with a more complete and abstract understanding of what the Infinite really is.

This is the normal way in which most people succeed in evolving into the higher spiritual worlds. There are, of course some shortcuts, I shall say, which

213

can be included and which can save numerous and painful life experiences. Being reincarnated into the flesh and living these experiences out, in the more normal reactive measures of these lives, can indeed be quite painful and distressing, and can also carry the element of danger that we may incur certain types of blockages which will precipitate us down toward the more ultimate and disastrous end of oblivion. We can also incur very serious psychic disturbances which will manifest themselves in our physical anatomies, and in the surface consciousness of our various life dispensations as they are lived from one life to the next.

This evolution of consciousness is indeed quite complex if it is approached and realized in a more complete infinity within the present moment of consciousness; however, it does not necessarily need to confuse anyone who so approaches the Infinite, in the sense that these principles can be rationally integrated; we can form different necessary basic concepts, and above all we can assume a more completely dedicated purpose and intent toward the Infinite in our desire to incarnate into a higher life.

It is at this point that we should remember the approach to the Infinite must always be made, as it was described by Jesus, "as little children". In other words, we cannot approach the Infinite with very definitely formed convictions which we have derived from other lifetimes in the past. We cannot constantly compare the Infinite with that which has transpired in our former earth life experiences, or with any other previous affiliations or denominational orders. We cannot classify the Infinite in generally accepted terms of relationship with political systems, religious dispensations, credos, etc. The Infinite must always be considered as the Infinite Perspectus, that is, we can, at any time in our evolution, completely evolve our mental consciousness with the combined elements

214

of Infinity, as they are so presented to us, and not necessarily compound them from out of our past experiences into the present mental tense; or the recombinations of these various elements become a compromising dispensation of life which seems to flatter the immediate apparency of this life as it is understood by us.

From time to time we have had a number of students write to us in regard to their endeavors to understand Unarius; and in these respects they have reverted to this common and quite fallacious practice of trying to compare Unarius with other previous contacts which they have made with such religious or metaphysical orders they have studied. This is a common practice and one which should be dealt with quite strenuously, inasmuch as we must first supplant within our consciousness an entirely new concept of Infinity. Unarius is just another name for Infinity; it cannot be classified in this respect with any other existing interdenominational orders; it cannot be classified as a religion; and it cannot be classified, in the material sense, as a material or third dimensional science. Although it is scientific in nature and does include the basic elements in our material science, it must be remembered that material science, in turn, has merely included or borrowed from the Infinite, certain basic concepts or principles which have made this physical science possible up to this point. Unarius, therefore, can be considered to be something like a large slice of watermelon taken across the entire section of the melon, and in this section we can see the various formations wherein the seeds are held firmly within the fleshy portions of the melon. Unarius, in a sense then, is a cross section of the Infinite and the beginning of your understanding of the Infinite.

At this point we can also make another analogy; we can say that your approach to the Infinite, through

Unarius, is, in all respects, an attempt upon your part, to again be born into the spirit or "born of the spirit." Being "born of the spirit" means much more than being consciously aware that such a thing as a spiritual world exists; or that there are heavenly kingdoms or mansions as Jesus spoke of them. In order to live in these more highly developed or evolved ways of life, it is most necessary that we understand them. Mere recognition does not give us the power to live in these higher worlds; we must become thoroughly acquainted with the entire proposition of life in a higher world in a sense that it is a definite reality of existence. Therefore, if we look back in our own present lifetime to that day when we were born, and we began a whole new system of reorientation into the present life with some of the more basic elements of life which we have lived from past lifetimes, then the first six or eight years of our lives— classified by the psychologist, as being the formative period of life—were indeed trying times for us, just as they are for all children.

You had to constantly, day by day, hour by hour, orientate yourself to various different emotional values and experiences which came to you, or through which you passed in this developmental process. However, as the years passed such things became familiar to you and you developed sort of an automation to them. You immediately adjusted yourself to them and, as a whole, this continuously variable form of constantly readjusting yourself to the new circumstances and experiences of life, comprised your life. The same situation is quite true in your approach to the Infinite, and as Unarius is your first fundamental and basic approach to the understanding of the Infinite, it is therefore quite conceivable that it may necessarily be quite complex to you. This is so because it also presents to you the unknown. For up until this point you have not had any reality with this Infinite, therefore, it remains rather intangible to you even though you have, to some degree, recognized or envisioned within your own mentality, the possibility, or even further, the various forms and attitudes of life which may be lived in these higher worlds. This however, does not make it possible for you to live in these higher worlds; so again we have the same approach, the same subconscious human frailty of constantly reverting back into the past and taking numerous extractions and derivatives from past emotional experiences and compounding them with the present time. If this is done and constantly practiced in your approach to Unarius, you cannot hope to succeed very realistically in the different integrations of the numerous and rather complex elements which comprise your approach to the Infinite.

It always must be approached without the conviction or without the comparative emotional reaction to these various past dispensations. You cannot say that this is similar to some other order of expression which you formerly studied or of which you were a part; you cannot say that Unarius was derived from any of these expressions; in fact it is the reverse. These other interdenominational orders or numerous other infractions of religious expressions or metaphysical groups, which you formerly studied, were, in themselves, only the acknowledgment of the Infinite and an attempt to verify the Infinite into a system of justifications based on the emotional values of earth lives. This is quite the reverse in Unarius. For we must, at this point, begin to understand the Infinite as a basic system of evaluation wherefrom, all different dispensations of life are extracted, not the reverse as has been just previously described.

In this sense then, Unarius can be considered to be completely in reverse to any and all known religious systems or orders; it is also in reverse, so to speak, with all known material dispensations of life, because

217

it has immediately transferred the point of focus from the physical or earth world to the adjacent and adjoining dimensions where it properly belongs. Therefore, from the varied points in the basic elements of understanding the Infinite, we can make all the necessary compensations and evaluations as they should most correctly be made, and without the constant subconscious reversion back into the past and the emotional complexes which have substantiated life to us, in these former expressionary elements.

One more point which should be interjected at this time is that other common frailty of human nature, which is simply this: when we arrive at some particular position in the various intellectual processes in which we are involved, the thinking processes, or the evaluations which we make, we must always remember that we are constantly, to some small or large degree, being dominated or subverted by the subconscious, or we cannot make a constructive approach to the realization of the Infinite. These subversive values will always exist until we learn to recognize them as they appear on the surface of our consciousness; they immediately can be recognized if we desire to do so. This does however, in all effect, tend to completely tear down the past understanding; it also tends, in a sense, to deflate our own personal egos, inasmuch as ego is the common derivative of all known and understood factors of your present lifetime.

The understanding of the Infinite, therefore, makes this ever-constant demand, that it cannot be influenced or intimidated; it cannot be subverted from the past. The conscious surface of your mind and the various inflective thinking processes are oscillating wave forms which are so necessary in forming the constructive picture of your analyses. These must always be predicated upon the re-emphasis of the future, as they are so reflected into your consciousness from the higher Superconscious Self, in conjunction with the sundry suggestive factors which are included in the lesson courses, the taped messages, etc., as they are being explained to you.

Here again in our analyses we have arrived at that most inevitable point—and a point which is constantly recurring in all of our various analyses and introspections—that our old self is our worst enemy. Inasmuch as we cannot eliminate this old self at any time, we are therefore our own worst enemy. When this fact is fully recognized by all people in their varied daily life introspections, they can be considered to be persons, individually speaking, who have taken the first definite and tangible step in the right direction, whereby they eventually can be born into the spirit and live in the higher spiritual worlds.

For life in these higher dimensions, as has been previously explained, is quite different than these earth lives. The various factors which involve life in these higher spiritual worlds, to a large degree, are quite unknown to most of the earth people. There is, at the present time, a small minority group of earth people who recognize the possibility of these higher ways of life; they recognize the possibility of the higher spiritual worlds, but as yet, it has not become a reality to them in the sense that these concepts can be justified, or that they can be realized in the different lifetime dispensations which are lived from day to day.

Therefore, the material man will, for some considerable length of time or for many hundreds of earth lives in the future, live such similar earth lives as the one in which he is presently engaged. This is the true evaluation of karma: the constant and never-ending repetition of certain cyclic paths of life as they constantly recur in the various patterns of daily life of these people. They wear different clothing, they may read newspapers, or have electronic apparatus, etc., which may not have been in existence in these previous lifetimes; yet the psychology of their existence is basically the same. It is an elemental psychology based upon the reactionary values of each life experience and as emotionally biased creatures, they must react to them. In this respect, the common man, as he is seen in the material world, is no better than any of the other animal creatures which inhabit this planet. He is different from them only in the respect that he has begun to recognize or to envision in his consciousness the possibility of a higher way of life; and in this respect he has erected the sundry systems of deifications which are called religion. These however, are not necessarily true; they are merely attempts at sublimating some of the various otherwise unexplainable values in the generally accepted frame of reference of earth life.

If you would be "born of the spirit," then do not attempt to preface this rebirth upon former extractions or derivatives in the emotional values of your previous life. Unarius or Infinity is one and the same; they are synonymous. Therefore, Unarius cannot be classified as a religion or any other particular type of dispensation which may be familiar to you at the present time. Unarius is a complete abstraction of the Infinite, wherein this Infinity is explained in a practical and realistic manner. Your approach to the Infinite can be fully realized; also it can be very strongly supported from the extra transcendent energy which is always at the disposal of the various students who are entering into these studies. For, at any time they so desire, the complete rebirth can occur; and when this moment does occur there will indeed be a tremendous and intense emotional experience, wherein the different past lifetime dispensations are, to a large degree, completely dissipated and cancelled out.

In fact, the entire vibrating rate of the atomic constituents of the physical body are again reinstated into a much higher rate of vibration with the Infinite.

Here at the Center, we describe these various processes as "work outs" wherein the students, who have reached this particular climax in their studies of Unarius, have manifested numerous major or minor physical and mental reactions, to the degree that partial or temporary physical incapacity is entered into. This is so because there is a definite misalignment, to a degree, with the former past lifetimes, as they were lived through the various portions of the psychic anatomy. As these different portions are so cancelled out, or they are rebuilt, there is quite naturally the consequence of temporary misalignment until realignment can occur in a higher dimensional respect.

It is interesting to note, that all students who have entered into the study of Unarius and who are so actively connected with the Center, have entered, more or less, into this climactic position in their working out periods. In this sense then, we see many of these students again actually being reborn in the spirit. They no longer have the same relationship to the physical world; the former strong appetites and the various expressions which they considered most necessary in their worldly life are no longer dominant factors in their daily lives; they have become indifferent to them. The true values of the higher spiritual world, in turn, become the more dominant factors of their existence. Yes, under these conditions even the most valuable of earth life condiments or expressions are almost wholly lost. They can be lost to the extent that it becomes a rather difficult proposition to live the remaining years of life upon the earth. They must constantly be compromised in various attitudes, manners, and ways in which Unarius so explains in the entirety of its science.

In fact, the whole concept of Unarius as a philosophical approach to the Infinite, does supply more than these cancelled out elements of daily life.

Therefore, in the future, if you personally enter into this phase of relationship with your studies, where there is a definite strong psychism which enters into your life at some particular point, that you feel like your physical body is coming apart, that your legs are like rubber, that you have crying spells, etc., do not be alarmed, but rather, feel joyful that this is an occurrence which is called being "born of the spirit." It is most necessarily severe at this time because a great deal must be accomplished in a short period of time. The contact with Unarius has given you great power over these past lifetime dispensations. In this effect, through your studies you are canceling out the negative quotient of these countless millions of life experiences as you formerly lived them.

Remember also, at all times in these various manifestations, that you have the constant and never-ending support of millions of highly developed spiritual personalities who can, and do, constantly project very strong mental energies unto you; energies which will help you in all ways, manners, and forms, to overcome the old self, and to be "reborn into the spirit." For this does, in effect, mean truly that the old self must die; you must be reconstituted in entirety, in concept, in manner and demeanor, and in all ways and forms, to the higher way of life. It cannot be otherwise. For these higher spiritual worlds are entirely different from any of your realizations of the material world. They are relevant in principle, only when we derive the basic abstraction of principle as the regenerative function of Infinite Consciousness.

# CHAPTER 22

## God's Only Begotten Son

One of the more classical utterances frequently used by the religionist, the preacher, or the evangelist, is that very familiar cliché extracted from the Bible, "The Lord so loved mankind that He gave His one and only begotten Son." Now, this may appear at the moment to be a deceptively innocuous religious expression, and it may seem to be reasonably supported from the various artifacts of the religion itself. Also it may include the very prominent subconscious suggestion which is interconnected with all religious dispensations, and which, in turn, gives the religionist his miasmic attitude toward the reality of creation and the Infinite Intelligence which is, in reality, the true God. The supposition that "The Lord gave His one and *only* begotten Son," immediately suggests certain intimidations which are not wholly supportable in the entire deistic concept.

The begotten Son, in itself, suggests that God must somehow be a being which possesses sex organs and does indeed give birth to living young. How this process is concluded must be done, of course, in a bi-sexual way; that is he possesses both male and female parts, otherwise the creation or the birth of the begotten Son must have some sort of a magical wand-waving proposition, wherein God somehow contrived by a bit of magical hocus-pocus to immediately bring into this world the entirety of Himself in the form of His son. In any case however, the unreality of this supposition is immediately apparent when we start to analyze it, and try to evaluate it on the common derivatives of scientific expressions, or even in common sense attitudes, as they exist in our present understanding of life. Therefore, we must understand that this classical cliché of religious expression, while it is neither realistic nor intelligent, in itself, does, however, in a parabolistic form as an extracted derivative, contain a certain basic element of the regenerative expression of life.

In the lesson courses of Unarius this has been described as an abstraction of the Infinite Intelligence; or God, or the Lord, etc., as it is called by the religionist; this facsimile or abstraction of the infinite expression is immediately available throughout Infinity; this means in essence, that it matters not upon whatever planet we may be living, or in whatever spiritual world we may be living at the time, we can, at any moment, put forth our mental finger, so to speak, and immediately contact the entire Infinite. This is done as it is explained in the more scientific presentation of harmonic attunement; the Infinite is constantly regenerating in numerous dispositions the entirety of Itself through the various dimensions and the interplay of vortices as they so compose the Infinite macrocosm.

Your contact with the Infinite, at any time therefore, will be determined by concept, or how well you can personally contact the Infinite on the basic elements or derivatives of conscious expression as they reside within the concept of the psychic anatomy. Always these various concepts, as they are abstractions of the Infinite, must come through that facsimile of the Infinite which is called the Superconscious

Self. The religionist has called this Infinite Intelligence "Christ," and he has further subverted this "Christ" into the common expression of the personal being as Jesus so lived it 2000 years ago. This whole supposition, therefore, immediately disassociates the common man with Christ. It also disassociates the common man with the Infinite Intelligence of God; in fact, it makes us, in a sense, spontaneous creations or merely bastards of existence; and up until some theoretical point in the future when we are "saved," as it is said, by "intercession," we really have no part in the scheme of Infinite Creation, other than the fact that we were born in "sin," as it is called by the religionist; he believes that sex is a cardinal sin and not an expressive quotient of life as it should be more properly understood by the material man.

When God, or the Infinite gave his one and only begotten Son, it merely means that as we personally contact the common abstractions of the Infinite, in various integrated relationships of daily life; these, in turn, polarize the exact facsimile of that same quotient which is pulsating or regenerating in Infinite Consciousness. When this is achieved we, in effect, make this part of the Infinite our personal property; we have compounded it within that dimension of the psychic anatomy which is called the Superconscious Self, and there it will remain forever, or at least, forever as we can understand it in a material way. It is in this way that the Infinite Father, the Infinite Intelligence, or God, does give Himself to each and every one of us, and creates from Himself His begotten Son.

In the more ultimate destiny of each human being, we can assume that there are a large number of these abstractions—and as they are polarized by our own personal expression with the Infinite, we develop a personality capable of evolving into the higher state of consciousness which embodies the entire concept of Infinity. When we arrive at this point where we can envision the whole Infinity in its true basic relationship to us, then we can truly say we are a begotten Son of God; we have been created in His true image, and we have been created from the substance of the Infinite God in that never-ending regenerative process of intelligent harmonic relationship which is constantly taking place.

If these scientific principles were more thoroughly understood by the religionist, he would cease to babble these inane and nonsensical suppositions which, through the strong dominant qualities of his personality, submerge the more realistic or factual understandings of his followers. He demands that his belief, his supposition should be the paramount virtue in the present life expression of his adherents; however, when he has so understood these principles, he will then cease to be such a dominant personality. Likewise, his religions and the various constituents which supported him in this manner of expression will, quite naturally, vanish; the adherents who followed him in this blind and sheep-like attitude will also vanish.

In general, through the same process of analysis, introspection, and a recombination of diverse and obvious elements, depicted not only in many Biblical portrayals and descriptions, but also portrayed in different attitudes which are deistic in the life of the average earth man at this time, to the extent that they supplant the actual reality of his existence, thus man has been relieved of the use of his brain in solving these important issues for himself.

Man is inherently lazy in the respect that so long as he can find ways, manners, and means to justify a certain release in the mental processes with which he is involved, or as these mental processes recombine to form such aspects of life with which he is familiar —he becomes evasive or demands ways in which he can dodge or circumvent them. He can, in all manners and forms, be said to be an escapist; for man, as he lives today, truly is an escapist. He is trying to escape, not only the fears, the degradations of the material life, and the fear of death itself; but also he is trying to escape the mental processes which are most necessary for him to evolve from his present carnal and animal-like state of existence. How thoroughly indoctrinated he is in these aspects of life can only be envisioned on the terms of his understanding of the evolutionary pattern of life as it is lived from one life to the next.

The dominant characteristic of human expression is survival. Like all other animals and creatures of the earth, at any moment of his life, man is most vitally concerned with survival. He is so dominantly concerned with it that he will procreate in the same manner and form as do all of the animals of the earth; he procreates because in bestowing life into the birth of a child, he does, in effect, envision in this child a continuity of his own life. He hopes to escape all of the ramifications or complexities of his material world which are climaxed or culminated in the moment of death; for death is the unknown, the unreal factor in his life which he never succeeds in sublimating. He only partially succeeds in alleviating this most basic fear, the most elemental fear in his religious deifications—that he is supposed to be saved—he is supposed to be elevated or otherwise cleansed or purified to live in a way or manner which is free from his former vicissitudes and emotional turmoils; above all he will be freed from the constant and never ending stigma of death.

Religion therefore, as it concerns every individual, remains the greatest of all hypocrisies; for it is, in itself, not only a deistic misconception, but also it forms the core or nucleus of the general escape mechanism which is practiced by all human beings in their hope to escape from the various and most certain of all earth life dispensations, the eminent fear of death. This fear of death is the destructive force and intent of the primitive world in which man finds himself; for as he has so survived from life to life, this entity of personal consciousness, as he has evolved it within himself, remains imperishable. Yet, he has not conceived the reality of this dominant characteristic of his nature, because he does not understand that evolution can and does support him from one lifetime to another.

He knows that he can live from one day to the next with the interval of sleep or nighttime in between. He does not conceive, however, that he also can live from life to life, and that the interval in between is sort of a trance or sleep-like state, the vague and unreal spiritual world. It is unreal only in the sense that he does not understand it; he has not yet evolved into that consciousness where the spiritual world is a reality, which could be lived very realistically just as he lives his present physical life, minus all of these fearful and emotional vicissitudes which have enabled him to live from one day to the next, or from one life to the next. This, as a whole, must remain a more complete abstraction in personal analysis.

In effect, we are, through these various life to life processes, not only being born of the spirit, but also the Infinite Intelligence is, in Itself, reciprocating an equal or a more dominant factor in each evolutionary concept. This is the way the Infinite Intelligence, God, the Father, or the Lord does give His only begotten Son, for, in a sense, each begotten Son is each individual who has ever lived, or who is living, or who can conceivably live in the future.

For the expressionary element of Infinite Intelligence is not necessarily confined to numbers; It is not emotionally concerned in Its creation. If it were so emotionally concerned, creation could not exist;

for the conflict of various emotional values would superimpose many false images in this otherwise super-intelligent being that people have called God. This would render Him as inept and as inadequate as is the earth man in solving the most obvious of all his differences. There is only one way in which the Infinite Intelligence, the Supreme Creator, the God deification can exist. He exists because He is not emotionally motivated, He is not emotionally concerned with any of the creations of Himself; they are all either a large or a small part of Him; and the whole passes all understanding or conception on the terms that we can evaluate it within the confines of a third dimensional mind. We must, for the present at least, be satisfied with the basic elements of this Infinite Creation, with the principles involved, and clear up some of the mists and illusions in which mankind formerly has been involved.

Do not be confused by the apparent numerical superiority of the atheistic expressionists as they exist today; for all people are atheists, despite the fact that they may proclaim to be religionists. They still are atheists until they understand the true Infinite God, until they understand the true procreation of mankind as a fundamental factor of regeneration which is constantly expressed from Infinite Intelligence. We cannot deify these things. We cannot remove them from the immediate apparency which is contained within the concept of our own minds. In all cases, and in whatever dimensions in which we so find ourselves, or in whatever lives with which we are so concerned, these basic elements will always remain paramount and dominant. They cannot be violated, they cannot be superimposed by any of our own personal facsimiles. We must ultimately be concerned with the complete resolution of these basic elements and principles within the ways, means, and manners of life as it is lived by us individually. As it is lived individually it becomes a pattern which is universally expressed by mankind.

It also must be remembered that, if at any time, we divert the more objective and abstract realizations of concept within our own minds into the more common and dominant physical expressions which may seemingly mandate their inclusion in our introspection, then we are lost—at least for the moment. We cannot form basic equivalents from such infractions as are commonly expressed by our fellow men, for these are merely the more primitive values extracted from the evolutionary process which sponsored them from the beginning of their more elemental and barbaric past.

Such equalities as are supposed to exist in any democratic system of government, for instance, are actually nonexistent, and the concept of equality is most obnoxious and should be avoided at all costs; for it does not exist, either in the concept of Infinity or in its expression. There are no equalities, and should we attempt to explain our own position as equal with that of any or all human beings, then we are approaching the tideland of mental vicissitudes wherein we shall be swallowed and made mentally inert.

As the Infinite is infinite in Its expression, so we, as individuals, must also become infinite in our expressions. We cannot, at any time, ever hope to express the same relationship to Infinity as does any other human being. We have not succeeded in doing this in any past experiences, and we shall never do this in the future. As individuals we shall always remain an individual creation of the Infinite Intelligence; and we shall, as personal beings in that creation, express the same quotient of Infinity as is the basic principle of Infinite expression.

To say that we are equal to someone else who may have a different colored skin, or who may have some other political or religious belief, immediately arouses many complexities in this analysis which can never suitably be equalized, no matter how far we carry this hopeless form of personal analysis. We can say that equality exists only in the common basic elements of expressive quotients or principles of expression as they are constantly regenerating in the infinite macrocosm and microcosm. In the full abstraction of evolution, each individual must realize that his evolutionary progress will give him equality in the scheme of Infinite Creation. It does not give him equality with any or all human beings no matter how he has so contrived his political or religious systems.

As a matter of fact, the constitution of the United States definitely expresses the ideal that everyone is entitled to live the way he chooses; then on the other hand it defeats the entire content of this expression by presupposing that equality exists in the common relationships wherein man can mentally conceive himself as living all aspects of life in a similar manner to that of his neighbor. Man has not realized that these individual expressions are most valuable to him, no matter what his religious beliefs, his political affiliations, that he has a different colored skin, or any of the other different factors of relationship which so vitally concern him at this present time. For each and every one of us, everyone who has ever lived or is so living, or hopes to live in the future, is at all times, most vitally concerned with that constructive process of becoming one of the begotten Sons.

The complete entity of creation is expressed in the mental consciousness of every individual; the Infinite arrives at a new plateau of Infinity in the net extracted quotient of an Infinite number of human beings who are constantly re-expressing Infinity in the way, manner, and form in which they have learned to evolve Infinity in their own consciousness—not that they are all similar in all respects in their relationship to the

Infinite, but rather that they present to the Infinite a different set of concepts—a different way in which they understand the Infinite, but always basically motivated, basically integrated, and expressed in the cardinal principle of regenerative creation.

This is the way the Infinite lives in such dimensions wherein we can envision mankind living in diverse and sundry brotherhoods or different aggregations as they should be more commonly understood. The more highly developed, the more highly evolved, the less desire there is to divide, to segregate, or to classify individuals into various groups, or to feel that the expressions of one group are necessarily superior to those of another group. Instead, there will be a gradual inclination or clemency to universally express the Infinite on the same cardinal principles of Infinite Regeneration; principles which will eventually, in more highly developed and more highly evolved states of consciousness, give to these various personalities the general consensus of universal brotherhood; a brotherhood which can be shared as an infinite proposition; a creative sublimation which carries on into the most remote phases of human expression.

Yes, man, as he exists today, is basically an animal, but he also is much more than an animal, at least in one respect; he has already begun to incorporate in his recognition of various deistic configurations, the more ultimate sublimation of consciousness. In the evolution of consciousness which will verify, enlarge, and solidify this Infinite Perspectus, he will, in a sense, be helping the Infinite Creator to create the one, the only begotten son in his own image, within the fabrication of his own psychic anatomy. In that day of realization he will not be confounded with the configurations of deistic expressions, he will be able to understand the Infinite as It exists, and he will not subvert the hard-earned and hard-fought-for mental horizon at which he has arrived, by trying to compare it with his past life experiences. He will not be confused by the proclamations of various priests or religious adventists; he will not be confused by political miasma; he will not be confused by the vague differences in political systems, or the differentiations of social structures and their so-called sciences. The economies of the world will remain as they should be, merely passive elements of expression, rightly or wrongly used by mankind; and this too, is the process of evolution into the higher worlds where man does become a begotten son.

# CHAPTER 23

## Karma

It is without a doubt that the most misunderstood concept of metaphysics is contained in the ideology of karma. This is quite true whether we are concerned with people who have studied occultisms or various other religions, or that we are considering the layman who has accidentally bumped up against some expression of the word karma in his daily life. The term karma is derived from such occult expressions as are portrayed or lived in many Eastern countries such as India, China, etc., and these occultisms have been so lived for perhaps several thousands of years. They are usually derivations of such concurrently expressed deifications as Buddha, who is the prime reigning deification at the present time; however, Hinduism, in itself, embraces perhaps a hundred million different gods, and the confusion among the Hindu cultists can be considered to be extremely varied, to say the least.

Karma, as it is understood by the Eastern mind, is a connotation which relates directly to reincarnation; and in reincarnation these people have derived some rather weird and fantastic suppositions. For instance, if they commit some sort of a crime, self-flagellation is necessary; they will pierce their flesh with hooks or skewers, lie on beds of nails, and do other strange and weird things in order to punish themselves for some crime which they believe they have perpetrated. Other expressions in this same vein include the supposition that if they harm or hurt an insect or animal they will, in a future lifetime, reincarnate into that particular animal form. This, of course, is also quite ridiculous. Furthermore, the Western minds, such as various people who are studying these cultisms in this country, have abstracted some of these similar weird transformations of this ideology into their own studies.

In order to clear up these different indispositions about this extremely misunderstood concept, we must go directly into the vein of pure science. We cannot hope to understand karma in a sense that because we perpetrated a crime against one of our fellow human beings, we will have to reincarnate and, in reverse, the same crime or sin must be perpetrated again. If someone had killed one of us in a previous lifetime, it makes no sense that we would come back into some future life and commit the same act against the same person, or any other different version or transposition of experience which we might envision within our consciousness. I have used murder as a concrete example of one of the more heinous forms of crime which has been perpetrated by mankind since the beginning of his evolution.

First, let us go back into the more basic understanding in a scientific vein, as I have suggested in the different liturgies of Unarius, and, in particular, to the construction of the psychic anatomy. If you remember, thought is an active oscillating wave form connected and interconnected within the psychic anatomy with hundreds or thousands or even millions of other wave forms which are harmonically attuned to it. Therefore, in realizing this most important principle, you are at any given time, here or hereafter, the sum and total of that which is contained in the psychic anatomy. It is constantly, in all ways, man-

ners, and forms reflecting back into your consciousness, into your physical anatomy, just exactly that
which has been impounded there in previous experience quotients. It cannot be otherwise; by the same
analysis, even if we think a thought and we do not
follow through with a physical action, the result is
just the same; we have impounded this particular
little concept or this thought as part of our psychic
anatomy. As a wave form it has gone into this structure and oscillated with other existing wave forms
harmonically attuned to it in such similarities of life
experiences, to form one or more of the numerous
vortexes of which the psychic anatomy is composed.

If we think about this for a moment, then we can
look back into history, so to speak, and see ourselves
in various other different life configurations. If we
have been soldiers in a previous lifetime, and we have
hurled our weapons, or plunged our swords, or fired
our guns into the adversary, we cannot justify or excuse this act of aggression against mankind on the
basis that it was most necessary that we do so to pre-
serve intact, our way of life, or that we were commanded to do so by the king, the emperor, or any other
ruling personality. Neither can we justify our acts if
we were merchants and each day we did a little plain
or fancy cheating, or any one of the many different
types of experiences which were impounded in these
previous lifetimes.

As we progressed through these various lifetimes
and different experiences, most of the little acts of
aggression stockpiled, as it were; they piled up to
form some of the more numerous vortexes within our
psychic anatomies; then, as we began to be spiritually
quickened, when we lived in the spiritual worlds in
the lives in between earth lives, we became increasingly aware of these situations. We must remember,
at this point, that we are also concerned with a very
definite and a dynamic principle of evolution. As we

progress into the future, that which we are doing at the present, or have done in any given moment in the past does become a negative quotient in our consciousness in the future. This is quite true in whatever manner or form of life experiences we so live at any given time.

It may be true that at this moment you are studying Unarius, you are actually stockpiling some negative energy wave forms, because you are subconsciously or consciously realizing that you are still not capable of understanding its full import and its breadth and scope. Also, you may not be, at present, actually practicing or putting into effect the different principles which have been explained to you. But from whatever point of introspection we wish to derive an analysis, we are always confronted with this inescapable fact; that so far as the future is concerned, the present is always going to represent a certain negative stance, or it is going to be negatively biased to this future at any given time.

Therefore, so far as this future is concerned, we must always immediately be concerned with the dynamic proposition of evolution as it concerns thought consciousness or experience at any particular or given moment of our existence. As you are today, a student of Unarius, you are reading this Message; you can look back into your past life or even into numerous past lifetimes and see yourself, figuratively at least, in numerous experiences, and while they were part of your daily life at that time, and perhaps, even in a way, were considered the ordinary manner, way, and form of life about you, you were a citizen of good standing in the community, yet the fact remains that because of the difference in evolution from that point to this point, whatever it was that you may have done in this previous earth life experience, it is now negative to you; it has, and will always continue to present a certain negative bias in the general conflux of energy wave forms which oscillate into the conscious form of your mind.

This, then will give you a sense of guilt, and the sense of guilt is always proportional to the distance you have traveled into the future. If you have approached that threshold, about which I have spoken many times, then this sense of guilt is much greater than it would be under ordinary circumstances; and, at this point, when we become so obsessed with this sense of guilt, we begin to do many strange things. No, we do not lie upon beds of nails nor stick skewers into our flesh, like the Hindu might; but we do use other strange and devious ways to try to detract from our conscious reality, the sense of this guilt within us. We are always avoiding the inescapable fact that sooner or later we must have to face this past guilt realistically. We must learn to cancel this guilt out and to superimpose into our consciousness the scientific mechanics of evolution, so that we shall be enabled to travel into the future dimensions of time less hampered by the reactionary way in which we have formerly lived.

When we have approached this threshold, we have, as I have said, become more and more conscious of these various guilt forms in our past experiences; this is approaching a certain dimension of consciousness which the Christian calls repentance. Now, repentance should not be misconstrued with some of the practices which are presently in effect in Christianity, no more so than repentance should be confused with the practices which are taking place in India in the manner and form of mental and physical flagellation. For the sense of guilt gives us a certain degree of recrimination, and we should not, at that moment, resort to any common practices which will involve us in an even far worse situation. A guilt complex, when it is supported or entwined with a persecution complex, is indeed a horrible monstrosity! Many people attempt various forms of mental or physical flagellation in order to escape the reality of facing this guilt mechanism which their daily life has engendered from the past experiences.

The manners and forms of these inversions or subversions are perhaps as numerous as are the number of people; for each person seems to be particularly adept at starting his own way, manner, and form of self-flagellation. The degree of self-punishment may range from very mild and deceptively innocuous practices, to some of the more perverse manifestations which can and do lead people into mental institutions. A feeling of self-pity or recrimination, if it is continued or practiced, can lead to disastrous results; for self-pity is a mental venom which is far more deadly and dangerous than that which is given off by a cobra. Neither should we, as have many religious people of Christian faith in the past, renounce the world to become celibates in a sense, nor indulge in other weird practices, such as proclaiming that God is punishing the world or punishing ourselves individually, nor any other strange and unrealistic attitudes and presuppositions.

There is only one way in which we can cancel out guilt and that is to understand the scientific mechanics of life as it is being portrayed to you in Unarius. When you begin to do this and it becomes a factually related science, then guilt is cancelled out as it is incurred in the day-by-day experiences. If you have done something in the past few days, which at the present moment does not seem right to you, then you can, by understanding the scientific mechanics of evolution, almost immediately—or to a large extent—see that this experience was a parallax or a justification of consciousness which occurred because other different and particular experiences were activated at that moment. In this sense, as we superimpose this concept of science in our daily acts and thoughts, we will then become increasingly less intimidated by the negative quotients from these life experiences. They will, in effect, so far as their negative biases are concerned, be cancelled out and they will not have that insidious guilt imposition which they have formerly incurred upon us. Moreover, we will also progressively advance; we will be less inclined to perpetrate these smaller or even larger crimes against ourselves; for with the increasing understanding of the science, the mechanics involved in evolution and the Infinite principle of creation, we will also superimpose in our consciousness a much higher degree of expression. The form or expression of life is always tantamount and relative to our understanding of how well we can conceive the principle which is activating the moment of consciousness. This brings us down to the reality of the present moment.

Just how well you understand the principles, which have been described to you in the lesson courses and books, can be easily evaluated when you scan your life at this present moment so that you can objectively analyze your present position in your lifetime. If you have achieved some concrete results, if you can see that your life has changed, and that you have a much broader and a greater degree of understanding, then you have at least made some progress. If you have not achieved, however, there is no one to blame but yourself; it means that the sum and total of these large or small biases, negatively speaking, which you have interwoven into your psychic anatomy in the past, are, at the present moment, exerting their same pernicious effect in your consciousness; you have not objectively realized that this is true. They are there, nevertheless, and when you succeed in eliminating these biases in their various inflections, you will advance proportionately as to how well you achieve the removal of these negative wave forms.

Now, should you, in the course of the future days,

suddenly achieve a more complete adjustment, then you will indeed have a great working out; and the sum and total, so to speak, of all of these different interpolations of life, the life experiences negatively biased, will, in a very short period of time, be largely cancelled out; this has a rather pronounced and seemingly drastic effect upon the physical and mental consciousness at that moment. You will recognize the symptoms immediately as to the moment and the hour you have achieved this parallax of consciousness, wherein you are working out and canceling the various negative wave-forms which have been impounded from these past life experiences. Your physical body will be rendered partially or completely incapacitated to the extent that you may not be able to walk across the room; your legs will feel like jelly or rubber; you will cry hysterically, perhaps for hours. This is a rather drastic moment, in a sense, but one which is not to be feared; for it merely means that you are leaving behind you many of the old friends that have supported you in your day by day existence in the past. It means that, as they are being cancelled out, you are left, temporarily at least, without a life raft; this may seem to you to be a moment of great unreality and, perhaps, if you are not forewarned of these consequences, you could be negatively biased or fearful at this occurrence.

However, do not fear it; it is the way in which you are being reborn into the spirit as it was described by Jesus to Nicodemus. It means, in effect, that you have, in those few hours of time and in this great psychic purging and working out, accomplished that which might normally require thousands, or perhaps hundreds of thousands of years to accomplish in the ordinary reactionary way which most people reincarnate or evolve in these future day by day, life to life experience quotient patterns. You can easily see that under these circumstances, by this great purging, this

241

great working out, you have made a proportionately large degree of progress. You must always remember too, that as an active Unariun, consciously dedicated to a better future and to reconstruct yourself into a better attitude toward the Infinite Creator, you will always be supported in whatever activity in which you may be presently concerned. There are at all times a very strong and positive number of energy wave forms which are being psychokinetically projected unto you. You will be helped, you will be encouraged, and you will be protected in all ways, manners, and forms; when you are asleep at night, you will be in the classrooms and will obtain new information, new teachings, and new contacts which, in the following days will make themselves very evident to you.

Briefly then, in this message we have accomplished a number of purposes in our synthesis. We now understand what a badly warped and distorted configuration of life the average Hindu is involved with in his understanding of reincarnation; we also understand how it is that the Christian has further degraded this degraded concept, and in its place has postulated the concept of hell, fire, and damnation in direct opposition to the principle of the so-called concept of divine intercession which is also nonexistent.

Divine intercession occurs only when we have approached the reality of a certain threshold which the Christian calls repentance; or it is the direct acknowledgement that we, and we alone, are responsible for our present position. If we do not like our circumstances there is only one person who can change them—that is ourselves; we, individually, are the only persons in the entire universe, the macrocosm or the microcosm, who can bring about a change. Any other supposition is entirely erroneous. It is up to us, individually, to change our course, and as Jesus said, "By their fruits ye shall know them," so that by our fruits we shall know ourselves. A constructive and objective analysis is always immediately mandated of every experience through which we pass. We must always constantly strive to look into the more objective scientific mechanism which has sponsored this act of consciousness; for we must remember that, so long as we are in this material world, we are going to be, either to a small or a large degree, directly influenced and concerned with the material world. This we cannot escape until we pass on into the spiritual worlds, and we have, in these higher worlds assumed a more realistic life attitude toward them.

Then we can say we can truly and objectively analyze the material worlds; they will no longer coerce or intimidate our thought patterns; but for the present you are constantly being intimidated in all ways, manners, and forms by this world in which you are so living. This is inescapable, for the diverse wave forms of energy which come to you as sight, sound, etc.—or that they are remanifested through your five senses are constantly an ever-present tempter. They will, in a sense, ring various and similar configurations of energy wave forms into your psychic anatomy and there will always be a converse effect in consciousness from them. This is inescapable, until we escape the dimension in which they are perpetrated.

At no time should we ever enter into this proposition of the future as an escape; it must always be a proposition which is dedicated to the best intents of all of life's purposes; to become a creative effigy of Infinite Intelligence, and to manifest in this effigy a direct facsimile of the Infinite Intelligence; in this way we have re-created the most objective development of Infinite Consciousness; and we have supremely manifested and reinstated this Infinite Intelligence in the most ultimate of its dispensations.

# CHAPTER 24

## More on Karma

Let us continue our exploration into the world of karma. In the foregoing chapter we have discussed some of the more pertinent and relative factors, some of the principles involved in this concourse of life, termed evolution, which constantly reinstate themselves in the principles of evolution as our day-by-day consciousness. However, there are many aspects to this all-important subject, inasmuch as karma, in itself, can more broadly be conceived to contain the very elements of evolution. There are many ways in which people work out the different experiences which they have incurred in previous lifetimes. We have discovered in our previous discussions how these various experiences constantly reflect a certain insidious or negative quotient in our day-by-day life expression.

In this respect, let us go directly into a further connotation of this expressionary form of karma which, in itself, as an experience, so reincarnates into our lives. If we have in some past lifetime experienced a great psychic shock, we do, from life to life create for ourselves a similar situation whereby we can again go through this same facsimile, as it were, of the previous situation. We are attempting to prove to ourselves that the reality of this experience is no longer true; it is not in effect; it does not hold power over us; or perhaps we may be more directly influenced by some knowledge gained in the spiritual worlds whereby we believe that we can institute, at the moment of recreation of this experience, some sort of a controlling or dominating power to cancel it out. Again, the experience from the past may simply recreate itself, apparently without substantiating any continuity, which could presuppose that we were intelligently concerned with working out this situation.

In other words, "as a man thinketh—so he is," and again in the Bible, it says, "The sins of the fathers are visited upon their children, yea, even to the third and fourth generation." However, if we consider for a moment, we can understand the possibility of becoming one of our own relatives in the process of evolution. Through incarnation we can actually become a grandchild; or we can vicariously be involved in various experience quotients with our parents. Assuming that our parents are in the spiritual worlds and are also involved in the same working out process of previous indispositions or life experiences, we can easily see how it is that the previous experience can also reincarnate itself into a facsimile in our present lifetime. We do then, in effect, seek out or find ways and means and various manners and forms to try to work out these previous experiences. Also it can be said that the experiences are the dominant motivations for these re-creative effigies in which we have involved ourselves.

We must always bear in mind that the higher forces are not working against us at this moment. The Intelligent Beings in the higher spiritual worlds are not looking down upon us and frowning because we have committed acts of indiscretion; they are all wise in the purpose of life and realize how invaluable the personal entity of consciousness is; for there would be no purpose, there would be no use for creation itself, unless the Infinite Creator could recreate some part of Himself through every conceivable manifestation, form, animal, vegetable, or mineral; even in the gases of the air or in the supposedly vacuous spaces of space itself, there is still Infinity; while we may not see the completeness of the all-encompassing Infinity, it is there nevertheless.

Our immediate problem is in discerning the mechanization or the principle of the Infinite and how we, as expressive entities, are concerned in a singular fashion with orienting a singular experience as a compound or substance form in the structures of our psychic anatomy. This, in turn, forms our future, and this is the true meaning of karma. The ways, the manners, and the means in which our past can re-inflect itself into our present, or into our future, are even more numerous than are the ways in which these experiences so propounded themselves in our past lifetimes; for we are always concerned, at any moment, with the law of harmonic interplay. As one set of circumstances in the past can, comparatively speaking, generate a large formation of energies within the psychic anatomy so that the interplay of this configuration can and does in the future reinstitute other conformations which, while they may appear dissimilar, are in essence quite similar to their originating source, which is this vortex I have just discussed.

Briefly, it can be said that not only does the experience re-create itself, but also it is quite capable of re-creating any one or a number of effigies or facsimiles which ring harmonically with the original entity, and we are indeed lost until we can picture within our own minds, the complete mechanics involved in this extremely complex problem. For, it is complex in the sense that each wave form, each harmonic, and all of the various interplays are directly connected to any and all formations of the Infinite Intelligence Itself. They are indeed as much a part of it as any other formation which we could visualize at the moment.

The discussion of karma could not be complete without including the concept of good and evil. Good and evil are, in themselves, inseparable from karma, for karma always does involve what is supposedly the evil conformation or configuration of experience in evolution or reincarnation. The concept of good and evil, in itself, is extremely pernicious, for never, at any time, can we sublimate the life processes in science and of Infinity until we destroy the illusion of good and evil. It is, in a sense, a frame of reference, which we have previously discussed, known in the more common phraseology as equality. The concept of good and evil is always a plane or base of reference which the average earth man uses to evaluate a certain circumstance or a certain something which has occurred or is happening to him at the moment.

However, he is not wise enough in his way to realize the complete ramification of any experience, whether it is good or whether it is evil. He has not conceived the entire entity of consciousness in this very broad portrayal of the Infinite. The Infinite is, in itself, the sum and total of all things visible or invisible—and by invisible we mean just exactly that; it includes all of the various intangible elements which are the direct cause of the experience itself; and whether it is good or evil, it makes absolutely no difference whatsoever. It is all part of the Infinite Consciousness. The struggle between good and evil in the mind of any man is age old, and it will exist until he can supplant this erroneous misconception with a much broader and a more generally understood functional process of Infinite Intelligence.

The religionist, and particularly the Christian, has attempted to vindicate evil on the pretext that God created evil in order that man could become good;

and, in a sense of the word, this is somewhat true. However, the Christian did not further explain that we must learn the mechanics of these various expressionary elements before we can overcome their intimidating or their coercive effect upon our mentality. Even the presentation, the acknowledgment of evil, in itself, is sufficient warranty that we will always incur evil as long as we can conceive its possibility or its occurrence in our lives. We can, in a sense of the word, psychokinetically re-create a facsimile of some circumstance which we had, in a previous lifetime, considered evil. The facsimiles here are harmonic in their regenerative abilities.

It then resolves into one basic fundamental objective; in whatever manner, or form, or way in which we can conceive some form of consciousness in any of our five physical senses, or in the more paranormal aptitudes of the psychic centers which always oscillate, not only into Infinity, but also in our third dimensional world, we must always be concerned with the complete proposition of Infinite conception. If we conceive less than this, then again we are embroiled in all of the various karmic subtractions of previous earth life experiences which we care to analyze or upon which we might philosophize.

As it has been postulated in diverse teachings of Unarius, the average human being in all form and essence, can be considered to be an electronic instrument. His five senses or other paranormal senses are merely ways and means in which he can differentiate the various wave forms which are impressed upon him and come to him from the varied earth life experiences. In this respect then, the reverse is true; for as he is an inceptive instrument, likewise, he is an instrument which will rebroadcast or re-create the facsimile of all of these various impressions which he has received in previous lifetimes. Broadly speaking, this is the concept of karma; as we relive each day, we have, in effect, re-created the karmic intent of yesterday. It makes no difference whatsoever how we attempt to subdivide the experience as it is so concerned at the particular moment; we can always derive from it a direct connotation into the past whereby either one or a large number of other experiences have so regenerated these harmonics which are presently appearing upon the surface of our consciousness.

As I have stated, the ways, manners, and means in which these facsimiles, these harmonic regenerations, so reappear and recur are as infinite or even more infinite than their originating sources. Each experience, therefore, mandates immediate scrutiny. We must analyze it; and we must include all possible factors of relationship as they encompass the expressionary principles of regeneration which have always sponsored our lives and which have always sponsored the regeneration of all conceivable forms and objectivisms.

There is only one other factor or element in this process of life which, at the present moment, does warrant discussion; this is another danger which is always imminent and present whenever we encounter a karmic experience, and whenever we do not have a complete co-relationship to the understanding of the experience. It is that dimension of objectivism called obsession; for, always in past life experiences, we were intimidated by obsessions. These obsessions ran the gamut, so to speak, from the various superficial social structures, political systems, etc., to the more unrealistic and intangible obsessions which directly involved the astral underworlds, or the remanifestations in consciousness of some entity, on a lower astral plane, who was trying to subvert or dominate the individual, or the group of individuals at that moment, or at any particular moment in any given lifetime.

It could be pointed out, at this time that there are

perhaps thousands of different obsessive forms which have taken a strangle hold upon the minds, the life processes, of millions of people who inhabit the face of the earth today. Religion, in its entirety is an obsessive form which has been reincarnated and is karmic in its intent, just as are all other aspects in the common denominators of physical life; for man is so supported in this physical life by the constant resurgent thought patterns or formations of consciousness which come to him from out of the past, he is always directly or indirectly related to them, and he is always incurring any particular bias so superimposed from that previous moment into the present.

So far as obsessions are concerned, we must learn to analyze and to be consciously aware of the possibility that we are being influenced, coerced, or dominated by an obsessive thought form consciousness which we have derived from a previous life or other lifetimes lived in various plateaus of expression.

The political systems of today, as they are being currently expressed, are merely new forms of the age-old political systems which have been used in the past. The President of the United States has only assumed a somewhat different relationship to the people of this country than did the king or emperor of previous lifetimes; and going back further, we can actually see the chieftain or the leader of the clan, the sheik, or any other differentiation we care to bestow upon these various manifestations of previous life expressions. The ruling or dominant entity of a political system is always the superimposed form of a previous incarnation; it can never be otherwise, until people, as they comprise the nation which is so dominantly influenced by this figurehead, can individually and collectively conceive, within themselves, the entire concept of Infinite Creation. When they do so, they can be considered to be relieved of the obsessive form of the age-old proposition of social structures, political systems, religious effigies, etc.

For, in all manners, forms, and ways of life in our present day, John Q. Citizen, whether he is American, Russian, English, or any other nationality, is going through the same hallway of karma. He is, from day to day, from life to life, re-inflicting upon himself the constant and never-ending burden of his previous suppositions; he is hopelessly lost in the miasma of the material world, in its karmic expressions. He will do this until he realizes the entirety of it; until he reaches that threshold, which I hope, at this moment, you have reached. When he does so, in that great moment of truth when he is again reborn into the spirit and into a higher way and consciousness of life, and when there is suddenly a great realization, a baptism, if it can be called such, in which he is immersed completely in the waters of pure spiritual consciousness, he will be cleansed and purified.

The karmic intent, the negative biases of the previous lifetimes will be cancelled out and washed away. As I have previously described, if this moment of truth is being lived, as it has been so lived by other students of Unarius, then you, too, will go through that tremendously emotional experience which defies description—a sort of passing through no mans land in unreality—for indeed, all old forms of consciousness are being purged of their intent and of their dominant factor of negative bias in your daily life. They are being changed and, in a sense, you also are being completely changed; yes, even the atoms in your body, after this baptism, will have assumed a new rate of vibration. You will have ascended, so to speak, into a higher dimension and form of consciousness, and it will always remain with you. You, alone, can nullify its effects in the future should you renege upon these life-giving life-sustaining principles of science which are being explained to you.

In this circumstance you, too, can wander down

into the astral underworlds and become one of those parasitic versions of mankind who prey upon the consciousness, upon the various vicissitudes of the earth man as he lives in his carnal expression of life; or you may even reincarnate into one of the earth man's expressive forms and become a destructive entity which will bloody the pages of history.

Let us never renege; let us resolve, at any given moment, and be firm in our resolution, that we will carry forward, that we will be completely dedicated to the better way, to the emancipation of personal prerogatives in that all-inclusive interdimensional concept, which includes the Infinite Creator as the tangible reality of life; not a disassociated demigod who rules through a very strongly, emotionally biased complex, as it is expressed in the Old Testament, or as it is even being purveyed at this present time. Instead, you will have a factual reality of the Infinite Intelligence, the sum and substance of all things; and the sum and substance will always be the ultimate resolution of consciousness within your own mind. This is the determinant factor of what you are at any given moment, and it will always determine your future.

For in Infinite conception, as it has been described to you, in becoming an entity of consciousness, a facsimile of the Infinite, you have achieved the most ultimate of all purposes of Infinity; and in effect, creating yourself into this God-like image, you have completely vindicated the entire purpose of your existence or the existence of anything which you may care to enumerate; the existence of the solar systems, the suns, the universes; the existence of all known and unknown things can then be fully vindicated and justified as part of this all-inclusive entity of consciousness which we call the Infinite Creator.

To sum up our discussion, we have now delved into the mysteries of karma; we have discovered that good and evil are synonymous in all respects; we must have sin in order that we can have good. There would be a complete lack of evaluation, for the primitive man, at least, or the material earth consciousness, unless he had the facsimile of each and every intent in his life so conversely presented to him. He must always choose and be selective in his endeavors. He must always have, within the consciousness of his mind, the mechanics involved in this presentation of consciousness, and when he has achieved this he has destroyed the illusion of evil; he has, in its place, reinstated the concept of constructive evolution. For when we have conceived the entity of this Infinite evolution, good and evil are no longer supported as reactionary oppositions. They become analogous to each other. They are, in effect, a different presentation of the same objectivism. However, this is beyond the dimension of the materially minded man who has not arrived at this point of introspection; we do not mean to mislead anyone or confuse him by saying that we are condoning or approving of evil in the sense that we fail to recognize how it is evil. If we possess the mechanics to discern it otherwise, if we possess all factors of relationship which can destroy the illusion of evil, then as we have destroyed it, it no longer has any effect on us. All thoughts and actions will of course be more intelligently constituted as part of this evolutionary principle of consciousness. This then is karma, the underlying and overplaying principle of life as it regencrates itself in evolution. The future will be made clear and known to you by the acts of your present day, by the acts of your present consciousness, by whatever you constitute within your own minds as your more ultimate attainments and objectivisms.

# CHAPTER 25

## Judge Not, That Ye Be Not Judged

Let us enter into a discussion concerning one of the more classical utterances of Jesus, contained in the Beatitudes of the New Testament. He said, "Judge not, that ye be not judged." If we wish to analyze, to the fullest extent, this utterance, it is quite obvious that when He spoke these words, He, no doubt, had in mind a more esoterical meaning, a more complete philosophy, or a more complete objectivism of human conduct than was normally possessed by the average earth man. We cannot conceive, even in our daily life or in any past day or epoch of history, that people, as a whole or individually, could ever have abstained from the process of judging. There is no act in daily life, either past or present which has not included, in its usual manifestation of the various acts of consciousness, the determinant reactionary motivations of life, which are always predicated upon judgment.

When the housewife goes into the grocery store and purchases articles of food, she selects certain articles on the basis that she believes them to be superior and therefore, renders judgment against those which she believes to be of inferior brand or quality. The same is true with the man who selects an automobile; so we can continue on into this introspection in whatever particular act of consciousness we see going on about us in our daily lives. People are all actively rendering judgment against various and sundry things which appear upon the surface of their lives. This is the common type of reactionary motivation which sustains all different forms of life expressed by the earth man. He knows of no other life, and he is therefore, in this constant interplay of judging and counter-judging, sustaining the common elements of his mental equilibrium, just as he has done through the many thousands of years of his earth life.

The proposition of judging or not being judged also carries other implications which are quite obvious in our analysis; if we think for a moment, this somehow suggests the old law of Moses, "an eye for an eye or a tooth for a tooth;" for in both cases, the objectivism here is, that some particular dispensation or reaction in life will always occur if we do something. This is the basic reactionary concept, and so far as man is concerned, this concept has been constantly motivated by the most carnal of all fears which sustains animal life upon the face of the earth. This is the primitive law of the jungle—the law of survival—the necessity of survival and the inclusion of all artifacts in consciousness which can instigate and continue this survival on to some indefinite date.

We can say that the judging proposition is also another indirect way of determining the so-called law of cause and effect, or casting bread upon the waters, etc.; but at whatever individual analysis we arrive, we will find there are the same basic motivations, the same basic reactions, and the same determinants which do actually motivate the conscious form of all reality of all mankind. If we select and vote for a particular figure, then we are rendering judgment against the other political figure. If we say our democratic system of government such as it is, is superior to the communistic form, we are rendering judgment against those people. Also, we must remember, whenever these judgments are so rendered, that we must consider the fact that we are not determining the value of these judgments as they appear, but we are, in actual reality, setting in motion a whole host of various harmonic wave forms which do tune and retune themselves in many different ways within the structures of our psychic anatomies; this is the true meaning behind the concept of not rendering judgment, and, no doubt, it is that which Jesus had in mind when He spoke these words.

For the implication of rendering judgment on arriving at some personal system of equality will, in all cases, involve the individual in certain negative ramifications. It makes no difference if we reject something because we believe that it is not good, or that it is inferior; it simply means that if we have become conscious of this particular objectivism, this certain thing, and we have become conscious of it in a negative way; we have reacted to it on the common basis of interplays in harmonic attunements and constituents as they have always existed with us; then we have indeed made this a part of us in all cause and effect, despite the fact that we may have consciously rejected it. In this sense then, as we have incepted the configuration of this inferiority within our own mentality, it does, in all effect, re-create its inferiority in these various interplays of harmonic structures and the effect here is quite similar, in many ways, to that which is obtained when we actually accept this particular thing, whatever it is, without the stigma that it is or is not inferior.

In all cases, the situation is quite the same, the effect is just as pernicious; and in this way we can say we have rendered judgment against ourselves. It is not to be considered for a moment, that there is some system of spiritual government or some great god who renders this judgment against us on the basis that we are naughty children, or that we have done something which is not condoned in the eye of this great god; or that when this act was perpetrated, he made a little mark opposite our names in his book of life. It means in effect, that in this scientific interplay of harmonic structures, which always occur whenever we incept something in consciousness, we always render judgment against ourselves on the basis that it is a non-progressive entity of consciousness. If it is a constructive or a progressive entity, then we render judgment in favor of ourselves and so conversely elevate ourselves in an equal quotient of expression.

Now, you may wonder how it is possible that you, yourself, or any individual can consciously recognize the various evils and vicissitudes, the interplay of emotionalism which are going on in the world about you today, and yet, not incur these disastrous personal effects of consciousness by recognizing, or reading about these things, or in other manners, ways, and means, sense the interplay of this vast international emotionalism. There is a way in which we can view all of these various and sundry emotional expressions without becoming involved in them, to the degree in which the average earth man is so presently involved.

To the earth man these diverse appearances are all very necessary parts of his life to the extent that they are harmonically attuned, in some manner or form, with numerous past dispensations which he incurred, either in this lifetime or in previous lifetimes. It matters not that they may be called by different names, or that they may involve different kinds of people; the basic principles which instigated these reactionary forms and artifacts are just the same as they have always been. If the average materialist or earth man reacts in the customary or normal way to the different emotional artifacts of his international civilization, of the survival situation, and of his community as a whole, then he has indeed recreated the old emotional content with which he has always been involved.

On the other hand if he has progressed to the point in his evolution where he can see the basic principles and elements which constitute and motivate these reactionary artifacts, he is, in a sense of the word, insulated from them, to the degree, that they do not emotionalize him; they do not harmonically attune him with the various negative quotients of his past, and he can view them introspectively. He can place them in the constructive scale of evolution; he can see that these are the necessary inequalities of existence which supply the necessary drives or libido for humanity as a whole.

The systems of equality, as they are posed in the diverse dispensations of our civilized life, are, in all effect, nonexistent; for equality cannot exist. Equality is a personal proposition in every person's mind whereby he attempts to equalize the sum and total of his consciousness in relation to the outside world. So far as the outside world is concerned, however, he does not, at any time, arrive at a point in this differentiation process where he can establish an equality. This, in itself, is the determinant qualification in that progressive scale of evolution, for, sooner or later, the individual will begin to arrive at some more definite conclusions in his evolution. In conjunction with various quickenings of the spirit, which he experiences, from time to time, in the spiritual worlds, in the lives in between lives, or various other inspirational values which are constantly recurring in his life, he will then begin to recognize these other basic elements in his daily evolution, and as he learns to recognize them, he will gradually inseminate, in his consciousness, the more basic principles of creative evolution, and he will, as a consequence, gradually cease to become emotionally involved in them, as he was formerly.

As it has been stated before, the system of equality,

included as a basic concept in our form of government, is, today, the cause of much racial strife and distortion. It is also the cause of international strife. For the proposition of equality of mankind, is not founded upon such concurrently accepted artifacts of civilization as are contained in the appliances he has in his home, and the manners and ways or differences in his voting systems, or in any of the different aspects of governmental systems which are currently in force in these different countries. The basic and relevant elements which should always be considered in these differences are the progressive basic concepts of evolution which we have discussed. The formation of the individual intellect, as a selective entity, as a functioning entity with Infinite Consciousness, can and does objectify form, motion, action, etc., without the common form of the emotional reaction. It is done in a more intelligent manner and form; it is done constructively because all elements of this interplay of international brotherhood are understood. Instead of saying that all men are born equal, or that they are created equal, we must say that all people, individually and collectively, have their own individual chance to achieve immortality on the same basic frame of reference that we have; and just as we have done, they should be allowed the full interplay of their own consciousness to determine these various aspects of their future—assuming, of course, that these things can be done constructively without intimidating their neighbors in a destructive manner or form.

At this point, we must revert to some of the more elemental principles of life as they are sustained in our present civilization; in our educational systems children are not taught the fundamental and basic aspects of life; there is too much accentuation on the diverse conformities confronting them. There is too much of the rote system whereby each child is forced, so to speak, through the same hole in sort of a uni-

versal sieve; he is made a conformist, he is regiment-
ed; and in all ways he is taught to act and conduct
himself along certain very rigorous lines of demarcation.

This is all well and good up to a certain point, but
it does not include the various intangible introspections. It does not include the metaphysical principles
of life; it does not include the basic elements of a
progressive evolution. No child is taught the full import of his moral responsibility in the scheme of creation. His religious system only vaguely supplants this
more esoterical understanding by inflicting upon him
the karmic sin of being born in an evil circumstance
and the eventual judgment day etc., another one of
these fear-ridden philosophies which are character-
istically expressed by mankind as a whole.

More than this, however, the child as he grows up,
is constantly being exposed in numerous ways, manners, and forms, to the complete dereliction of his
civilization. In many different ways the various emotional vicissitudes of mankind are constantly portrayed
and activated upon the surface of his consciousness.
Through the movies, TV, etc., he witnesses thousands
of murders during his childish years; he cannot con-
sole himself with the fact that this is merely a re-
enactment or a farce. The emotional content of wit-
nessing this murder and its destructive intent, as it
is superimposed in the psychic anatomy, is there
nevertheless.

It is granted that during the material or earth life
phases of incarnation, the average individual does
come up against a host of situations which involve the
more destructive potential of human expression. But
these different emotional vicissitudes and destructive
intents should not be made the dominant expressive
quotients of life. They should not be made the denominators whereby fame, notoriety, or other personal
forms of identification can be exploited to the extent

that the child is intimidated by them in forming his own basic course of evolution. Also, when these different emotional vicissitudes are constantly played upon the surface of his consciousness, he is confronted in different manners and forms, in his daily life, with the various pressures of his civilization. The hopeless automation which is usually the heritage of most people who are growing up in the world, the inescapable numbers, manners, and forms of these different interplays, as they are superimposed as negative happenings, in his consciousness—the newspaper accounts, the ways, manners, and forms in which his parents conduct themselves—the systems in which he finds himself involved during the teenage years—his activities in high school and in college—are all dominantly activated by these subconscious conformations, which he has woven for himself, from out of the fabric of this interplay of emotional vicissitudes, which he has witnessed in his growing up period.

Small wonder it is then, that in this present day, crime is rampant; in fact, in the past year, 1960, there was an increase of more than 14 per cent of the total number of crimes committed in the United States; and in California, this increase was 21 per cent! If we are to continue in this ratio of increase, it is conceivable that in a few years time, everyone will have committed sin and crime to the extent that he has become involved in the law. This is an alarming situation; fortunately the government of the United States does recognize the seriousness of this situation and is spending some time and money in trying to discover various ways in which these evils can be alleviated.

Unfortunately however, despite their well-intended efforts, they quite likely will come to naught unless they can include the progressive elements of constructive evolution which we have presented to you in these Unariun concepts. We must always analyze personal behaviorisms on the basis of what they

261

formerly were in previous lifetimes; we cannot re-institute various and different ways, manners, and forms of life which will aggravate or reinstate the more negative propensities of consciousness to these individuals. We must have different manners and means to cancel out or to gradually help the individual eliminate them from his own individual conscious-ness. In short, it means that we must institute some system of personal psychology which can be actively inducted in the early and formative years of the child's life. Psychically speaking, he can be analyzed on the basis of what he really is. His propensities and attributes, which are constructive in nature, can be emphasized in his future life and the negative indispositions can be more correctly dealt with and reasonably assumed to be more correctly eliminated from their emotional or repercussive effects in his daily life.

Our civilization cannot sustain itself on the cur-rently existing artifacts or the emotional values which are presently in force. To build this country up to its present position was not necessarily mandated by these emotional portrayals of consciousness; there were much stronger and more basic elements of evolution involved in the formation of this country. We have reached a certain point, we shall say, where-in there is a diminishing effect on these stronger values, brought on by the pressures of an enlarged population; the dominant factors which relate to the incarnations of many hundreds of thousands of indi-viduals, who cannot reinstate themselves in a pro-gressive form of evolution, all add to the stresses of our present time.

The picture is indeed complex; it must be dissect-ed individually in order to find out just where each one has erred in forming his way and manner of life; he must include certain constructive dispensations in his future relationships, and he should exclude others because they are destructive. However, at whatever particular dispensation mankind arrives in the future, it is quite likely to be the same destructive and constant never-ending recurrence of the emotional values of his life. He will always be confronted with that never-ending succession of evaluations, based on the emotional plane, whereby he attempts, in general, to equalize the world on the basis of his own personal evaluations. He can also conceivably be so biased and predicated in his evaluation of the Infinite, if he ever arrives at such a point that he can view the Infinite. However, when he does so, he will have had to leave behind these old reactionary evaluations, the ways, manners, and forms of which Jesus spoke, when He uttered those words, "Judge not, that ye be not judged." For the judgment which each person renders against or for the different values in his life, does surely intimidate him nevertheless. Despite the fact that he may reject them, they are still with him and they will remain with him to the end of his evolution; unless, in placing them correctly in the scale of evolution, he succeeds in evaluating mankind in the scheme of created and re-created regeneration which is the sustaining principle of the Infinite Intelligence.

Let us look for peace of mind in our own hearts and in our own consciousness. The obvious facts have been presented to us in our constructive evaluation of the future, as it is contained in the concept of Infinite Intelligence, and also in our relationship to Infinite Intelligence, as an entity of consciousness which does live beyond the bounds and circumference which man has, in his earth life, circumscribed for himself. We are in form and consciousness immortal, and if we sustain an immortal consciousness, surely, we shall live forever.

# CHAPTER 26

## Good vs. Evil
## An Emotional Judgment

In our discussion in the foregoing chapter, we entered into some of the more reactive elements of common everyday thinking as it is so ordinarily expressed in our present world and just as it has always been currently expressed. We have compared this in a manner and form in which we were rendering judgment, and, principally, the judgment, because of its emotional value, was against ourselves. We based this introspection upon the commonly accepted denominators which were derived from classical interpretations of the New Testament. In this same vein then, to continue on into these objectivisms of personal psychology, we cannot neglect, at the present time, the presentation of different religious forms which, while not strictly orthodox in the commonly accepted frame of reference, claim themselves to be metaphysical or the expression of some different relationship in religious aspects than are commonly denoted in the other church systems. These metaphysical groups—one of which is particularly strong in this respect—teaches that to be absolved from sin, guilt, or evil, one must not be conscious of this sin or evil; it is nonexistent; it is not a part of God;

God created only good, and evil occurred because we abstained from the more pure objectivism of God in our consciousness. These people, as a whole, do not express the fundamental and scientific relationships that human beings should have with the Infinite Intelligence or God; they do not possess the necessary scientific knowledge which always should be currently expressed by every human being, therefore, they have only attempted in this fallacious interpretation, to make some compromise in what must otherwise be a very fundamental and basic concept.

It is neither scientific nor factual to say that evil, or the appearance of evil circumstances, or other differences in manners, ways, and forms of life, which we might render judgment against, are nonconstructive; neither can we say that these things are not part of God. If we begin to reduce God, or Infinite Intelligence down into the common denominators which are understood by the earth man, we have destroyed the entire entity of Infinity. We have destroyed the ability of man to rise above these inequalities; in short, we have become Godless creatures because we have reduced God to an emotional creature who is rendering His various interpolations of life on the emotional basis.

For good and evil in any person's life can be truly considered to be an emotional experience; it will remain an emotional experience until this individual is able to constructively analyze the experience on the basic elements of progressive evolution and to envision the Infinite Intelligence as being the principle, the sum and total of all things. Whether or not we consider these experiences good or evil makes absolutely no difference so far as the Infinite Creator is concerned because, I shall say in a broad sense, the Infinite Creator is conceiving the concept of man. It must be realized that for man to so conceive—if he is to become god-like—he must necessarily include all of the qualifications of immortality as they exist in this Infinite Consciousness.

Therefore, at any given time in a personal evolution, when any individual was vitally concerned with all of the elements of Infinite expression, he had the choice. He could choose that which he wished to choose and gain the constructive or the destructive evaluation from this experience. In this way he will gradually evolve into a state of consciousness whereby the determinant qualities of his character will be constantly activated and automated by the knowledge of this basic interplay of Infinite Intelligence.

Ninety some years ago, a gentleman, by the name of Karl Marx, attempted to re-evaluate the basic constituents of human behaviorisms as they were propounded in governmental systems; this became a documentary which has been, and is at the present time, the basis for a communist system. I am referring to this individual in particular and also include the various philosophical adventists who have appeared throughout the Middle Ages—yes, even back to and before the time of Socrates.

These individuals, collectively speaking, have all made the one obvious mistake in their philosophies; they did not, at any time include the scientific aspects of human relationship with Infinite Intelligence; therefore, after a certain point has been passed, their philosophies can be considered entirely sterile and invalid. They are not relative to human conduct, but they are only relative to that person's individual consensus of various material values of life and how he has succeeded in making certain determinants in these reactive values. He will, therefore, in the course of history, attract to himself and his philosophy, harmonically speaking, different adherents who have found the same basic plane of reference in their daily introspections of life.

This does not mean, at any time, however, that

because these systems have attracted small or large numbers of adherents they are, by necessity, considered to be completely valid and the all-inclusive or dominant principle of life; no more so than can the numbers of adherents in any system of religion be considered the dominating and impelling reason why we should incept this type of ideosophy into our daily conduct. The difference here must be strongly emphasized and re-emphasized; that in Unarius, we are, for the first time in many thousands of years— or at least since the time of Jesus 2000 years ago— attempting to reinstate in consciousness the connection between each individual and the all-Creative Infinite Intelligence as an interdimensional aspect of human evolution. These factors are all scientific in nature. They relate to the interplay of different energy conformations which have constructed, not only the atomic constituents of our material world; but also the other dimensional forms which constitute our life relationships with the present world and any conceivable future incarnations.

Throughout present history, there is not one single instance wherein any philosophy or expressionist in the past, and before the time of Jesus—with the exception of Jesus—has included a scientific explanation of the principles which relate the individual consciousness with the Infinite Creator.

Here is a rather paradoxical equivalent into which we can enter: man, in all his numerous strife's and emotional turmoil's, his living in the past or in the present, his striving for these principles has inherently, within himself, as it is contained in his psychic anatomy, already been alerted to the consciousness and the possibility of immortal life lived in the higher dimensions and of his position with the Infinite Creator. His good and constructive expressions in his daily life, are all inspirational values instigated by the subconscious acknowledgement in these acts of consciousness. He does, in a sense, subconsciously know of all the things we are trying to explain; he knows of them in a vague and undetermined sort of way, but he has already had the quickening of the spirit, nevertheless.

It is this quickening of the spirit that has made him different from the animals and other forms of life which inhabit this planet earth; for, in this struggle for survival he has already begun to achieve, within the circumference and dimension of his life, the possibility of immortality in a higher kingdom. The next step in his evolution is obviously one which should include the dominant characteristics of life which can elevate him in this position of immortality. These dominant characteristics are the scientific elements of life, which have not, heretofore, been explained in any philosophy regardless of its source or origin.

Even Jesus, in His own time, did not explain these principles of life scientifically, and it is quite obvious, that at that time in the Holy Land, people would not have understood them, had they been so explained. However, in this day and age, even a small child has some understanding of chemistry, physics, or electricity which makes this child vastly superior, intellectually speaking, to any of the age-old philosophers who formerly expounded their own particular types of philosophies. Any child who graduates from high school or college is a hundred or a thousand times wiser than were any of these age-old prophets and seers, in the respect that the curriculum of the educational systems include, in a scientific way, the various artifacts of this civilization. Of course, we cannot degrade these old philosophers and their systems for, in a sense these people, too, were spiritually inspired; they were old souls reincarnating into their world, and with their philosophies attempted to indoctrinate the minds of people with a formulative plan of evolution, which would form one of the more basic steps in this progressive flight into Infinity.

The sad mistake which mankind universally makes, in his position and in regard to these different philosophies, is that he considers them to be the criteria of human expression. As a matter of fact, at least two different governmental systems have been quite recently erected upon the fabrication of two of these philosophies; these were, in point, the totalitarian form of government, expressed by Hitler, called Naziism, which was formed from the philosophy of man and superman compounded by Nietzsche; and, the communist or socialist form of government which was, to a large degree, compounded by Karl Marx. We can also go back to the formation of our own system of government, and we can include very similar objectivisms, held by the writers of the Declaration of Independence, which are in the Constitution and are quite similar, in certain socialistic respects, to this general tenure as it has been expressed in these philosophical contexts. In short, it is the struggle within the dimension or circumference of mentality of the earth man to achieve a more Utopian position in his life. He is constantly looking forward to the time when he is relieved of all these different turmoils and vicissitudes of earth life.

In his religious systems mankind has conceived the possibility of living in an immortal city completely freed from the necessities of life, and in this sense, every person does have an escape mechanism which has been engendered and formed by these different pressures. A Utopian condition of life can never be achieved by any individual; furthermore, it is not to be desired; it is to be the least desired of all situations or relationships in our daily lives. It would be incomprehensible that any human could, in any future time, be reinstated in some civilization wherein people lived without any cause or effect; they lived purely because they were living; they had no comparative systems of evaluation whereby they could say that this was destructive or constructive, that it was good or it was evil. They would not have the necessity to eat or to wear clothing; they would not have any of the other libidos or drives which they currently understand and to which they react in this present circumstance. In short, they would be completely stripped of all the necessities of life which always have, either constructively or destructively, occupied the consciousness of the individual; and they would have neither purpose, manner, nor form of life in such an Utopian condition.

We must always remember that man, individually and collectively, is a creature of evolution, just as is every other form of life in the world about us. We should also remember that this evolution is not necessarily contained in the third dimension or earth world; but this third dimension or earth world is merely the beginning point in some form, of the evolutionary progress of any given number of species of plant and animal life. The same condition exists throughout thousands of other planetary systems throughout our galaxy and our universe, and it extends into a countless number of planetary systems in other galaxies and in other universes.

These forms of life, and their manners of conduct pass beyond the boundaries of your comprehension; but nevertheless, they exist. They also exist by the same dominant basic principles of evolution which form and reform the various contexts of your own personal relationship to the Infinite. That is why it is most necessary in all our introspection to subtract the entity of consciousness, as it exists in a form, and supplant the obvious necessity of this form and its emotional values with the more inward complete visualization of it as it exists in evolutionary progress. Its form was so constituted by the same basic elements which have created all other expressions of consciousness.

In other words, we are not concerned with the form; we are concerned with only the principle and with the substance which created this form. In all cases this substance, and these principles are exactly the same, no matter what configuration they assume in our consciousness; therefore, the proposition of Infinity is not a religion; it is not a social system; it is not a national system. It is a personal proposition as to how well we can inseminate in consciousness, and *put into active force*, the dominant principles of re-creative evolution, which are formed from out of the energy substance which is the mind of the Infinite Creator Himself.

These facts have been stated and restated and I hope that I am never to be accused of repetition; but this repetition is a necessity, because of the obvious fact that your approach to the Infinite will indeed be complex. It must be constantly reinstated in your evaluation of the emotional experience as it comes to you on these basic elements of Infinite regeneration. If, at any time, you stray from this course, you will become emotionally involved in the circumstance, to the point where all past experiences in your previous lifetimes, will come into a great resurgence within your psychic anatomy; and again you will have re-created, in essence and in form, all of the sum and total of your past elemental vicissitudes, your turmoils, and your strifes. You must remember at all times, that, up until the present moment, these different emotional values always constituted the determinant qualities in your life; you were never more nor less than you could conceive within the dominion of your own mind and your reaction to these values in your evaluation, as to whether they were good for you or whether they were destructive in your expression of life.

271

It was in this reactionary interplay that you continuously got into trouble because of the obvious fact that you always intensified the negative proportions of these emotionalisms in conjunction with your past experiences; and in constantly reinstating them, in their negative quotients, within your consciousness, you gradually built them into horrible monstrosities which dominated the various aspects of your life; they even reinstated themselves into diseased conditions in your body. They warped and distorted your relationship to the world in general. They impeded your progress, and in more advanced cases, as we see people who are incurably ill in hospital beds or in mental institutions, these people have gone almost beyond the point where they can be helped.

Your own position is precarious enough and will remain so until that time when you have, in a sense, rebuilt and remolded your psychic anatomy and eliminated from it the reactionary values of these numerous past lifetimes and their countless millions of emotional experiences. For each one of them is like the small snake, cleverly hidden in the grass, ready to strike out at you, mentally speaking, any moment that you place yourself within reach of them. They are like hidden destructive beasts or other unintelligent and destructive entities of consciousness which you have incurred in the emotional values of your life. They are much more destructive, as of today and this hour in the position which you now occupy, in your introspection; their effect, if you place yourself within reach of them, will be even more destructive than had you not conducted yourself in the first inductive processes of the Unariun principles, or that you had not quickened yourself to the higher life. For the contrasts, and the oppositions in these contrasts, are indeed much greater than they would have been, had you gone on into the future in the more material sense of values.

Your future, then, will be entirely formed and re-formed in the manner and way in which you can induct, as the basic principles of life, the scientific factors which have been explained to you. Life, instead of being a constant repetitious summation of various reactionary values, becomes a place where we see the interplay of cosmic and intercosmic energies; we see in the thoughts of every individual, the psychic evolution of consciousness in the interplay of numerous wave forms which are reacting in his psychic anatomy. We see the earth in its many dispensations of life, not as the old form of consciousness which sustained us in these previous lives, but instead, it is also a part of this vast cosmic and intercosmic interplay—the interdimensional formations of consciousness which have manifest themselves within the dimension of your thinking processes as an inductive formation of life about you. When you have so conceived them, you will quite naturally be evolving into a higher state of consciousness; you will be passing, in effect, into the higher spiritual worlds.

For in the higher spiritual worlds, life is lived in such a manner. People are conscious of the oscillating principles, the inductive relationships of these oscillating wave forms in their daily lives. They do not objectify their lives in a series of conformations or configurations, either in their personal relationship to the world, or in any political systems, or any church systems, or in any other ways, manners, or forms in which you are presently involved. Life in the spiritual worlds is a more complete introspection of the interplay of cosmic energies, the cosmic energies which are the *substance* and the *principle* of Infinite Creation. And even in these higher worlds do not look for a Utopia; that is an idle thought on the part of many people who are influenced by an escape mechanism.

In these higher worlds, you will find an expressionary element in your daily life which is just as relevant to you as were any of your former expressions of life at any given time. They will be even more important to you in many other ways than were any other previous life dispensations, because they will be much more inclusive in the interdimensional stance which you will have acquired in this higher way of life. Your Utopia will be found in the security which you will have by realizing your position to the Infinite, and your function and purpose with the Infinite, as an oscillating entity of creative expression.

# CHAPTER 27

## Five Wise And Five Foolish Virgins

From time to time these messages (composed on the tape recorder) have been taken from various depictions in the Bible, from the Old Testament and, in particular, the New Testament as it relates to the teachings of Jesus. In this respect, I have accomplished several purposes. First, I have proven the unfactual, the unrealistic composition of modern Christianity and how it has been distorted and malformed into a devilish symbology; I have also proven, so far as Jesus is concerned, that His philosophies and teachings are as valid and as good today as they ever were. Furthermore, I am reinstating these teachings in the idiom of the twentieth century science and thereby removing from them the stigma of mysticism; for in the future, the people of the world, as they are dominantly scientifically minded, must understand their religion in a scientific way.

Also, I am compiling irrefutable evidence in the scientific dispensations of Unarius—its entire Infinite Perspective—explaining its relationship to mankind in general and in various other ways, I am making the reality of a progressive evolution a realistic concept in your minds. Realizing all of these various implications I shall, at this moment, take another of those classical interpretations or parables of Jesus', and re-establish this parable in a more scientific abstraction and present it to you in a more realistic concept. This is the parable of the five wise and the five foolish virgins. These virgins were supposedly going to a wedding feast; the five wise virgins, having oil in their lamps, were admitted to the feast, and the five foolish virgins, who had no oil in their lamps, were unprepared and could not go.

Now, the moral implication here is quite obvious; it was intended to convey a certain sense of responsibility in preparing for the future and in this respect, too, preparing for a future life in the spiritual world. Of just what this consisted, was not explained in the parable, and it has been generally taken for granted that it was in essence abstracted from a general recognition of these spiritual worlds, which was further re-emphasized by existing Christian dogma, consisting of the time-worn, inept, and erroneous supposition that Jesus died for our sins, and the recognition of His death and the blood he shed would wash away our sins, etc.

The sum and total of these suppositions are not only unrealistic, but also they have, to a large degree, made mental and spiritual criminals of almost everyone who has professed Christianity; for somewhere within the intricate confines of the subconscious, there is a deadly machination which takes place constantly. They are excusing their various iniquities, whether they are mentally conceived, or whether they are actually perpetrated by that which they think will bring a more ultimate conclusion to these injustices; their sins will all be washed away, or they are automatically forgiven, even as they commit them.

Now, the hypocrisy of this supposition is immediately evident, and it is felt throughout the various social structures of all Christian adherents in their intent and purpose of life. In order to more constructively analyze the "oil in our lamps"—which will

276

give us virtual admission into the spiritual worlds and into a higher life—let us re-establish the whole context of spiritual emancipation—progressive evolution, in a more scientific idiom, minus the slantings and derelictions which previously composed this concept. We can say that, as of today, every human being has a lamp containing oil and also a wick; at the end of this wick there is a small flame burning. This has been true with all people who have lived on the earth. The oil in this lamp however, is not that which I shall call spiritual oil; it is a material oil which has been extracted from the very fat of their bodies; the wick of their lives is their mental concept, supported by the various ego structures they have composed from their reactionary evolution. Almost needless to say, the flame, which burns on the end of the wick, is a general manifestation of consciousness, which has been generated from out of this oil through the wick and burns in a material atmosphere.

In the same vein, the oil which you will use in your future evolutions—if it can be reasonably supposed that you will evolve into the higher worlds—must be an extraction of Infinite Consciousness; it must contain all of the various additives which compose Infinite Consciousness. The wick will be, of course, synonymous to the wick of the old life; it will be the way and manner in which you will manifest a portion of this Infinite Consciousness oil to the terminating point; or the expression of your life, which gives rise to the flame upon the end of the wick, will be quite different from the flame which formerly burned in a similar manner. This spiritual flame will not need the atmosphere or the environment of the material world; it will not be limited in its light, as was the material flame, because this material flame could only light a very limited circumference of life about the individual who carried the lamp. Your spiritual flame will burn so brightly that it will reach into the Infinite vistas of space, so to speak; it can shine, not only into some of the more sublime or the higher reaches of Infinite Consciousness, but also it can shine a very strong and radiant light into the astral underworlds. And, in a sense, these people can, by seeing that light which burns so brightly on your wick, actually be enabled to follow that light out to its source.

We have presented the more esoterical value of the spiritual oil extraction of Infinite Consciousness—the wick and the flame of life which burns from out of that oil of consciousness; let us now see exactly of what that oil consists. It can be reasonably supposed to be, not an extraction of fat from out the material life or the material body; but it is an extraction of all forms of consciousness which live in the higher spiritual planes. All forms of consciousness are expressing and re-expressing themselves in that constant, never-ending, oscillating process which has regenerated all forms and is constantly regenerating an infinite number of structures of consciousness. It is harmonically attuning all forms of consciousness unto each other in some reasonable facsimile wherein we can see a continuity of expression in a forward progressive and dynamic evolution.

First, in order to understand the most basic element of this oil, in its expressionary element, we start with the sine wave. The sine wave is an interpretation of the material dimension which is constantly re-expressing the content of all manifestations of your present physical life in the same form and in the same relationship, except that it becomes a cyclic or a circular transposition of form. The same continuities or facsimiles of expression can be envisioned as the dynamic interplay of this infinite expressionary energy conformation which I have constantly attempted to describe to you.

Within the lesson courses a factual presentation has been made in these various expressionary ele-

278

ments; they have been diagramed, and they form the basic concepts which will enable you, in the future, to travel into the higher spiritual worlds.

At this point we must enter into a third dimension of consciousness in relationship to ourselves in order to find out just exactly how much these things mean to us. First of all, it is most necessary to understand that even if you have recognition of the higher spiritual worlds, or you assume to know something of these energy formations of harmonic interplays, does not necessarily conclude that you have a sufficient amount of this knowledge to guarantee a more complete evolution into the future which can be reasonably supposed to elevate you successively into higher states of consciousness.

There is still another element, which, up until this point, is somewhat missing and perhaps has gone unrecognized by you; it is this: that in the recognition of all these presentations, even if you can envision the enormous concept of Infinity and Infinite Intelligence, you are still an earth creature. This is because you have not yet reconstructed your psychic anatomy to its complete and entire content. You have started, and perhaps, it can be granted, you have made some progress; but not until that time when your psychic anatomy has been completely rebuilt in these concepts can you say you are progressively situated in the higher spiritual worlds.

It might be mentioned at this point that the concept of baptism, being born into the spirit, receiving the holy ghost, and all the familiar Christian clichés can be directly interpreted as part of the true meaning of this general conclusion and abstraction which I am making to you. Being born into the spirit, being baptized, receiving the holy ghost, etc., means that time and day when you can conceive the entire concept of Infinity, the Infinite Creative Intelligence, not just a vision, or as that something to be attained, or

279

even a realization in a conscious way; but it means that you will have actually reconstructed your psychic anatomy to the degree that it will include, at least, all of the basic elements of this Infinite Creation. The newly reformed psychic body will be in a position to more correctly oscillate with this Infinite; it will also, on the surface of consciousness, give you a much greater and a more complete degree of mental consciousness which will be far removed from your present environment. In this sense then, your flame of life is burning brightly in those far off spiritual worlds.

Now, the problem at the moment is to recognize your position, and, by recognition, I do not mean that you should try to inflate yourself with pre-suppositions that you are a creature of God, etc. We must realize, at all times, what our position to the Infinite is. There is only one way in which we can attain a relative idea as to what our position to the Infinite is, and where we are on the scale of evolution. This is realized through the common ordinary symptoms which we manifest in our daily lives; these are all evident if we wish to objectively analyze them. They cannot be objectively analyzed by anyone who is using an escape mechanism, or who is attempting to create a smoke screen to hide behind, or by a person who is trying, in various and devious ways, to escape the reality of himself. If you have problems, fears, insecurities, illnesses, etc., then, these are tangible symptoms; they should be objectively analyzed as to their origin and the manner in which they can best be eliminated. This must not be attempted in the customary reactionary way of elimination; but must be done by realizing the entirety of a concept which places you on the infinite scale of evolution in regard to Infinity. When you envision this position, you will realize how intangible, how inconsequential, and how utterly stupid are some of the different problems, the various suppositions, and the many ways of life in which most people live.

When you arrive at the point where the material world seems to be some kind of an asinine, unrealistic dimension, in which people live a kind of an animal-like existence, then you can reasonably assume you have gone beyond the point of the material dimension. You are then already in a position to incept some of the higher principles and concepts of life; you are then, in a position to begin that practical re-fabrication of your psychic anatomy in a much more constructive way. In that moment of truth when you realize the full import and intent of Infinity stretching out ahead of you, you will also realize how inconsequential these symptoms are in your own daily life.

In this Infinity, time and the consequence of motion, in any position in regard to time is less than the slightest tick in the consciousness of the Infinite. All of the years of your life are less than the slightest tick, or even all of the thousands of years during which you have evolved back and forth into the planet earth in the numerous lifetimes, would not even make a split fraction of a second in Infinite Consciousness. By the same token in this full realization, you can assume that the future will be quite the same, so far as time is concerned. It means that we can, constructively, place ourselves in consciousness at any given point in our scale of evolution merely by the process of conception. When we have conceived what is at that particular point, then we are in truth and in entirety, an active participating entity of consciousness in that particular dimension. That, in essence, is the long and short of our personal metaphysics.

In your present position upon the earth today, in whatever set of life patterns, problems, or fantasies you are presently involved, you are at this moment, at the exact point at which you have placed yourself in concept, in that great cycle of evolution which can transcend you into Infinity. If you will remember, in the future, that whatever problems you encounter, these are always fantasies from out of the past; they are only presuppositions at which you have arrived, and they can be as intangible in the future as you will let them become; then you will have formed one of the more basic elements of your evolution. No, I do not suppose that you can adopt one of those hedonistic attitudes, or the Pollyanna attitude, as it is more commonly known, and ignore the reality or the existence of your problems, no more than you can ignore the reality of the earth on which you live. But the reality will pass just as surely as does the concept of its reality.

However, at no time must you attempt to remove a reality from your consciousness by assuming that it is not there. You must take an entirely different relationship to this all-important proposition. You can recognize the reality without it being a reality. Now, that may sound strange, but it is exactly right. If you think for a moment, you can envision in consciousness a distant city. That city is, in all sense of the word, a reality; still it is not an element of your consciousness in the various artifacts of your daily life; you are not concerned with that distant city in respect to the fact that you have to consider it when you eat your meals, or go to bed, or do any of the other apparently necessary constituents of your daily life.

Life in the higher worlds is lived in full consciousness. You maintain a full consciousness in these higher spiritual worlds; you will always remember your material lives, and you will remember, in a sense, the various experiences through which you have passed. But they will not maintain that coercive and mandatory expression which they now have over you; as a consequence, you will not suffer from the many repercussions which are involved in the interplay of these dominant subversive characteristics carried from the past into your present. That will be, when you have—as I have said—reconstructed the psychic anatomy in a manner and form which is not subject to the coercive effect of these past experiences. In other words, it will be harmonically attuned in a different way, to another dimension of consciousness. Like your radio, while it can, in a way, sense all the other hundreds or possibly thousands of radio transmitters which are broadcasting at this moment, it, however, plays but one of them at a time; simply because the component in the circuitry has been brought into resonance with one particular broadcasting station.

However, within the first stage or the first antenna coil of the radio and in the antenna itself, there are vibrating all of the other different radio stations which are broadcasting. The same principle holds true in the spiritual worlds. You will have consciousness of all other dimensions through which you have passed, but they will not have that coercive effect upon you, because you will be out of tune with them, to the extent that you will be more positively attuned to a higher dimension of consciousness. They will, in the language of the scientist, be out of phase in your present form of consciousness.

So you see, dear friend, at whatever terminating point of these various constructivisms we may arrive in our analyses, we always come to this inevitable conclusion: if we are going to get anywhere in the spiritual worlds or amount to anything in our evolution, if we are going to get rid of this karma, which we have carried from life to life, then we must do all of these things scientifically. We must have a scientific knowledge of how this is done, and fortunately, you and others who are directly concerned with life, have at this moment a great advantage. The twentieth century science has placed at your convenience, the understanding to achieve the first primary inductive

283

principles of energy which will form the hard core of inception of your objectivisms and various other additives which are most necessary for you to evolve into a higher plane of consciousness.

No, perhaps you may not become a scientist or a physicist, in the sense that you can quote or write algebra to explain all things; for mathematics in any form—calculus, trigonometry, algebra, etc.—is only a crutch used by mathematicians to arrive at a certain point of that which would otherwise have to be a complete mental function. It is a crutch and never, at any time, does it supplant the true dimension of consciousness at which we must ultimately arrive. For consciousness cannot exist as a mathematical formula; it cannot exist as any of the other age-old subterfuges, symbologies, or various things which have been used by people since the beginning of their evolution. None of us are immune to the principle of life as it is expressed by the Infinite.

Neither the priest, the rabbi, nor the minister can give you these things; they are not contained in your Bible. They are not contained in any other written work of mankind or in any man's eye until he has evolved into the complete consciousness of the Infinite; evolved by first inducting the principle of Infinite Consciousness, contained in the sine wave as an expressionary element, which is the configuration of all expressed forms of energy as you know them through the five senses today.

In the future, mental telepathy, clairvoyance, astral flight, and all of the other usually considered, mystical or paranormal functions will be just as natural to you as are the acts of life in present consciousness; and you will not attach any importance to them, to the degree in which you are now presently concerned with them.

# CHAPTER 28

## Insecurities = Diversion & Deception

Let us, at this time, enter into a discussion on some of the elements of personal psychology. Sometime ago, while walking upon one of my garden paths, I inadvertently startled a mother bird who was nesting nearby in the bushes. The frightened bird flew out of the bush, where her nest was situated and tried, by the age-old ruse of dragging her wing and limping, to lead me away from this most treasured spot; she tried to impress me with the fact that perhaps she was crippled so that I would pursue her. This, of course, is a well-known and very obvious device which has been used by birds and animals as long as they have existed. However, as I walked away from the spot, I could not help but muse that the countless millions of people who had inhabited planet earth and who are living at the present time, are all to some extent, practicing this same old device of deception which had been used by animals and birds for so many countless ages.

Of course, these people for the most part, did not know they were using some sort of deception and no doubt would have been quite surprised and perhaps even angered had this most obvious fact been pointed out to them. It is a provable and foregone conclusion that all people in the world do, at some time or other

—some more frequently than others—revert to forms of very obvious subconscious deception. In this manner they hope to detract attention from some deeply rooted subconscious insecurity complexes derived from unresolved past lifetime experiences and from the time they were born into the world up to the present moment, as a natural product of evolution. The sum and total of these insecurities would, of course, largely determine just how much deception and how obvious was the deceptive device being used by any particular person.

Typical of these various devices are such attitudes as can be called subtle or strong exhibitions wherein any person attempts, by bragging, by various other exploitations, or expressions, to try to succeed in impressing his fellow man with what he considers to be the most obvious virtues of his own ego. Proverbially, the small, short man is known to puff himself out, to strut, or to otherwise try to portray, ostentatiously, a much greater degree of physical and mental prowess, in lieu of the obvious deficiency in his stature. The same, in reverse, is true with the tall, thin individual who tries to make himself, subconsciously speaking, a little shorter by stooping, by drawing in his chest, and assuming some sort of an introverted attitude. In either case, where we consider the more ostentatious display—the extroverted form of ego, or the introverted form—these are devices in which the individual is attempting to divert attention from the sense of insecurity which subconsciously, he knows he has—the sum and total of various unresolved insecurities from which he has suffered in his lifetime.

Sometimes, however, these insecurity complexes exert themselves much more strongly and in different forms and manners. A person may become an extrovert to the extent that he will be an actor or she will become an actress; and again people often enter the field of politics, or such professions as teaching, the clergy, or the priesthood; in fact, any and all walks and occupations of life have these, either introverted or extroverted persons who are attempting to conceal and to divert by the obvious aforementioned devices, the attention of their subconscious feelings of insecurity which arise from these insidious complexes. Then, too, we cannot fail to consider the more extreme cases where an individual can actually become a dangerous criminal, or even a person who assumes such strength and power that he becomes an emperor or a king. Hitler was one of these extroverted persons. It is well known, biographically speaking, that Hitler suffered a tremendously introverted childhood.

Unfortunately, in almost all cases, people who are so introverted or extroverted fail to recognize the symptoms within themselves; they fail to analyze or take suitable action whereby they could hope to attain solvency from these various psychic differences which lie deep within the subconscious portion of the psychic anatomy. So long as these numerous inadvertent or malformed wave forms exist, and while they may not oscillate to the exterior surface of the conscious mind, they, nevertheless, do exert a strong and pernicious effect upon the varied oscillations which are currently expressed. This gives rise to the many deficiencies or otherwise plainly exhibited forms of this most familiar of all subconscious behavior, the insecurity complex. No individual can ever hope to achieve supreme control or dominance over these countless subversive forms of consciousness which thus exist. For, as rapidly as they are cancelled out, the processes of life very often give rise to new forms, and subsequent developments of new inferiority or insecurity complexes.

So far as the present existing insecurity complexes are concerned, the individual who is attempting to attain a better way of life and to free himself from some of the mental and physical vicissitudes, which most necessarily accompany any person who is not primarily concerned with the innermost functioning or workings of his subconscious nature, must attempt, at all times, to keep close watch over his various emotional differences which may arise; he must display a plain and evident concern and awareness of the many propensities of subconscious workings which are going on within the deep recesses of the psychic anatomy.

In this respect we can refer to one of those classical bits of philosophy; "evil is in the eye of the beholder." It is sufficient to say that anyone who feels more than the ordinary or temporal sense of distress or emotion, should such forms and expressions reassert themselves in a continuous fashion; or should there be a habitual train-like consequence of varied emotional differences or obvious habit conformities, which so clearly indicate that this subversive form of subconscious interplay is in constant or periodic activation, must realize that it is high time something constructive was being done to eliminate this condition. We cannot overlook the obvious facts of reality and assume or adopt a Pollyanna attitude and decry that which some metaphysical concepts try to teach us to do; we cannot merely shrug off the reality of some particular annoying circumstance or some happening which may have an emotional value to us. Such things do exist and always present the immediate conformity of reality.

However, the point in question here is within ourselves, how much of this emotion remains and reconstitutes an activated resurgence of emotion within our own particular consciousness; these emotional vicissitudes so reinstate various other habit or mental conformities which are so classically distinguished by a psychological approach, or by an analyst who can learn to distinguish these various differences as they are displayed upon the surface of human consciousness. Self-analysis, by any individual is indeed dangerous, unless it can be done completely honestly and objectively, without the taint of personal conformities entering into such judgments of jurisdictions or objectivisms, which any person may attain in his self-analysis. This honest approach of self-analysis is extremely difficult to attain, and more so because the immediate demands of any objective analysis centers upon one pertinent fact which is this: how well you can objectify, within your own mind, that it is you yourself as an individual, who is involved in this emotion; who is involved in this consequence, or this extrusion of consciousness which has so complicated your life. It does not, in a more abstract sense, exist outside the dimension of reality, as it presents itself in consciousness to you individually.

If one is hypnotized, he cannot consciously objectify any particular thing unless it is suggested by the hypnotist who is controlling the person who has been so hypnotized. In a sense too, we can say that such emotional differences which appear upon the surface of our minds are, in consequence, autosuggestively stimulated by the appearance of some reality which is just beyond the immediate confines of our more normal level of introspection, as we proceed in our various daily life activities; and, such as they are, should the appearances of these countless realities suggest or autosuggest to our consciousness some facsimile, as it so conforms in attunement with previous lifetime experiences which are so attuned into these numerous subversive elements of inferiority or insecurity, then we immediately have a chain reaction. We become antagonistic; we become fearful; we develop many other types of emotional duress, customarily exhibited by people who have these more firmly entrenched or advanced sensitivities, engendered from these insecurity complexes.

There is no excuse in saying, "well, everyone has

them"; we cannot justify the emotional vicissitudes, existing in our own minds, or other consequences which may be incurred from these many emotionalisms, by resorting to this old subterfuge that everyone else has a sin, or everyone has his own weaknesses— we must have some too, etc. Such mental processes are not justified; they are not intelligent, and they will eventually lead to moral decay and the more complete destruction of the personal entity in the various integral values which have largely sustained him in his evolutionary process. We must reach in the hole, drag the lion out by the tail, and slay him before he consumes us. Sometimes this process is indeed difficult for we must remember, in all cases, that of whatever these insecurity complexes consist, they were impounded by ourselves in the active integration of various processes of life, not only in the immediate lifetime in which we are so living, but also, we can reconnect them into possibly hundreds of lifetimes, or even back into the reaches of our more primitive beginning.

As a matter of fact, the material world is largely constituted and motivated by sundry fear complexes, and it is to be expected, in this carnal law of the jungle, wherein fear exercises the more dominant libido or drive, that various insecurity complexes, can and do, very quickly and easily arise to the surface of everyone's life. Individually speaking, these complexes make people very unhappy; they make them emotional; they give them the innumerable drives which we have described; such subterfuges which, like the little bird, are merely attempts to divert the attention away from the weaknesses we subconsciously feel from these diverse insecurity complexes.

In one of the previous chapters of this book, we entered into some discussions regarding recogni tion of the old self, and the old self as being the most dominant enemy any person ever has. The constant struggle with the old self, in its variant continuities into the present, always contains the adverse potential, as it is compared in the progressive cyclic movement of evolution; the old self, indeed, gives rise to the many inequalities of everyday life. The old self and the method of its recognition are similar and parallel, in all respects, to entering into the various psychological aspects of everyday life, (as we are discussing). Briefly then, the turmoil, strife, hatred, jealousy, lust, fear, and other emotional vicissitudes are poisonous in their content and in their intent; they are destructive and coercive in all the many interplays of harmonic attunement with any of the more progressive elements in our personality complex.

It is, therefore, most important that we immediately recognize these reactions and emotions as they exist in our consciousness; we should take the utmost recourse to analyze such appearances, to immediately discern from whence they sprang; and in this personal analysis—if we are honest and objective—we will eventually triumph; we will succeed in establishing a sort of automation within consciousness which takes over, so to speak, like an automatic pilot which will, immediately, divert consciousness from the extremes of the emotional complex, as it is exerting itself; it will also deflate or discharge the strength of this emotional complex.

Then, we will, consequently, in a few moments time, feel completely passive with whatever this situation was, or whatever gave rise to this emotional difference. When we have attained this position of automation, wherein the more philosophical, the sane, the logical, or the introspective qualities of our personalities can always be dominantly reflected, and we can manage to control these numerous situations, then it can be said, we are attaining mastery over ourselves; we are attaining mastery over the old self, and we are also attaining mastery over the physical world.

Needless to say, until such mastery is attained, we will be constantly victimized by the many emotional differences which constitute the way and life of this material world. Mastery over the material world is mastery over self. It is the instituting of a personal philosophy which immediately equates all abnormal differences, all emotional complexes, and various subversive introverted fear complexes into their proper perspectus. They can no longer survive in the atmosphere of logical and philosophical objectivism; and speaking in the scientific idiom, we can say, that in this superior mental atmosphere, we have generated out of phase wave forms, which, when so generated in the present tense in contrast to the time element in which they were incurred, cancel out these sundry, insidious, negative vortexes which remain, and have remained unobserved and undetected in our psychic anatomies.

This will result in a general purification of the psychic anatomy; it will also constitute and enable us to rehabilitate or rebuild the psychic anatomy into more suitable configurations of wave forms which result in an overall intellectual superiority, a broadening of the mental horizon; and, in a true sense, we will gradually evolve into a higher state of consciousness, which actually means that we are oscillating more infinitely with the Infinite Intelligence.

Therefore, it should be immediately resolved by any and all people who are so interested in attaining immortality, a future and better life, to immediately start to reconstruct this future for themselves, to do so upon the sound psychological, scientific approach which demands the conquering of the old self and its many emotional vicissitudes; they must conquer the former way of life in which they have always lived, and begin to try to re-establish life in a continuity and form which is progressively superior in all respects, manners, and forms; so that it is not emotionally constituted, but instead, it resolves itself into the philosophical and scientific conformities which form the Infinite Intelligence.

Personal psychology is relatively simple if we are honest and objective; it does not need to entail the nomenclature used by the modern psychologist or psychiatrist. It is simply the more ultimate resolve that we, ourselves, are our own worst enemy; and so far as our past lives are concerned, these are the dominant elements which we must always strive to conquer. They will introduce and reintroduce the content of various emotional strifes and turmoils until we would find the proverbial "snowballs in hell," if we let them. Our problem is to dissolve them before they dissolve us!

The dynamic principle of evolution is predicated upon the progressive mental stance of each person who so wishes to live in a progressive future. This dynamic, progressive principle should always assume the predominant position in everyone's life; he should always envision himself so biased that he will progress into the future. And so, as each life is lived, it presents the never-ending, the never-ceasing problem of a future conquest of this life in another time and in another dimension; for, such is the nature of Infinite progression; it is the constant contrast, within one's self, of the emotional values of experience, until such time when a person can so resolve the more ultimate configurations of the Infinite Creator as an oscillating process which does *not* entail the emotional content.

# CHAPTER 29

# Identical Twins

During the summer months of 1961, a certain event transpired which made medical history; it also became a news item in different newspapers throughout the country and eventually became a nationwide TV broadcast—one hour in length—depicting this event in its entirety, and in extensive detail. This event was, specifically, a human kidney transplant. Identical twin brothers, who, at that time, were forty-seven years of age, had this operation performed, and one kidney was taken from one brother and transplanted into the body of the other brother. The operation was sufficiently successful to enable these two men to eventually return to their respective positions in their community.

Now, aside from the technical skill involved and other factors to be considered in such an operation, it is of great value to us in our introspection into the processes of human life, that we should enter into this explanation of a kidney transplant to more fully understand what is basically concerned in our own progressive evolution in the future. A kidney transplant is possible only on the basis that the two people involved are identical twins; as a matter of fact, even such a common thing as skin transplanting is not possible unless the two people involved are identical twins. For, in the case of a severe burn where skin is taken from one person and placed upon another, the skin apparently grows and becomes normal in many respects for four five, or possibly six weeks; then it sluffs off, and new skin has begun to form in its place. This poses a great mystery to the doctors; they realize that somehow, within every individual, there is a definite potential element called individuality. They have their own name to define this particular aspect, but so far as getting either to its origin, or to the reason for the existence of such things, they are still as mystified, as to these vital and important facts which concern human welfare, as were the cave men in the primitive days of evolution. They shall never arrive at a suitable or a compatible science in medicine until they can envision—as it is placed in the Unariun Concept—the entire psychic anatomy and the human body, not as a common ordinary chemical function, as it is posed in the metabolism of human anatomy, but they should more ultimately realize it as composed of different electronic constituents, seen as oscillating wave forms, which are forming and reforming the physical anatomy as well as the physical consciousness; forming them from out of the various impounded wave forms within the psychic anatomy, just as we have described it to you so many times in the lesson courses.

The situation of identical twins means that in the course of insemination, or at the moment of conception, the ovum or the egg within the female womb, began the process of complete separation; instead of growing normally, it in effect, split; instead of one normal fetus, growing from out of the egg, two individual human anatomies began to form; that is, an exact replica or an exact facsimile of all that was contained in the numerous chromosomes or gene structures in the egg or ovum were, in a sense, withdrawn from each other to form an exact facsimile of each other.

They did not split, or divide in the sense that an apple was split by being cut, but rather a sort of regenerative process took place wherein an exact simile of each and every constituent within the chemical structure of the molecules of the egg itself re-formed themselves into two different anatomies; after birth the two babies would grow, as identical twins, and form respectable citizens in their community.

Skin could be grafted from one of these people to the other, it would be entirely compatible, and it would grow. Kidney transplants or diverse other feats of a surgical nature could be performed. Whereas, in the case of ordinary humans, such conditions would not be possible, and also even if ordinary twins were involved, for ordinary twins are not identical.

In order to understand this basic element of human differences, each human, while he may appear, in some respects, identical to another person may have the same R-H blood factor, he may exhibit other extremely close similarities, yet these are dissimilar in all respects. As it has been previously postulated in other discussions, equality in human nature or in such transpositions of human nature is nonexistent. Any person or community who so attempts to equalize its life on the basis of visual conformities, will always arrive at the inevitable result which is confusion and obvious disparity arising from comparisons of good, evil, etc. Only when the communities and nations of the world, individually or collectively, can conceive the entirety of evolution, will they reach a compatible level of understanding. Up until that point, as a whole, the differences in communities, as they are expressing the equalities which are now the presently existing conformities of our civilization, will always include these disparities, the obvious quarrels, and infractions which arise from these odious comparisons.

The situation of conformity, as it exists in various human dispensations, must be considered as a

296

product of evolution; there are no two people who are exactly equal, except, perhaps, identical twins. Here, however, while there are physical equalities in the human anatomy of identical twins, these two humans have already begun to form differences which will ultimately result in a complete separation of the entity of consciousness between these two people. Actually, identical twins have the same psychic anatomy, or more specifically, the same psychic anatomy which has been divided.

Let us go back into the beginnings of human evolution and again review the process of becoming a human being. We will say that in the fourth dimension—and understanding energy as we have presented it to you—energy is a cyclic motion, or a cyclic transference; that is, it revolves within itself. In order for it to manifest into the third or physical dimension, it must, in a sense, separate itself into the time element. In other words, the expression as it takes place in the third dimension must have a beginning and an ending, a terminating point. Therefore, when we look into the past and see the beginning of any human being, various entities of consciousness began to collect together. After they had become certain energy configurations—we shall say—which were somewhat intelligent in nature and had a relationship to life lived upon the planet earth, such as breathing, blood circulation, etc., they began to collect together and form an amalgamation which eventually resulted in a new and different psychic anatomy.

This psychic anatomy could conceivably reincarnate as one of the more primitive human beings and during the concourse of this person's life, when he began to sustain a personal or an ego relationship from one life to the next, in the manner and form that he re-oscillated into the third dimension, the constituents of this psychic anatomy then could be said to have become a human being, and this person would

297

be endowed with the usual propensities, attributes, proclivities, etc., which human beings normally and concurrently express.

However, here is a difference. All humans have not interpreted these various life-to-life relationships on the same base plane rate or the same time rate. In other words, all such energy inceptions, as they were related to any other similar inceptions of energy, were inducted into the psychic anatomy at a slightly different point in the evolution of any person; and they must be considered, therefore, to be out of phase with all other existing wave forms irrespective of any similarities involved. This out of phase condition which occurred in the formation of any psychic anatomy, whether it was an individual wave form constituent or a collective energy entity, could be considered to be, in all of its basic and elemental oscillations, out of phase with any other human psychic anatomy, even though the various constituents of energy wave forms could, and did remanifest themselves in consciousness in the usual conformities and similarities which we see about us every day. They were, in all respects, out of phase with any and all other wave form configurations; it is in this sense that each human being is different from every other human being because he cannot, at any time, assume the exact relationship with any other person, except in the case of identical twins.

Now, when the identical twins were in the process of insemination or conception, the ovum split and formed, in a sense, two different human anatomies; this occurred first in the adjacent or fourth dimension. If we remember—at the moment when conception takes place, the psychic anatomy of a human being attaches itself, by oscillating to the psychic anatomy of the mother and the father in various harmonic relationships, then the new psychic anatomy of the child to be, establishes itself in rapport with

the different elements contained within the chromosomes and genes which are to form the physical anatomy of this child. This oscillating condition will
be maintained until birth takes place; then there is
a more formal junction of consciousness of the psychic anatomy with the infant, to the degree, that now
the psychic anatomy can begin the process of reorientation with all of the five senses. However, if at the
moment of conception, when the psychic anatomy
begins to join in an oscillating manner with the egg,
as it is held within the womb of the mother to be,
there is some unusual circumstance involved which
will cause sort of a dissension within this psychic
anatomy; the psychic anatomy, in a sense, can be said
to split. This does not mean that it cracks in half and
so divides; it means that because it is an entity of human consciousness, it does maintain a sort of relationship with all other different psychic anatomies
and other vibrating elements in the fourth dimension
or spiritual world in which it is, at that moment, presently living; in that condition it can be influenced, to
a large degree, by these different interpolations of energy which are beating or oscillating about it at the
particular moment.

Therefore, it can be said that the psychic anatomy
does respond to these influential differences in the
sense that it still maintains a certain continuity of
human expression or the attributes of its common
human form; it is still a human being without a physical anatomy; and it can be influenced the same way
in the spiritual world or fourth dimension as it can
be influenced as a human being in the physical or
material world.

In this condition the psychic anatomy, or this soon
to be human, will come under certain dominant
forces as they are oscillating from these aforementioned centers of energy radiating around it. The
psychic anatomies of the mother and the father can

be a very dominant influence; other psychic anatomies or spiritual forms which are in contact with this person can also produce a dominant and influential force according to the manner or shape of its reaction to its spiritual environment. Under these conditions you can easily see that it can be, in a sense, divided against itself. It is in the same position in which many people find themselves on this earth world.

It is well known that when two people go through life together as a married couple, they develop a certain strong polarity between themselves to the extent that when one dies the other will soon pine away and follow the mate into the spiritual world. The same condition holds quite true in the spiritual worlds. At the moment of inception when there is a linkage to the soon to be child, this new spiritual form will, in a sense, be confronted with the inevitable fact that it must leave behind certain other affiliations; it may also come under the dominant influence of a very strong psychic anatomy in many other ways, and under these stresses and conditions it can easily be seen that in the extreme urgency, the psychic anatomy can actually, under these dominant forces, separate itself; it does not do this, however, by splitting down the middle. This means that all of the millions of entities of consciousness contained in that psychic anatomy will, in effect, separate from themselves and form two different sets of everything which is in the psychic anatomy, something like sitting down and dividing a stack of dollar bills. You take one bill from the pile in front of you and place it in number one position and the next bill will go in position number two, etc. This is the way in which two psychic anatomies are formed from one.

In a sense, they will always remain complete within themselves on the basis that they are oscillating together in harmonic frequency relationships. They are, and will always be completely in phase with each other in whatever physical or material world dispensations they may contact. That is why skin can be grafted from one of these persons to the other without the usual repercussive sluffing off effect.

We must understand that the compatibility of all cell structures, or that which is called the chemical synthesis of the human anatomy, must always be the result of certain sustaining oscillations of wave forms of energy which have been impounded in the process of evolution. It cannot be otherwise. When this simple and obvious fact is thoroughly understood, it will, in turn, explain all of the mysteries of the human anatomy and various other human indispositions and frailties.

So far as identical twins are concerned, we will have reduced the proposition of two human beings with identical individual propensities and attributes to the extent where medical feats, such as the transplanting of kidneys, etc., can take place in a manner and form, as was depicted in this TV portrayal.

The situation of the divided psychic anatomy presents some rather unusual objectivisms, inasmuch as here are two people who have the same psychic anatomy; it is divided into two separate entities of consciousness and so far as time and space are concerned, these two people will never be involved with a situation such as time and space in the third dimension. In other words, even though these two individuals may live thousands of miles apart, their psychic anatomies are still oscillating in complete unison and harmony with each other because they are, in effect, one and the same, even though they may be divided in their function toward the respective physical anatomies, as two different entities or two different sources of oscillating expression.

Therefore, the context of this discussion has explained to you one of the greatest mysteries and enigmas concerning human dispositions and frailties.

301

When you have understood the principles of this and similar discussions we have presented to you, then indeed, you will be wiser than the wisest scientist, the wisest man of medicine, or, for that matter, wiser than any other particular dispensator of human consciousness which you may care to envision within your mind. You will have many more of the ultimate secrets of life—as they are sometimes called—you will then be able to equate these inequalities, not on the basis of the usual conformities as they exist in civilization, but on a much more intelligent basis; you will see them as oscillating wave forms synonymous in all respects and in their effects, yet the equality of each human resides entirely within the dimension of his own consciousness. It is the equality which man has derived from the different portrayals of life, the experience quotients of his participation in these different elements of life; and while he is similar in some respects to all other human beings, he possesses one fundamental difference which gives him that individuality that is so thoroughly misunderstood by the man of medicine or the scientist.

The individual propensity or equality of human expression is always portrayed as a difference in phase relationship. This phase relationship is quite a difficult proposition to understand, inasmuch as it involves a complete harmonic interplay with the entire dimension of Infinite Consciousness. When we consider the number of harmonic structures which are involved in the differentiations of human experience, as they appear upon the surface of consciousness, as a result of that harmonic relationship with other countless and infinite numbers of similar expressive wave forms in the general content of Infinity tself, we must realize that they not only exist in countless millions of other human conscious forms, but also they exist in countless millions of infinite forms of consciousness which are expressed from

Infinity Itself.

This harmonic relationship is very important to remember, because it always gives the individual quality of expression to any experience or any extractions or derivatives of consciousness of the experience in *proportion* to the harmonic interplays or formations which give the additive dimension or perspective which is so necessary to evolve each individual constituent. In other words, if you are standing in almost the same place as your fellow human being and viewing a scene in the valley below, you are not seeing this as does the person standing next to you. You are incepting the wave forms from this scene in various phase relationships to your past experiences, which are in many respects, different in the manner and way in which they expressed consciousness by the individual standing next to you. Therefore, you are not seeing the scene as does this other person; you are seeing it with the differences which have been interposed or interjected by the harmonic interplay which always occurs at the moment you incept a wave form of consciousness. This is the determinant, or the point of differentiation in consciousness which every human possesses.

It gives the individual, not only the diverse factors of difference in the forms of consciousness in his surface mind, but it also gives the physical anatomy the same differences in these interplays from the psychic anatomy. While they may, chemically speaking, react in a similar manner in all respects, there is still the individual propensity, nevertheless. It is that constant interplay of the harmonic structures in the different portions of the psychic anatomy which are out of phase to other different interplays and wave form structures within the psychic anatomies of other human beings. Therefore, compatibility cannot be achieved because it must always exist in the psychic anatomy before it can exist in the physical

303

anatomy. This is, indeed, rather complex and a somewhat abstract proposition, but it must be thoroughly understood before you can hope to achieve the complete introspection, of, not only the human anatomy and human indisposition, but also as it concerns your own personal evolution into the future. It will form, in that future, more relative and more basic platforms or elevations of consciousness—to yourself in particular—than you have heretofore displayed in the reactionary concourse of this, so-called, civilized world in which you now find yourself.

Evolution in the future will be an inductive process; it will be progressive proportionately as to how well you understand Infinity.

# CHAPTER 30

## Fission, Time & The Life Cycle

In the previous chapters we discussed one of the greatest enigmas or paradoxes in our civilized science; this concerned the development of two individuals who have been called identical twins. Using the same principles implied in this objectivism, we can equate all of the numerous concepts of human life as they are so concurrently existing about us.

This proposition is quite necessarily complex, because it involves a personal demand of consciousness which is most relevant in the dimension of electronic science; you must develop the consciousness within your mind which can see life, not as it consists of the usual conformities of existence, as they seemingly appear to you in the constituents of mass and these different compounded infractions of mass, but, as it actually consists of the interdimensional forms of energy which have remanifested, for the moment at least, in this apparent physical or material world. These principles and their various re-expressive forms constitute the generalities which can be classified as evolution; with whatever form we are presently concerned, we must always resolve this appearance, into the principle of the regenerative aspects which engendered it. We must also be concerned

305

with our relationship to it in the way in which it is inducted into our consciousness, and on the basis of harmonic relationships with previously inducted wave forms, it forms the basic elements of concept as they again reform themselves in that regenerative process within the brain cells of the conscious mind.

Many years ago, two individuals, Darwin and Mendel, respectively, lived upon the earth. Darwin originated the specific evolution of consciousness scientifically known as evolution; he postulated the theory—and it was to some extent conclusively proven in our modern biological sciences—that there are certain determinate equivalents of progressive evolution from the lower to the higher animal forms. Mendel, too, as an adjunctive relationship, postulated a theory of these inductive processes which stemmed from organic constituents of cells within the human anatomy, or within any physical anatomy which have been classified in the various genetical references as chromosomes and genes.

However, neither Darwin nor Mendel was aware of the fact that in whatever form these appearances so manifested themselves, there were always the inductive relationships of energy conformations which stemmed from an adjacent dimension; so far as animals or plant life which appeared upon this planet was concerned, there was a psychic anatomy involved in any and all cases. It was this psychic anatomy which was regenerating the entire purpose, or intent, or the conformity of these wave forms within itself into the conscious configuration into the material world. Evolution and genetics always expressed the inductive relationships which were so harmonically attuned in these different evolutionary inceptions from the quotients of experience which, in the future, always determined and re-determined these expressive elements on the basis of harmonic relationships.

In order to clarify this situation, let us explore, for

306

a moment, into the microcosm, the more primitive forms of life on this material planet, and we shall find in it the first formative regenerative concept of evolution as it concerns the bacteria or germ life inhabiting or infesting this planet earth. Now, a germ is a very simple little creature; it has one cell and is usually too small to be seen with the unaided eye. If you can, picture the life cycle of a germ somewhat in the form of a circle; the germ starts at some particular point in the circumference of this circle and, in living its life, or its cycle, it will in the future terminate or die at the point where it began.

Now, we can see that at the point about halfway between the beginning and the ending of this cycle, the germ will regenerate itself—this is because it has a psychic anatomy. This psychic anatomy is linked and re-linked in different harmonic structures in that regenerative process of evolution which contains the net sum and total of all the various infractions of regeneration; the germ will then, by necessity, procreate. It will do this very simply by dividing itself; this is more technically known as fission, and it becomes two germs. This does not mean that these two germs are going to have exactly the same life expectance. One germ will die in exactly half the life span of the other; even though it was originally one half of the germ which formed the two subsequent germ formations.

Now, this is a mystery to the scientist, but in the same ratio, the creation and recreation of germs can, therefore, conceivably multiply into great numbers, which they do; because each succeeding germ, which has split away from the parent, lives twice the life span of the parent from which it so sprang. The context of information as to how the germ lives its life expression, what it does, its function; and how it procreates in this fission process, etc., is all contained in its own particular psychic anatomy. It is that constant

never-ending, regeneration of energy wave forms—
cyclic in motion—living in that timeless fourth dimension that make the germ possible; it is because the
one-celled creature, which the scientist calls bacteria,
is merely the surface product of this regenerative process.

The act of fission, therefore, or the splitting of this
germ means that it has reached a certain point in this
oscillating process, whereby there are formed several
other different junctions of consciousness in this
psychic anatomy, and in this formation or junction
of formations there will be a parallax. This parallax
re-expresses, in the content of its motion, as a series
of oscillating wave forms, a direct composite form of
the expressive element which is the cell or germ
living in the third dimension. This will constitute the
fission process because, after this attainment of
consciousness is manifest in this tiny psychic anatomy, the physical germ cell can then split and form
two new and different constituents. As the new germ
is formed and oscillation is again sustained in the
parallax which originally formed it from the originating psychic anatomy, the parallax will, in turn, grow
in the usual conformity of the psychic anatomy which
was identical to that of the parent psychic anatomy.
It will, in all forms, manners, and ways re-oscillate
with the original parent psychic anatomy, but it will
still remain an individual psychic anatomy because of
the obvious fact that its outside surface manifestation,
the cell into which it is expressing, is out of phase in
its relationship to the parent.

Numerous configurations of expressive intelligent
motion within the energies of the psychic anatomy,
were all expressed by that regenerative principle
which contained the basic elements of harmonic
structures; we must remember how harmonic structures are created; these harmonics are direct multiples, a mathematical formula approximately two plus,

or minus two; this determines, to some extent, the harmonic itself. While this harmonic may contain all of the information from the originating or the basic wave forms which engendered it, it is still, on this basic time level reference, out of phase with the original wave forms, and it will, therefore, maintain its individuality; it will not again remerge or become part of these original wave forms because it is now out of phase with them, even though these wave forms did induce this harmonic in a relationship which was harmonious in its original intent. This is the commonly expressed condiment or relationship of time which always must be considered, because the relationship of time merely resolves itself down into the expressive quotient of energy which is terminated and again resumed; or it begins and ends at a specific point of relationship. In the third dimension, time is a beginning and a terminating point as a straight line reference; whereas, in the fourth dimension time is expressed as a cyclic motion of reference.

However, time is a quality of fourth dimensional expression, just as it is in the third dimension, with the exception that it must always be visualized as a complete entity of consciousness within itself; and as such, it is constantly re-expressing itself in that so-called timeless dimension. Its expression can be linked and relinked with other cyclic wave form motions on the basis of this harmonic relationship which has been explained to you.

Now, we have arrived at that point in our introspection, where we can say that although regenerative wave forms, can and do, in their cyclic motions within the fourth dimension, regenerate a completely new set of harmonic structures or cyclic motions which form an entirely new entity of consciousness, they can be considered to be vibrating elements with their original formative constituents, their original parent wave forms, yet they will always be individual expression-

309

ary elements irrespective of whatever other conditions come to pass in their general expressive wave form quotients. This is the principle of infinite regeneration; and as it has been previously postulated and re-emphasized, the Infinite Intelligence—that which the ordinary earth man calls God—is the sum and total of all things which are constantly regenerating; we can now see how important it is to understand regeneration and the interplay of harmonic structures. As these various formations are so reconstructed in Infinite Consciousness, they are also given that certain particular quotient of expression called individuality. Harmonically speaking, while they are to some extent, attuned to their parent or originating sources, they always maintain that individuality, because the out of phase relationship—which does not permit them to remerge with their parent sources--still exists; and if these formations were to constantly degenerate, we would not have a single existing form of consciousness in the third dimension.

Therefore, Infinity must always be progressive; it must always be progressive in the sense that the Infinite is creating a succession of new and different forms of expression, and while they may be basically constituted in all originating concepts and conformities of expression, yet each new expression is, in itself, different. It is individualized because it is out of phase, so to speak, in the inclusion of time in its aspect of expression; it is still out of phase or out of time with the parent sources. I am emphasizing this concept because, while it seems to be very complex, it is actually very simple if we take the time and effort to constructively analyze it and place it in our minds in a manner and way that we can understand it. The success of your future evolution depends upon how well you can begin to understand the different regenerative processes which are the intelligent expressionary forms of Infinite Consciousness.

In the case of identical twins, such as we explored in the previous chapters, the individuality of these two persons could be considered to be immutable, and they would continue to re-express their own individual concept of life irrespective of the fact that they were oscillating in harmony with their respective psychic anatomies. The psychic anatomies, in this harmonic oscillation, could be considered to be one psychic anatomy; yet these two could not merge because of the out of phase relationship which had engendered the original separation. In other words, each of these men, living hundreds of miles apart, married, having different aspects of community life, different jobs, etc., has the same conformities of their physical or material world oscillated into his psychic anatomy, and these formed the same basic relationships in the two psychic anatomies. In this respect, the two psychic anatomies were identical. However, they were separated because of a great stress which had been previously imposed on the original psychic anatomy, and in this great stress, all of the different wave forms so contained in the one psychic anatomy regenerated on the spur of the moment—so to speak —and formed an entirely new set of wave form expressions, or an entirely new psychic anatomy which expressed itself into the womb of the parent as two different individual human anatomies.

This is exactly the situation which exists with the tiny germ we have previously inspected. The germ, in effect, regenerated the entirety of itself in a new psychic anatomy which again relives in that part of the cell which separated from the parent cell; however, as was previously explained, the entire time content in this expressive element was different, the parent cell would then die much more quickly than would the offspring. The offspring would again repeat this same process because the psychic anatomy which was expressing this cell in the third dimension would, quite naturally, be considered to have exactly the same wave form conformations and expressive elements. Now this same basic principle holds true in any expression of life in the world about us, and the same principles are inviolate for any species of plant or animal life; they are always contained in those expressive regenerations. Their harmonic expressions and reconformations which are generated and regenerated in the out of phase relationship to each other give the definite potential of evolutionary expression.

It means that there are basic derivatives of expression whereby a species of plant or animal can evolve into another species because wave form expressions, in any respective psychic anatomy, can and do regenerate certain harmonics; therefore, in this process of regenerating respective harmonics, they are synonymous in all respects to their originating and parent sources. These harmonics also regenerate harmonics in other wave form constituents with which they are immediately surrounded.

The environment of the spiritual world is completely filled with all forms and all kinds of expressive wave forms. Any element of expression, as a wave form which is pulsating in a cyclic motion within the fourth dimension, is always immediately concerned with all other existing wave forms or expressionary motions in the fourth dimension, on the basis that it is, or it is not, harmonically attuned to its own particular expressive wave form contained in its cyclic motion, the determinant quality of time as it expresses itself within this cyclic motion of interpretation.

A species of tree, plant, shrub, or animal can, therefore, conceivably be said to evolve into the respective formations of psychic anatomies in this constant process of regeneration, by reinstituting new harmonic forms which are conformities, in a sense, with experience quotients engendered from the usual life manifestations, forms, or conformities; these regenerations constantly reintroduce and form new harmonic structures within the respective psychic anatomies. As these different conformities of wave forms are so instituted, they will, in a general sense, again regenerate within themselves certain base plane references of interpretation which give a new form of expression to the outside exterior or the physical conformity, and, therefore, the species then can be said to have readapted itself to a new environmental situation with which it has been confronted. This is evolution; it is the science of evolution, and it must be realized to be an extremely complex electronic process; electronic in that frame of reference whereby we can visualize all forms of life as expressive elements of wave forms and harmonic structures.

In the Unarius lesson courses the presentation of these scientific facts was, quite obviously, made comparatively simple; your approach to them had to be made in a simple form because it is not generally known, either to science, or to many of the so-called, higher forms of educational curriculums on the earth today. As the science which we are explaining to you is not generally known, it cannot, therefore, be presupposed that you, as a student, would know of these truths. The approach to this science, which is currently being expressed through Unarius, had to be made in a more gradual inclination. It could not reasonably be assumed that you could incept the complete concept of interdimensional science in its entirety from the beginning of a material consciousness. You would quite necessarily have to have a considerable amount of spiritual conditioning and awareness or quickening of spirit to understand the possibility of this entire consciousness of the Infinite as a regenerative formation which is Infinite in nature.

This, too, is your approach to the Infinite in that never-ending process of evolution; for each idea, each readaptation of various conformities in your physical

313

life is quite necessarily evolutionary in nature. They, like all other forms of energy which go into the psychic anatomy, generate their own respective harmonics; and in these respective harmonics there is again regeneration, which can conceivably link up the entire originating inception of energy wave forms to the entire Infinite Intelligence. Through harmonic structures there is sort of a highway in which all conformities, all ideas, and all manifestations are linked and re-linked in that never-ending regenerative process which is Infinite Intelligence.

# CHAPTER 31

## The Electronic Man

In the Advanced Lesson Course, and in various other places in Unarius teachings, the electronic process of life has been repeatedly mentioned; these depictions have struck certain parallels between existing electronic devices and those occurring in the concourse of life in every human being. In other words, every human is basically and essentially quite similar to a radio or TV set. The earth scientist has, in the construction of these electronic devices, struck an exact parallel configuration with the complete electronic essence of the Infinite Creator, or with the principles in which the Creator so expresses Itself in that never-ending regenerative and reconstructive process.

In all fairness to both the student and Unarius, and in consideration of more highly trained or developed personalities who will, in the future, contact Unarius, it is best that we explore more deeply the mathematical processes, the manner and way in which life, with every human, is made possible and is constantly created in this evolutionary pathway. We shall be able to see that every human being, just as yourself, is basically an extremely complex electronic instrument which, at any given moment, is actually conducting these various and intricate processes of energy configurations and radiations within, not only the physical anatomy, but also the psychic anatomy; for, indeed, it is the psychic anatomy which can be considered as the larger portion of this expressionary form of life.

Therefore, let us take, specifically, one of these electronic devices—the common table radio which you might have about the house—and I shall describe to you just how it functions; then I shall describe the parallel configurations through which life is made possible for you in the different manifestations of consciousness or the experience quotients in which you are presently involved.

This radio is, quite naturally, one of the more popular models which is called super-heterodyne. The word heterodyne, in itself, relates to an important function of electronic wave forms which, when they beat against each other, re-create a second harmonic frequency which is called heterodyne. The table radio functions in this manner because the designers, the electronic technicians who so constructed the entire concept of this radio, had to consider certain purposes—these are selectivity and amplification. On the basis of selectivity and amplification, the different configurations within the radio were so conceived and designed, and they became a functioning entity of purpose. Within your radio there are a number of different kinds of coils; a coil is a very thin wire wrapped around a type of spool and connected with other devices called capacitors; these are merely two different sheets of foil with an insulating separator between them, and these are wound very tightly so there is an interchange of an alternating or an oscillating current between these two plates.

However, we are more concerned with the windings of wire, called coils, or inductances. The inductances within your radio consist primarily of a certain type of configuration known as an intermediate transformer; that is, two small coils of wire are wound closely together and tuned together by the capacitors so that they form a resonant or a tank circuit. This resonant circuit functions at the base plane rate of about 600 kilocycles per second. In order to make this frequency operative, a second set of coils is brought into play with the necessary tube function; this section is called the oscillator. In this function the oscillator sets up a second radiation which is vibrating at the rate of 1400 kilocycles per second. When this 1400 kilocycle vibration comes in contact with the 600 kilocycle vibration, a second harmonic is generated, which is the ratio of two and one-half,* between these two fundamental vibrating wave forms and is mathematically equated at exactly 460 kilocycles. It is this 460 kilocycle wave form which is used as a carrier through the other stages of intermediate frequency amplification and finally terminates into the second detector.

Now, these radio frequencies which are oscillating in this radio are too intense or pitched too high for your ear to hear; they vibrate in regions of thirty or forty thousand cycles per second, and the second detector, therefore, serves a purpose—it demodulates these frequencies or steps them down, so they become audible to your ear and they can be picked up and re-amplified to sufficient strength before emerging as sound from your loud speaker.

Now, while this process may, to some people, seem very complex, it really is basically very simple if we stop to analyze the situation. We must always consider that which the scientist calls phase relationships, and also some other very important factors which are connected with this generating and regenerating process. If we recall, there is a difference in polarities of

317

the common horseshoe magnet; the north pole and the north pole repel each other, whereas a north and a south pole will attract each other. Therefore, in our analysis of the wave form, we can say that as two waves meet, they are oscillating in their respective frequencies—positive and negative—each time the wave changes in its up and down motion; and if these polarities are similar to those of the horseshoe magnet, that is, a negative and a positive spot on the wave or the negative and positive place where it bends, then the two wave forms can be said to be inphase; that is, the phase is, in itself, 180 degrees. This means that in this phase reversal of 180 degrees we have presented one positive and one negative configuration to the other wave form with which it is presently involved.

However, should these two waves come together so that the two positive polarities are in junction, then they are out of phase and they will cancel out each other. Whereas, in the case of the inphase wave forms, they would regenerate and be enabled to form harmonics which contained all of the original information of these waves and carry them on into a more ultimate purpose. In the case of the out of phase wave forms, these out of phase conditions would, as I have said, tend to cancel out; however, we do not destroy energy. In the canceling process where these two waves met in opposition there would be a break-up in their content; that is, they would generate a certain set of out of phase harmonics, and these out of phase harmonics could conceivably regenerate into other out of phase harmonics, and they would eventually completely dissipate the entire energy information which was contained in the two original wave forms. It is this principle which is in effect with any person who is tuned in, negatively speaking, to the Infinite. He presents an out of phase wave form condition to the Infinite Intelligence, and, therefore, everything he does will constantly regenerate negative, or out of phase wave forms which will eventually destroy him. Whereas, if a person is always positively tuned to the Infinite Creator, then he is inphase to the different wave forms which come to him, and in turn, these will regenerate constructive harmonics in his life.

In order for you to more specifically see how it is that these inphase and out of phase wave form conditions can and do affect your present life—even though they were impounded in your psychic anatomy hundreds, or even thousands of years ago—let us go into a more complete analysis. Remember, that in the fourth dimension a phase is 360 degrees or a complete circle, whereas, in the physical or material world a phase is 180 degrees. However, this is a point of academic interest, and in all cases the effects will be the same.

For simplification we shall confine ourselves to the 180 degree wave form conditions, remembering, of course, that we must, so far as our psychic anatomics are concerned, always visualize that wave forms within the psychic anatomy are in 360 degree wave form conditions; there they will, in a sense, have time interwoven into them, and they will not be concerned with a stopping or a starting place; they can be considered to be imperishable in nature. However, we can analyze them more simply on the basis of the 180 degree wave form condition.

Now, if you will turn to that part of Lesson Number Five in the Second Course where we have a diagram of the psychic anatomy, you will see that there are three different portions of this psychic anatomy; the subconscious, the mental, and the Superconscious. The subconscious—as you perhaps know—is the result of the formation of different wave forms which have occurred since the moment of your conception;

and in the moment of conception, your mentality, posed from the psychic anatomy with which you were most vitally concerned in the spirit world, began to beat against the various wave forms within itself. At the moment of conception, combined with other wave forms in a telepathic communication system with the mother, father, and other members of the family, you began to develop the first elements of the newly forming subconscious part of your psychic anatomy.

At the moment of birth this constructive process would be renewed and intensified with the complete function of your five senses, and telepathy would to a large degree be abandoned. However, telepathy would exist but more subconsciously than before; so, as you grew up through childhood and into adulthood, you would, in effect, be constructing the subconscious, and at the moment of death this subconscious would begin to deteriorate.

In different Eastern philosophies connected with the Yogi and in Western versions of these philosophies, this subconscious has been called the astral shell of the soul. The subconscious is a system of oscillating wave forms and centers which must be constantly sustained in the acts of consciousness of your daily life; when this sustaining process is suspended after death, the subconscious begins to fade. However, all of the many content forms of the subconscious have, by that time, been impounded in that part of the psychic anatomy which is called the mental consciousness. In this compounding process, there is a condition which is very similar to that which goes on in your table radio.

In order to visualize this more clearly, let us re-create a scene. Let us say that in a previous lifetime, some three or four hundred years ago, you drowned in a boat accident on a lake. Now, at the present time, it could not be reasonably supposed that you would remember the details of this drowning accident; you would, however, have a vague fear of drowning, especially when you were confronted with the necessity of getting into a boat. The reason for this can be analyzed quite simply. In the act of drowning in the previous lifetime, let us say that your subconscious was oscillating at 600 kilocycles per second, just as in the case of the radio; and the mental portion of your psychic anatomy was vibrating at 1400 kilocycles; therefore, in the oscillating process and in an *inphase* condition between these two parts of your psychic anatomy, there was, as I have mentioned before, a beat frequency set up which was the sum and total difference in the ratio of these two wave forms.

This was called the basic frequency harmonic; it was upon this harmonic that the different energy wave forms—of the drowning experience as they came into your subconscious at that moment—traveled into the mental part of your psychic anatomy and were impounded there in an entirely different frequency to that which they originally came into your subconscious mind. There, in that mental part of your psychic anatomy they would remain, because, as I have said, they were revolving in a cyclic form of 360 degrees. Therefore, when you were reborn into this lifetime, you carried the entire content of this drowning experience, along with all other experiences which were incurred from any other previous lifetimes.

However, in this lifetime you would not consciously remember that drowning because the wave forms which composed the drowning experience were in an out of phase condition with other energy wave forms oscillating in your consciousness at the moment. But, if you went to a lake and embarked upon a boat, there would be a condition set up in conscious reality which would regenerate certain wave forms into the subconscious, then oscillate on the beat frequency or

321

the heterodyning into the mental consciousness where they would again come in sympathetic resonance with the original drowning wave forms; in turn, as they oscillated together they would be repeating the intelligence or the information of this experience which would regenerate a third set of harmonics that would then go into the mental consciousness or the brain cells.

Now, these brain cells are exactly like the detector circuit in the radio description. The brain cells are rectifiers, that is, they pass the electrical impulse in one direction, but they refuse to pass it backwards; and in the various layers of the cortex or the surface of the brain, there are different types of cells which perform a certain particular function; they determine certain frequencies which they will pass and other frequencies which they will not pass; they are linked and relinked to each other with different nerves. The whole system, then, can be said to be a sensing device. In other words, the passage of these countless impulses or wave forms of energy back and forth, between these cells as they are being brought into play in that moment of excitation on these different wave forms, will create the sensation which was, in effect, the exact facsimile of the original sensation which performed the same process in reverse. Therefore, the wave forms of vibration which contained the information of drowning, as they stemmed into the conscious mind, were considered as biasing wave forms; that is, they gave the energy information or whatever was contained in the wave form in the way and manner they vibrated to the brain cells, which, in turn, could then react according to these principles of regeneration and according to the mathematical formula, I have described to you.

When you realized that these little wave forms of information containing the drowning experience, were oscillating in your brain cell, the sensation of fear of drowning would again be created; it would be fear because within the different portions of the brain structure there would not be a complete junction of consciousness which is necessary to complete the memory process as it would have been so completed had you consciously remembered this drowning experience. Therefore, you would, in this incomplete consciousness process with the oscillating information, be only vaguely aware of a dread or a fear of the boat and the lake.

Now, if I were with you at the moment, and tuned back into your past by the same process of doing exactly that which the radio does; I would, with my antenna—which is my form of mental consciousness —be able to pick up the radiations of these vibrations as they were resonating in your psychic anatomy, and I would be able to describe to you just how you drowned in this previous lifetime. That would immediately set in motion a certain "in-phase" condition within the subconscious portion of your psychic anatomy. In other words, it would now become a reality to you; and while this "in-phase" condition was oscillating into your subconscious, the subconscious would, in turn, reoscillate as it was so oscillating with the mental consciousness in that heterodyning principle. The condition would then regenerate a harmonic of wave forms containing the information of the reality; these would then go into the mental part of the psychic anatomy where they would be in an "out of phase" condition with those previously impounded in the actual experience, as I described it to you. Since they are of proportionately equal velocity or strength in this out of phase condition, they would cancel out the negative part of that oscillating wave form condition by virtue of the fact that out of phase wave forms cancel out each other.

They would blow apart these different wave forms and degenerate them into other and less destructive wave forms, because they were less destructive and also out of phase with each other; they were out of phase with other different wave forms in the psychic anatomy and, therefore, could never again regain their former potential or strength in regard to this in and out of phase condition. However, at this point you must also remember that, in the same and exact process of heterodyning, you had within your Superconscious that drowning experience; the Superconscious is a heterodyne or an oscillating circuit which creates the heterodyne principle with the mental part of the psychic anatomy, and in the same process which occurred from the subconscious to the mental conscious, the harmonic of the drowning experience was carried into the Superconscious and there it polarized certain wave forms. That is, it reconstructed the information in an entirely different dimension, because in this higher dimension there was an exact facsimile of this energy already vibrating in its entirety. In polarizing this experience from out of the mental conscious into the Superconscious, you merely changed it in its course or direction, or in its cyclic path and made it a part of the Superconscious, in respect to the fact that it was now, in an inphase condition; but it was out of phase with the lower portions of the psychic anatomy, such as the mental and subconscious.

Therefore, in the future, when you viewed the lake or you were in a boat, you would no longer have fear with it. The drowning experience wave forms in your mental consciousness were, to a large degree, dissipated in their inphase condition to you; and the fear would not be in your conscious mind because you would have extracted the reality of the situation. You would now be able to remember it through the subconscious; therefore, you would have automatically instigated an inphase, out of phase situation, a simultaneous condition which gave equilibrium to the entire experience; therefore, it was negative to you in respect to fear or any intent or purpose.

You could, from the Superconscious, say that the information contained in that drowning experience was also coming into your conscious mind as an added form of bias which would give you, at the moment of reflection, a certain positive quality of introspection, whereby you would be able to see this drowning experience as a constructive element in the process of life. You would have seen that it was a repetition of a karmic circumstance; in the analysis of this experience, you would be enabled to form a constructive entity of consciousness with it, and therefore, it would add to the general tone, or structure in a positive manner as to all other forms of consciousness in the entire psychic anatomy.

By now you can see that the process of life or each act of consciousness is an extremely complex process which involves the heterodyning or the beating against each other of literally hundreds of thousands or even *millions* of wave forms which are contained in the different portions of the psychic anatomy. In the regularity of these mathematical formulas which have been incorporated in such electronic devices as radios and TVs, and inasmuch as we have this same mathematical regularity in the same principles impounded in our psychic anatomies, we, therefore, function inviolately; we are, in essence and in effect, an electronic instrument. We are always tuned to the Infinite in the direct ratio and proportion of these different wave form formulas. We are also immediately attuned with any and all wave forms which we have impounded in the experience process in any or all of our past lifetimes. This also adds to the tremendous complexity of the entire situation.

However, this complexity need not confuse you, if you remember the basic elements which are involved in these principles; that we have two or more wave forms which can be coming together, or beating against each other according to their harmonic frequency, or the times per second which they are oscillating up and down in that positive and negative fashion; when they come in conjunction with each other, if the polarities are negative to positive and positive to negative, then we have the inphase condition; and we have an out of phase condition if the polarities are in opposition; we can have regeneration constructively, in the inphase condition, and we can have degeneration or cancellation in the out of phase condition.

We must also remember that in whatever processes of life we are involved, even if we are completely idle and just letting our thoughts roam, the same complex system of oscillations and regenerations is occurring within this psychic anatomy. It is in effect, one of the most wondrous and complex configurations of energy wave forms which has been conceived in the Infinite Mind and in the purpose of Infinite Creation; because it is in this respect that, through man and in the formation and the *reconstruction* of the psychic anatomy, God *becomes* an individual being in every human. In the more highly developed forms of evolution to which any human being can aspire, man will, eventually, evolve into these higher states of consciousness if he can so conceive the possibility. Then this person is indeed, to all intents and purposes, somewhat of a God-like personality, very much like Jesus.

* The formula for computing the final frequency is rather complex, hence the more easily comprehended two and one half presentation. (Page 317)

# CHAPTER 32

## The Electronic Man, Part Two

Now that we have entered into some of the mathematical abstractions in this universal oscillating process, called Infinity, and as we enter into this more complete abstraction, visualized in its entity of consciousness as the Infinite Creator, we are most necessarily concerned with other factors involved in the evolution of man and, in particular, our own evolution. In all respects, however, wherever we find evolution, it is Infinite, and we will always find the same similarities in various configurations and wave form expressions.

The psychic anatomy of man is, therefore, basically and essentially, the same in its configuration as is the whole universal Infinite, or Infinity can be subdivided interdimensionally; it is in this respect, that it might serve a good purpose to explore some of the more constructive evaluations of Infinity and in a comparative manner set up a facsimile of consciousness within our own minds, whereby we can realize the entire entity of creation.

Up until this moment the psychic anatomy was largely pictured as a body or a formation more or less loosely compounded of different vortexes; however, this does need clarification. For, within the psychic

327

anatomy and with whatever structure we are involved, we shall find the utmost degree of regularity. There is, in resonance within the harmonic principle of regeneration, oscillation or the compound of harmonics which again re-expresses the parent sources. We find the same principle is also functioning in different aspects of interdimensional expression, so that they, in turn, form suns and planetary systems. Yes, indeed, they even form galaxies and universes, as they are presently determined by the astrophysicist or the scientists and even beyond the horizon of the five senses. As we have described to you, the interdimensional configurations of Infinite Consciousness do so infinitely fill space in the same precise and constructive manner as they are, interdimensionally speaking, linked and relinked to each other in this same configuration of positive to negative phase relationship which exists in the common table radio.

To form within our minds a more constructive configuration, let us take a long piece of wire from a spool and coil it in a regular fashion around our fingers; we will stretch it out somewhat and loop it about, so that it forms a continuous circle. Then we have a spiral of wire which is revolving around and around into a perfect figure of a circle. This is a fourth dimensional concept of the sine wave, and we can now determine positive and negative in respect to different portions of this circular configuration of wire. We will find that the negative polarity always manifests itself on the exact inside circumference of the wire at each place where the wire returns into a loop. On the opposite or outside part of that coil of wire, we will, in turn, find the positive polarity.

The psychic anatomy is composed entirely of such configurations which, to some extent, resemble vortexes. A vortex is not an exact configuration for a vortex starts as a spiral and terminates in a point. We do have, however, within these spiral formations of energy within the psychic anatomy, the same condition which we can liken to a vortex. As we have previously described to you, positive and negative must relate to each other in an in phase condition if they are to be constructively or harmonically regenerative in their purpose. In order for two of these different spirals or vortexes of energy to thus be constructive in their intent and purpose we cannot place them against each other, as two doughnuts laid side by side on the table with their outer edges touching each other, for we would then, in effect, have the positive polarities of this cyclic form of wire touching each other, and they would be out of phase; they would repel each other. How then would they regenerate or become in phase with each other? This is possible because of the various frequencies from which these configurations were formed.

In these frequencies we can say that we have a large doughnut which has a larger vibration, and we have a small doughnut which has a smaller vibration; if we place the small doughnut within the large one, we will immediately see that the positive polarities of the small doughnut are contacting the negative polarities of the larger one. In this phase relationship they can oscillate harmoniously together and regenerate harmonics as the base and same multiple of that ratio of two and one-half which I have formerly presented to you.

Now, at this point we must remove from consciousness the proposition of size, because size, in reality, does not exist in the fourth dimension; size and time are of the same quality of proportion. In other words, time, size, and space are synonymous; we cannot separate one from the other. If we say that something is of a certain dimension it means that we have to take a certain time differential from the place where we start to envision this object to the place where it can be left off or terminated. The time interval, therefore, is synonymous to the space or the difference between two points.

However, this differential does not exist in the fourth dimension, simply because all things are cyclic within each other. I have used the doughnut configuration merely as a convenient means to build up your consciousness to a point where you can envision the construction of a vortex; it is a manner and form which is constantly re-linking the different frequencies or the various kinds of oscillations in an inphase or positive relationship to each other so they can regenerate into constructive configurations of harmonic wave forms which will again relay or convey the energy—the information—to other sections of the psychic anatomy; they have done so on the same basis of frequency relationship and regeneration.

Now, every object in the solar system which you see as a planet, a sun, a star, or a moon, is, in effect, the center of a vortex, just as it was described to you in the Second Lesson Course. That is, we have in the fourth dimension a large number of varied sized doughnuts placed regularly within each other—if we wish to create the image within our minds—so that in their oscillating content, the positive and negative are constantly regenerating and oscillating constructively. As we look into the center of this vortex, we shall see that, conversely, the degree of oscillating frequency must decrease; that is, it does, in a manner and form, separate itself from the previous doughnut because it is not vibrating at exactly the same frequency. Therefore, it can place itself in the positive and negative phase relationship with the larger circumference of the different spiral energy configurations, which I have described.

As we go on down, so to speak, into the center of

330

this vortex, we have a centripetal motion; that is, energy is, negatively speaking, constantly precipitating itself into the center of this vortex; and, conversely, the same situation is true in respect to the positive polarities, they will increase as we approach the periphery or the circumference of this vortex. Therefore, in this constantly expanding outward and constantly increasing positive condition, we have regeneration into a new dimension or a new circumference, or a new entity of expression; and in the centripetal or the negative configuration we also have a more ultimate expression, which terminates into the center of this vortex as a sun, a star, a planet, or even a moon.

Yes, even the same configuration is used to describe each and every atom in your body; and, for that matter, all atoms which compose the planet earth. They, in turn have these same minute configurations of spiral wave forms which form vortexes of their respective psychic anatomies, and these are all pulsating in very regular cyclic motions from positive to negative within themselves, as these energy expressions are constantly revolving in that timeless fourth dimension, as Einstein called it. When we have somewhat mastered this concept within our own minds, we shall indeed have a true picture, and a true portrayal of Infinite regeneration—the secret which is now being sought after most assiduously by the earth scientist. It has to some degree, been envisioned as an esoterical virtue by the religionist; however, the religionist, whether he is Christian, witch doctor in the jungle, or any other intermediate expressionist, does not possess the scientific knowledge of the Infinite which I have just described to you. Wherever we may go upon the planet earth, we do not find people who possess this knowledge. In this sense then, Unarius is the "Second Coming," or the return of the "Christ Consciousness" to the earth; it is in respect to the fact that all creations have psychic anatomies, whether they are atomic, whether they are human, whether they are planetary, or even if it is a universe itself, for even the universe possesses a psychic anatomy.

If we look at the picture of a universe in a planetarium or in a scientific book of astronomy, we shall see that a universe—such as the one in which our galaxy is revolving—has a center core, and from this core there are radiating outwardly in a spiral-like fashion great arms of lighted energy; these arms of energy are following those same cyclic paths of motion—previously described to you—which occur within these cyclic motions of the great vortex forming the universe. This leads us to some of the more indirect expressions of energy configurations.

An atom does, in itself, express outwardly into the third dimension a certain electromagnetic field, just as the sun is expressing outwardly into the confines of the solar system, a great amount of energy which is a composite field of force—that is, it is composed of many kinds of energy, including the magnetic fluxes which hold this planetary system together and which relink it to the galaxy and in turn to the universe. The composite energy which is pouring outwardly from the center of the vortex known as the sun, is again retransferred in that magnetic stress condition which is called hysteresis, and is reconverted into such quantities of energy spectrums which we call heat, light, etc.

The same condition holds true within your body, and the same principles are as inviolate there as they are in the function of a solar system or a universe. Each atom, as it has an electromagnetic field, does, in proportion, radiate outwardly around it in its field of force either a direct opposition to other kinds of atoms, or it presents, in the 'inphase and out of phase' wave form motion of these electromagnetic fields, an affinity to some other atom. It is in this manner and way that molecules are formed.

Molecules are composite groups of atoms which have been somewhat loosely held together by the electromagnetic fields in their respective atoms. Now, it is quite easy to break molecules apart, but it is extremely difficult to break up atoms, for the reason that molecules are a third dimensional configuration held together by a somewhat third dimensional field of force, the electromagnetic fields; whereas, within the atom the different fields of force called by the scientist, electrons, protons, neutrons, etc., are actually exact facsimiles and configurations of the vortex which forms the atom; and this in turn, is relinked to an infinite number of vortexes throughout the cosmogony, or the microcosm and the macrocosm.

We can see that breaking even one atom apart is, in effect, the same in principle as breaking the entire Infinite apart; and in breaking up an atom, we have actually released, in a split fraction of a second, a certain potential of infinite energy into the third dimension, which could not have come into this dimension except in that evolutionary process of phase wave form relationships and the regeneration of electromagnetic fields, just mentioned.

When the scientist, the chemist, the man of medicine, or any other expressionist in the field of science understands the principles of magnetic coupling, or electromagnetic repulsion among atoms, in their more third dimensional expressions as groupings of molecules, then we will develop an entirely new science; it will be a science compounded from the electronic principles, which have been described to you, and not from the presently existing seemingly reactionary components, which are expressed in chemical reactions.

In the same way, body functions also can be dissolved and re-established in a more correct synthesis as an electromagnetic or an electronic proposition wherein we can see that even the food we eat can be inducted and reconstructed into molecular content in the human system, by the same inductive and repulsive conditions of electromagnetic forces as they are re-combined in these different polarity constituents. As these numerous energy configurations are thus expressing themselves in the general metabolism of the human system, we must also realize that through the nervous system and the ganglion of the nerves, as they are terminating in the different cell structures of muscles, bones, etc., of the human anatomy, these nerve cells are constantly pouring into the molecular structures the biasing currents which emanate from the same harmonic interplay in the psychic anatomy.

These biasing agents, in turn, are related in that timeless and spaceless dimension—the fourth dimension—back into the very beginnings of your evolution, or, for that matter, back into the very primitive ooze or the beginning of your existence, as it concerns even a simple one-celled animal. For even the germ life, the bacteria, or the protozoan which inhabit this planet, have developed from these same principles; they have the same psychic anatomies, the same regeneration and the same electronic automations as does every human in the entire universe.

Therefore, in your daily life, if you have become addicted to fads, if you are overweight, or with whatever manifestation of life you are consciously aware, remember that these are merely beat frequencies of oscillations which are coming to you from out of the past. It is here that we come into that all-important element of synchronization. For this is another scientific terminology which describes how two wave forms can either oscillate together or in opposition to each other. The element of synchronization is in the time in which these frequencies express themselves in that

334

regenerative process.

Therefore, if you are synchronized—and you always are at any given moment—in a general summation with all experience quotients which have come to you in your previous lifetimes, i.e. you may over-eat because a thousand years ago you died in a famine, or you may avoid meat because you have a sense of guilt from being a soldier and killing other soldiers in a war; these various configurations from out of the past have, in these different synchronizations, generated certain parallaxes, or, as they are called by the scientist, synchronisms or anachronisms, or whatever term you wish to use to describe these appearances of energy configurations. They are, in turn, any number of energy wave forms beating in that never-ending, never-ceasing process of regeneration; the opposition or the combining of polarities in their respective content; the relaying of the information which all wave forms do carry as their wave shape or as their oscillating content. They will convey and re-convey this information as they were so propagated, and as they were so constructed in the experience of the moment.

Fads and fascisms are merely the expressionary forms of past experiences which combined with certain pressures of this present civilized world. They tend to regenerate a certain form of psychic pressure which, in turn, will have to be equalized or stabilized by an escape mechanism. An escape mechanism, is, in a sense, a safety valve and is usually quite harmless unless such an escape mechanism builds up, and involves all of the essential and dominant qualities of the personality. If this occurs, the person is either extremely neurotic or he is extroverted and psychotically inclined. However, by whatever terminology we wish to describe a mental condition, so far as its appearance in the third dimension is concerned, we have the same automation of electronic constituents which are involved in the general conflux and the construction of different parallaxes as they are expressed into your present-day life.

Food, in itself, is merely one of those elements which you have incorporated in your psychic anatomy as a concept of living, just as are all of the other different configurations which form your present-day life. There is no reason to believe that these various incorporations of consciousness need to exist in the higher spiritual worlds for, as life is predicated upon a constructive evolution, we must always envision within ourselves, that all of these various forms of consciousness will, eventually, pass from us. They will become only a memory in the reality of the past.

Therefore, learn to constructively analyze your present-day life and whatever act of consciousness in which you are involved. Try to trace back in a direct connotation all of the differences in the psychic manifestations as they have been impounded in your psychic anatomy from previous lifetimes. If you will gain this constructive and objective thought process of self-analysis and do it without the limiting perspective of self-recrimination, flagellation, or other subversive elements of psychic masochism, you can attain a constructive evaluation of evolution in particular to your own position on the scale of Infinite Consciousness.

When this is done, you will have begun to constructively master life, for life is merely a symposium of constructive evaluations wherein we attain mastery; our most ultimate destiny is mastery over any dimension in which we find ourselves, and we always should be vitally concerned in this mastery. No indeed, mastery does not mean that we can wave some sort of a magic wand and create any kind of a condition we so wish, or that we have opened a bottle and loosed a genie. It does not mean that we can step up to any person who is sick or suffering and say, "Be thou healed," then watch the transformation occur. It means, instead, that we have a *regularity of consciousness* which is *sustained* through an *infinite number* of dimensions; *this is mastery*, mastery which *immediately objectifies* the *most ultimate conception* of *Infinite Consciousness* as it is contained in that *never-ending regenerative process* which is *Infinite Consciousness.*

When we have obtained the complete and absolute abstraction of this Infinite Consciousness and so applied it as the sustaining element of our lives, as the prime purpose, and as the motivating impulse of our lives, then we can be said to be masters in the dimension in which we find ourselves.

Do not be confused with "isms" and "osms" which come to you from outside in your material world; as Jesus said, "The Kingdom of Heaven is within," and this begins only when we can constructively analyze the entire intent and purpose of life as an evolutionary principle. This is scientifically interrogated and interpreted as the different interpolations and interplays of energy wave form configurations, either third dimensional or otherwise, which I have previously described.

It is almost needless to say that when you have attained mastery over any dimension, when you have a correct knowledge of the function of this dimension in its relationship to Infinity, then you will quite proportionately express mastery into the dimension around you. You will not be constantly pressurized by the impending impact of experience and your reaction to this experience occurring with you. Instead, experience itself will immediately resolve itself into a dimension whereby it can be introspectively analyzed and reaction will cease to exist.

God as the Infinite and all-creative Intelligence is

not emotionally activated. God is an inviolate, ever sustaining principle of life which is not subjective to the different emotional vicissitudes which are portrayed in human consciousness, as God is the sum and total of all things. The principle of God is incorporated as the functioning entity of all things; God therefore cannot be emotional. God must always remain the absolute and ultimate abstraction of all forms of consciousness, for if this were not so, there would be no reason, no purpose for the existence of either a sun, a planetary system, an atom or a human being. For the entire service of creation is, in itself, predicated upon the great motion of Infinite Creation sustained by that constantly regenerating principle, which I have so often described to you.

# CHAPTER 33

## Utilitarian Concepts And Values

Now that we have gained a somewhat comprehensive evaluation as to the differences in electronic potentials and in the manifestation of these potentials in that regenerative process of life, it might be well to discuss the more utilitarian concepts and values as to what can be derived in a practical realization and readaptation in our present life experiences. It would do little good to evaluate the Infinite on this constructive basis without including the obvious fact that we must begin to form the various constructive values of life with which we are constantly concerned. These principles, as all other principles which have been described, are inviolate in nature; they can be considered to be the all-inclusive principles, and the usage of them in our daily lives will determine the more ultimate ends of our destiny, whether we evolve into the higher spiritual worlds or whether we remain bound to the wheel of material karma, which has been and is the lot of the material man and to a large degree has been your lot since the beginning of your evolution.

This consensus of evaluations so far as our contact with the Infinite is concerned, means that we must participate in this universal progressive scheme of evolution; we must begin to utilize this proposition of Infinite Creation in our own daily lives, and we must do this, not from the old emotional plane of contact which was our material world, but we must do it in a constructive manner and form which at once implies, not only a direct knowledge of all principles and functions involved, but also the constructive usage and the utilitarian value of these things as they manifest themselves in our daily lives.

Perhaps you have been in contact with various so-called mental sciences which have tried to evaluate the principle of regenerative construction in life as one of concentration. This is quite untrue—concentration should never be attempted, for concentration without the proper knowledge and usage of all factors involved, is, indeed, a most destructive attempt to try to construct for ourselves something of value in this material world. If a runner or an athlete is attempting to win a race, he does engage in tremendous concentration in the manipulation of his legs or in performing some athletic feat; however, there is a terminating point to this concentration, and if it is continued too long it can result in physical damage, or even eventual death.

The value of concentration is only relative to the amount of knowledge of the principles involved, and to the average earth man who knows little or nothing about these principles, the effects in his efforts to concentrate can be quite deleterious, and in all respects can be considered to be quite incomprehensible; for no man can, at any time or at any place in his life, until he becomes Infinitely conscious, be considered to be the person who knows what he should have in this life. Because of the great inflection of subversive, subconscious elements which are constantly stemming into consciousness, no person, at any time, can constructively evaluate his life until he is completely aware of all factors involved in whatever pressurization he is attempting to automate in his life.

You have all had the experience of trying to think of a name or a word, and it apparently seemed to be blocked from your consciousness despite all efforts to recall it; it was on the tip of your tongue, so to speak, but you could not say it, the reason being quite simple. Referring back to that which has been previously discussed, we can easily see that in trying to concentrate on this word or name, we have, in effect, reinstituted a certain oscillating condition which is out of phase with that which we wish to manifest; and in this out of phase condition, we have temporarily destroyed this entity of consciousness; that which we wished to say, we cannot say until we relax this concentration and remove the out of phase wave form from consciousness; this will then let the subconscious oscillate freely and the word or name will then appear in our minds.

The same position is quite true if we have misplaced an article about the house, and we wish to find it. Most people start that reactionary process of searching; they will hunt and hunt until perchance, they may run across the object in question, whereas, all of this could be easily avoided if these persons would sit down for a moment and remove from consciousness the tension as to the placement of this object, then realize that this—as all other objects in the house or even the world itself—was of molecular composition, it contains a number of molecules. This object, like all other objects, was, therefore, radiating a field of force; part of this field of force is fourth dimensional and part is third. However, we are concerned with the fourth dimensional field of force; inasmuch as this is, in a sense, a spaceless or timeless situation, we can tune into this object from the psychic anatomy instantaneously, no matter where it is, then we can get up and walk directly to it; it will be as if someone had taken us by the arm and led us to the object. This is because we are following through, we are using the same principle which is being used in radar—the energy wave forms which we have connected in that portion of the psychic anatomy will, in turn, direct the conscious effort of movement into our limbs as we walk toward it.

There is no doubt that some of you, too, have heard reports or have been told that sitting and concentrating upon something would cause it to materialize. This is far from the truth, and any such practices are only a short step removed from some of the age-old practices of witchcraft, black magic, etc. The process of psychokinesis in the materialization of any object must always be substantiated conversely, by a great or a corresponding amount of knowledge of the function of spiritual values as they are contained in the knowledge of the interdimensional function of Infinite Creation. Perhaps you have seen or heard of someone who sat and concentrated in order to materialize, let us say, an automobile; and that as this concentration was continued for possibly several days, suddenly, it seemed that a car did appear. However, this may be, and is most likely to be entirely coincidental; the proof of this pudding would be—could this same person materialize one hundred cars in one hundred successive concentrations? If you think for a moment, this would be utterly and completely impossible.

The first car that materialized was, no doubt, something that would have materialized regardless, or perhaps it could be quite possible that a very strong astral entity, in the form of some human being without a body in the nearby adjacent spiritual world, was actually instrumental, to some degree, in materializing the car for this person, simply because he wished this person to continue on into a process which could easily lead to some disastrous results; and he would have an ulterior motive in influencing this person to continue these unintelligent objectivisms of concentration.

Irrespective of the different evaluations which may be found in individual attempts to use psychokinesis as a concentration in order to materialize various objectivisms in our daily lives, to remove sickness or mental conditions or whatever else is so desired to achieve, we must always imply and use a great amount of knowledge of Infinite function and Infinite Creation. If we do not we are quite likely to be led down the garden path, so to speak, and wind up in one of those blind alleys of mental introversion from which a considerable amount of time and effort is required to extricate ourselves, and which, in themselves, can be considered to be dimensions of karma. In order to obtain a more realistic approach to the function of life, and to the purpose of realizations in the personal evaluations of life, and as life manifests itself in the conscious form of reality of our existence; or, in other words, if we wish to be happier and more prosperous, these realizations cannot be obtained because we wish to objectify happiness or prosperity as a material value.

Happiness and prosperity are esoterical values which are always derived and result from the fact that we have obtained, within our consciousness, a more complete objectivism of the principle of Infinite regeneration and creation. It is quite useless to think that we are happy; this is that hedonistic or Polly-anna attitude of which I have formerly spoken; it is unrealistic. If we go about saying to ourselves that we are becoming stronger every day, or nothing harmful can come to us, or everything is positive and good— which was given, in a sense of the word, back in the early twenties by a French doctor named Coué—it makes no difference whatsoever in the form and manner of our lives. All of these things can be said to be hypnotic in their emotional intent in our lives; we are,

343

in all essences, autosuggestively creating a hypnotic condition within our mental consciousness which can blind us to the reality and make us unable to solve our differences in a realistic and a tangible manner.

Therefore, the proper way to realize a happier and a more affluent life is to realize that the entity of the personal self is a progressive entity; that is, it normally would be so, if we could properly inseminate the progressive principles of evolution as we progress along this pathway of life, from one pathway and from one lifetime to the next. The proposition of Infinite Creation, so far as we are individually connected to Infinity, is a two-way situation; that is if we can conceive in consciousness that which Infinity is and its principle, we do, in effect, at that moment of realization, project our consciousness into Infinity and from this position of projection where we have contacted Infinity, then it can in turn, re-oscillate into our consciousness. It will, also, in that general conversion of harmonic frequencies, previously described, reconvert energy into form and substance in your material expression, and you will have been, in a sense, directly led into that which you most wanted to achieve. You would find in this interconnection into the higher formations of Infinite Intelligence that in the converse ratio and proportion of inception or conception, Infinite Intelligence and creation would, in turn, in this two-way oscillating proposition, re-create the form and substance of the life you so desired.

However, this cannot be a selfish proposition in that we wish to acquire these things simply to relieve certain psychic pressures, or because we wish to live in the same manner and form as the Joneses, or that we wish to obtain power and dominion over our fellow man. For these subversive elements of consciousness, whether we recognize them or whether they are subconscious, if they exist, can deter and make it absolutely impossible for us to project consciousness, or contact the Infinite in any sense or in any proportion, that will make any materializations possible for us in our surface life.

The selfish or the grasping motivations of carnal existence, as they are lived by the earth man, are, in themselves, of a foreign nature; their frequency is so irrelevant to the higher frequencies of Infinite Consciousness, that a complete re-attunement, a complete remanifestation of consciousness is most necessary in order to re-establish a higher continuity of life and to establish a higher and more esoterical purpose, or a spiritual purpose, or even a constructive purpose *without* the intimidating taint of personality. The power of the Infinite within a more highly developed personality can be utilized to a degree and extent which, to the average earth man, would be quite magical; it can be very dramatically demonstrated by any and all of these personalities who have aspired and obtained a higher measure of purpose in their evolution into the Infinite Cosmogony. Whenever we come in contact with any one of these persons, we immediately sense or know that we are in the presence of some great transcending power. There is something there which sets this person apart from all other people; in fact, many different physical appearances of energy and the interconnection of energy will stem from this person and make him manifest in your own physical consciousness.

When you find or contact such a person, you will immediately recognize a very obvious fact; that he is not emotionally concerned with any or all of the more superficial values of life. He is not concerned with obtaining dominion over you; he does not have his hand in your pocket—so to speak—while he is trying to tell you something. As a matter of fact, you will find that whatever dispensation this person enters into, it has a certain constructivism and a certain

345

value of life which transcends any and all known material values of life; in fact, you will find this person displaying a certain mastership which is immediately apparent, if you care to so analyze such mastership, and it will not be limited in its dimension or in its scope. This person can take any artifact of any contrivance and suitably explain all known mechanical functions, all known electronic functions and he can in any other manner, way or form divert consciousness into a constructive entity of realization, even though he has had no academic training, even though the world itself does not know of these things, and, that in itself, is ample proof that this person, in his mental attunements, can and does materialize the Infinite Consciousness into some sort of a dispensation which can be personally realized by you.

Psychokinesis, or our attunement with the Infinite does assume many practical purposes, and to some degree psychokinesis is recognized by many people on the planet earth today. Barney Oldfield once held a certain portion of his car together while he finished a race, and it broke after he passed the finish line. In my own life I have used many instances of psychokinesis, not only to repair or prevent breakage in mechanical parts of my car or various other constituents of the mechanical phase of my life, but also psychokinesis has—even though I may not have been consciously aware of it—been functioning as a creative entity of intelligence, and, therefore, my life was led from one dimension, from one experience, expression, or demonstration—that could be considered at least extraordinary and many times miraculous in nature—to the next. I have found that if I let this Superconscious projection so manifest itself *without* the involvement of the conscious mind or the physical entity of consciousness in this projection, I had a much greater degree of success; and, therefore, life became a revelation of purpose as it was unfolded

346

before me, in a sense, that I, in my physical world, was merely an automation or a channel through which this more Infinite objectivism could be so expressed.

However, the more intimate details of these many hundreds of thousands of personal revelations and demonstrations will, to a large degree, have to remain until that day when a biography is instituted, and they can be recounted somewhat in their entirety. Sufficient to say at this moment, that while we are exploring the possibilities of a higher way of life and such manifestations as are called psychokinesis, teleportation, etc., these are all very scientific in nature; they are the resolutions of principle in Infinite expression that I have attempted to convey to you in the previous messages.

It is needless to say at this point, that the success of your future evolutions will depend entirely upon how well you can, within your consciousness, contrive to use these principles to refabricate your entire psychic anatomy; and to do this without the stigma or taint of various escape mechanisms which will always contrive to divert you from this purpose. For the old way is difficult to give up. It is the familiar way in which you have trod with your material feet through the centuries. The unknown always presents itself as a vague and a fearful aspect. Any person involuntarily cringes from the unknown; and, in fact, all deifications and religious systems have been compounded to relieve the psychic pressures engendered from the unknown dimensions of the spiritual world, which is realized by every person in the moment of death.

In a final analysis, to sum up this discussion, we can say that as all material forms in your world about you today are actually electronic constituents; that is, they are compounded from tiny little atoms which are solar systems of electronic energy; and as this electronic energy was compounded in the vast interplay of vortexal dimensions from a number of other dimensions that were part of the function of the Infinite Intelligence, it is, therefore, conceivable that to have a direct knowledge of this interplay, its function, its principle, and all of the different ramifications so involved will indeed imply a direct connotation of proper usage. Usage and knowledge in this respect are synonymous, and you will find that as you incept knowledge, you will, proportionately, have to inspire the thought and action of usage, for one could not exist without the other.

In the higher worlds and in those spiritual kingdoms that have, to some extent been described to you in the books, there is a great interplay of these principles in your own personal relationship to the Infinite. In fact, all manners and forms of consciousness will have to come to you directly and not indirectly as they do in this lifetime; but they will come directly as manifestations and as appearances or as materializations of consciousness in the forms in which you have respectively, in your consciousness, so conceived and contrived them and psychokinetically projected them into your life.

In other words, if you wish clothing, clothing will be contrived as a direct psychokinetical projection; you will use your mind forces instead of your hands to contrive the fabric with which you make clothing for yourself. This is rather a crude allegory, but it does serve the purpose that we are involved in the constructive fabrication as an entity of consciousness with the Infinite, and it will ultimately resolve within the confines of our own minds, as to how well we do this; how we will ultimately achieve the complete function of Infinite Consciousness, will quite naturally determine our evolution. It will determine, to some extent, whatever we can conceive as a reasonable terminating point; for in Infinite Consciousness there are no terminating points, and should we ever arrive at one, then we have immediately contrived to defeat ourselves in attaining a higher way of life.

This, therefore, is the proposition of life, to not only construct the entire effigy of Infinite Consciousness within your own mind, its principle function and purpose, but also that this effigy will become the useful instrumentation in your progressive evolution into the future.

# Other works by Ernest L. Norman:

## The Pulse of Creation Series

The Voice of Venus
The Voice of Eros
The Voice of Hermes
The Voice of Orion
The Voice of Muse

The Infinite Concept of Cosmic Creation
The lesson Course, (the key to the Unarius Science)

Cosmic Continuum
Infinite Contact
Truth About Mars
The Elysium (Parables)
The Anthenium         "
Magnetic Tape Lectures
Tempus Procedium
Tempus Invictus
Tempus Interludium Vols. I & II

Also a publication, now reprinted by
Unarius Publishing Company:
The True Life of Jesus of Nazareth
Alexander Smyth (1899)

(The Sequel): The Story of the Little Red Box